ELCHO
OF THE '45

ELCHO
OF THE '45

Alice Wemyss

EDITED BY

John Sibbald Gibson

THE SALTIRE SOCIETY

Elcho of the '45 published 2003 by

The Saltire Society
9 Fountain Close,
22 High Street,
Edinburgh EH1 1TF

A catalogue record for this book is available
from the British Library.

ISBN 0 85411 080 X

The publisher is very grateful to the Wemyss
Family Trust and the Earl of Wemyss for financial
assistance in the publication of this book

Cover Design by James Hutcheson

Printed and Bound in Scotland by Bell and Bain Limited

Contents

Foreword

Earl of Wemyss and March
K.T., L.L.D., D. Univ.

Another book about the '45! But this is really a rather special one. The author, David Lord Elcho, was not my ancestor, as I am descended from his younger brother, Francis, and the writer, Alice Wemyss, from an even younger brother, James, ancestor of the Wemysses of Wemyss.

David Lord Elcho was, I believe, fluent in French, as indeed was Alice. David's *Journal*, in French, covered the whole of his life; and in addition he wrote a closer account in English of the '45 itself. He was actually the victor of the last battle fought in England — admittedly a small one — at Clifton Moor near Penrith, before the retreat into Scotland in December 1745.

Elcho was a devoted supporter of the attempt to win the throne for the exiled King James, although he had a bitter and final quarrel with Prince Charles Edward. And unlike many of the other leaders of the Rising he never received a pardon, and died in exile in Paris.

Alice Wemyss, the writer of this book, was the daughter of Lord Wester Wemyss who was the First Sea Lord in 1918 when the Great War ended with the Armistice signed by him and others in the railway carriage at Compiègne. She was therefore very much of the Wemyss family and also descended from King William IV. She was completely at ease with the French as well as the English language and was rewarded for her studies in French Protestantism in the 18th and 19th centuries, with an honorary degree from the University of Toulouse. All of this made her uniquely able to translate Elcho's very long *Journal* and to write his life. She died in 1996 and this book, scrupulously fair, is her abiding monument.

It was a great stoke of luck that the well-known Jacobite scholar, John Sibbald Gibson, was willing to complete the work, and to prepare the manuscript for publication. We should all be most grateful to him.

I sometimes wish I could have been there to join Prince Charlie on the '45 effort. Had he had greater support from the French, and had he not turned back from Derby, much against his will, he might really have got to London and pushed George II out, back to Germany. Lord Elcho's account, which I believe to be fair and well-balanced, sets straight the record of what actually happened in 1745-46, and would surely have been welcomed by many of the scholars who have been concerned with these events over the decades. I wish they were all here to read the book.

Wemyss
May 2002

Acknowledgements

I am very grateful to Her Majesty Queen Elizabeth for the gracious permission to publish some documents from the Stuart archive at Windsor.

I owe to my many delightful conversations with the late Professor Gordon Donaldson a far better understanding of the Scottish past having worked in quite different historical fields up until then. Mr John Sibbald Gibson, the well-known authority on the '45 has been more than helpful in every way, whilst Professor Bruce Lenman has provided most useful criticisms. To these three eminent Scottish historians who have all read my manuscript I tender my grateful thanks, as I do to the Earl of Wemyss who furnished me with a copy of the letters exchanged by our great-grandfathers on the subject of the publication of the *Narrative*.

The pursuit of Elcho has led me into a number of Record Offices and Public Libraries both here and on the Continent, where I have always been treated with great courtesy and consideration; but it is in Neuchâtel, where Elcho's memory is still green, that I received the warmest welcome. Monsieur and Madame de Triboulet lent me their delightful flat, situated on top of the Neuchâtel hill with a glorious view of the lake and the snow-covered Alps, a view Elcho must have often admired when he stayed with the Earl Marischal in the nearby castle. Their son, M. Maurice de Triboulet is the archivist of the Canton of Neuchâtel, and as such unearthed many a document for my benefit, as did M. Rychner, librarian of the municipal library. M. and Mme Gabus, the present owners of Elcho's place, Cottendar were also most hospitable and helpful, whilst the late Mademoiselle Berthoud, a local historian, took me round in her car to the places once haunted by Elcho. I came to the conclusion that he was very lucky to have grown new roots in so delightful a place after his native ones had been brutally torn up after the Rising. Finally, I want to thank Mrs Elspeth Grisenthwaite for her patience and the cheerful way she has always responded to my numerous requests.

This book is dedicated to Mrs Pamela Adams, distant niece, like myself, of Elcho, to whose constant support and understanding it owes a very great deal.

Alice Wemyss
The Red House
Wemyss Castle Estate
Fife
December 1995

Sadly Alice Wemyss died in 1996. I was delighted to take on the task of completing her work and am very grateful to the Scottish International Education Trust for meeting the cost of my editing her manuscript, and to the Earl of Wemyss and the Wemyss Family Trust for financial and other support in bringing the work to publication.

John Sibbald Gibson
Edinburgh
January 2003

Introduction

This book is about a man, rather than an event; the man being David Wemyss, Lord Elcho; the event, the '45 with which his name is indissolubly linked and on which it throws important new light. It is based on two manuscripts in his own hand: *A Short Account of the Affairs of Scotland in the Years 1744, 1745, 1746*, usually known as the *Narrative*, written in English, and the *Journal* which is in French. They have in common that their language is plain, grammatical, and of the kind then spoken by the ruling classes. They are both factual without much comment or any trace of embellishment, and surprisingly accurate. Evan Charteris, who published the *Narrative* in 1907 with a long introduction drawn from the *Journal* tells us that he submitted it to W B Blaikie, the well-known Jacobite scholar of the turn of the century, who found that it conformed to his own research. In the intervening years, a good deal more has come to light about the '45 but Blaikie's approving judgement still holds good; for myself I checked every incident in the *Journal* which occurred on the continent to see if it fitted in with what was then taking place there at the time, and it did. This fully vindicates the description given of him by a young relative who visited him at he end of his life and who could not get over his astounding memory. But in other ways the two documents are very dissimilar. The *Journal* is a straightforward account of his life from his early childhood on to practically the day of his death. Indeed it would seem as if the pen had fallen from his hand as the manuscript stops abruptly. It was clearly written for family consumption, probably at the instigation of two of his nephews who spent many months in his company, both in Paris and at his place in Switzerland and who must have badgered him with questions about his past.

i

The *Narrative* is an eye-witness account of what happened between 1743 and 1754, and includes references to the Elibank affair of 1752 which had it come off would have led to the seizure of King George II. It presents some interesting anomalies, such as Elcho's use of French when referring to the cavalry, which obviously comes from his having received his training in France.

The question arises for whom was the *Narrative* written? Unlike so many of his contemporaries, Elcho did not often put pen to paper; he had no regular correspondence with friends or relatives as was then the custom, and the few letters to be found in the Stuart papers at Windsor Castle are, like the manuscripts, very much to the point. But he did write when strongly moved; his writings had always a purpose.

The *Narrative* describes what happened to the Jacobites between 1743, when the French decided on an invasion of England with a view to putting the Stuarts back on the throne, and 1754 by when Jacobite intrigue had had its final sputter. It is written in the third person singular, and it deliberately plays down Elcho's own role during the Rising, either because he did not want to appear boastful, or because he did not attach much importance to it, or because the person to whom the document was addressed was already well informed on the subject. The emphasis is laid on Charles Edward's behaviour towards the Scots during the '45 and betrays Elcho's resentment and sense of betrayal. Everything points to its having been addressed to some important Scottish Jacobite who wanted to know what really happened there, because there were many rumours on the subject. A close study of the document shows it to have been written about 1754. It was the time when the Prince was endeavouring to get Frederick the Great to back him. Seemingly the king, who had no love for his uncle King George II of Britain and Elector of Hanover, was showing signs of toying with the notion, but being prudent, he would surely not embark on so momentous an enterprise without first finding out more about Charles Edward, all the more that there were damaging rumours about his behaviour in Scotland. And who would he go to but to Marshal Keith, who had recently entered his service; and who

ii

would Keith consult but his brother, the Earl Marischal, now Prussian envoy in Paris and to whom Elcho was then acting as unofficial A.D.C.? All this is speculation, but could well explain the existence of this revealing document. However the whole thing soon fizzled out, the *Narrative* remained in Elcho's possession but was brought to Wemyss with the *Journal* after his death.

My first contact with the *Journal* proved a disaster. I was made to read it in an English translation made for Evan Charteris by the then chaplain at Wemyss. In my extreme youthfulness I found it dull. It seemed to consist of nothing but dates, places and people of whom I knew nothing and cared less. As far as I can remember I did not even finish it. It certainly put me off Jacobitism, a subject which I was careful to avoid for years. I even refused to read Sir Walter Scott's *Tales of a Grandfather* which I would have enjoyed, it being (ostensibly) written for a boy of much my own age at that time. I was therefore far from enthusiastic when my cousin, David Wemyss of Wemyss asked me, many years later, to check the accuracy of this English version of the *Journal*, as he wanted to have it re-typed.

My first impression was that old Mr Grant, whom I had known in my youth as the translator of the *Journal* was no French scholar, for he had occasionally gone so far as to reverse the meaning of the original! Then, as I plodded on, the *Journal* began to take my interest and I began to wonder what this distant uncle of mine could have been like. Except as regards his own bitter dislike of the Stuart Prince he had served so well during the '45 he certainly did not betray himself on paper.

There was a plethora of detail, often fascinating detail of *ancien régime* Europe as he saw it while in seemingly perpetual movement between France, Germany, Italy and Switzerland but it was only on reaching the account of his pathetically short-lived marriage, which ended in the death of his young wife and new born son, that I came to realise that he had, on the contrary, very strong feelings which a childhood spent amongst strangers had taught him to conceal. And turning back to chapters on the '45, I became aware of the violent antipathy he felt towards the Stuart Prince. This aroused my curiosity. He was clearly an unusual character, and one well worth studying, and so I began to read about Jacobitism, a subject I then knew nothing about.

What struck me then was the discrepancy which existed between the then long accepted heroic figure of 'Bonnie Prince Charlie' and the self-centred, self-opinionated, ill-educated young man, impervious to advice and so vulnerable to flattery, who comes out from the pages of both manuscripts. It is not an attractive picture, nor does it explain the Prince's early successes unless one takes into account his charm, that charm which commanded the devotion of so many Gaels, bowled over the women folk, enthused the more sentimental amongst his male followers, and was later to excite the Paris mobs to such an extent as to cause grave embarrassment to the French Government. But a long and intimate acquaintance (he had spent a whole winter in Rome with the Prince) had rendered Elcho immune. On thinking it over I came to the conclusion that writing, as he did, from first hand experience, he was probably fairly close to the truth, all the more that his picture of Charles Edward tallies with the latter's later behaviour which, to put it mildly, was 'unworthy of a Prince'

Unlike the *Narrative* which deals solely with Jacobite affairs, the *Journal* recounts Elcho's whole life from early childhood almost up to his death. We see him banished from the nursery for fear that he might pick up Whig notions, sent away from Scotland at the age of twelve, only to return after the Grand Tour, when he had been sent to Rome so as to act as companion to the two Princes, Charles and Henry Benedict. He became involved in a French invasion of England which never came off, then in the Rising where he was to make his name and in the immediate aftermath of Culloden was to have a heated row with Prince Charles which, for historians is crucial to any grasp of the '45. This was followed by forty-three long years of exile during which he rose from being a lonely, impoverished and friendless exile — he was at odds with both parties — to become a popular man about town, ending up a highly respected citizen of the Principality of Neuchâtel in Switzerland, where his memory is still green. As he was extremely observant, and always took a vivid interest in his surroundings, we do indeed get an interesting picture of the last four decades of the *ancien régime*.

The subsequent history of the *Journal* is illuminating about 19th and 20th century attitudes and is related in the final chapter. It is to be hoped that this present portrait of Elcho at full length will do his memory the justice it deserves.

After having visited many scenes of the '45, I thought I should see some of the places where he spent those long years in exile. Paris I know well, but I had never been to either Angers or to Angoulême of which he gives such a delightful description. Both places are charming, more especially the latter which must still be very much as it was in his day. But it is in Neuchâtel, where 'Milord Wemyss' is still remembered that I came closest to him; not to the angry and indignant Elcho of the '45, but to the kindly, hospitable and public spirited 'bourgeois' of Neuchâtel, who was ever ready to give a helping hand to his *concitoyens*. This gives us some idea of what he might have been had he finished his days as laird of Wemyss instead of as an unfortunate and homesick Jacobite outlaw.

CHAPTER ONE

The Wemyss'

'I was born at Wemyss in the County of Fife in August 1721. My father was the Earl of Wemyss, Viscount Elcho and Baron of Methil in Scotland, and my mother was Miss Charteris, daughter of Colonel Charteris of the English Guards.' It is with these words that David Wemyss, Lord Elcho, starts his autobiography, the *Journal* he wrote in French at the end of a life spent for the most part in exile. He goes on to give a somewhat boastful account of the family as was the custom in his day, but he does not exaggerate when it comes to its antiquity; it is indeed very ancient. We find Wemyss' settled on the northern shores of the Firth of Forth as early as 1165 as vassals of the powerful Earls of Fife, and alleged to descend from the legendary Macduff. By the 15th century they were living in a strongly fortified castle perched on a cliff overlooking the Firth, with the small port of West Wemyss nestling at its foot. They belonged to the higher baronage of Fife giving support to the Kings of late mediaeval Scotland. They also provided Fife with sheriffs and members of Parliament. In 1511 James IV erected Wester Wemyss into a burgh of barony by which means the lairds obtained judicial powers and the right to hold markets and fairs.

Wemyss-shire as this part of the country was called, stood in what James VI described as the 'golden fringe' which edged the 'dull grey mantle of Fife'. It owed its relative prosperity to the sea which furnished it with fish, and above all salt, a priceless commodity at a time when salted fish was the staple diet of Northern Europe and cattle had to be slaughtered before the winter, and it found a ready market abroad. It was produced by evaporating sea water in large pans heated with coal which was plentiful in the area, and it was exported for the most part to Holland from the nearby royal burgh of Dysart, known as 'little Holland'. The laird had as vassals fishermen, salters, colliers and craftsmen of different kinds, as well as farmers. They were independent-minded folk, but who traditionally looked to the Castle for defence, support and leadership.

The proximity of Falkland, the Stewarts' favourite place of residence, brought the family into closer contact with the monarch than may at times have been convenient, for the whole Court would descend upon them on its way to and from Holyrood, thus placing a heavy burden on its hosts. The Regent Mary of Guise was in the habit of seeking the advice of Sir John Wemyss, and it was at his home that her daughter, Mary Queen of Scots, first saw Darnley, whilst her ever impecunious grandson, King Jamie, proved a most demanding neighbour: would the laird lend him the horses needed to draw the coach of the French ambassador; lodge the Danish guests come for his wedding; escort the Queen down to London?

In 1633 another Sir John figures in a batch of Earls Charles I created in the vain hope of compelling the reluctant Scots to adopt the Prayer Book and conform to his authoritarian religious policy. However both the new Earl and his son, the first Lord Elcho, as well as their people were all fervent Presbyterians. The Wemyss' were among the first to sign the Covenant which coalesced resistance to the enforced changes in religion, and Elcho proudly noted that Wemyss was the first Kirk to appoint a minister without reference to the bishop. Father and son took an active part in the Bishops War, that precurser to the great English Civil War, and when that war spilled over into Scotland Elcho was in command of an army made up of miners and ploughboys which was routed at Tippermuir near Perth in 1644 by Montrose's Highlanders and his Irish.

Wemyss suffered at the hands of the Cromwellian soldiery who vandalised the Kirk, and the Restoration of 1660 found Earl David — as the second Earl is called — greatly impoverished but still powerful enough to ward off Episcopal interference, and the local

kirk went on much as before. He set about restoring the family
fortunes, building new saltpans, digging new mines — a work in
which he took an active part — and building a new harbour at
Methil from which he exported coal.   He was a good employer.
He never resorted to those iniquitous laws by which colliers and
their families were tied to their mines.   By the year of his death, in
1679, Earl David, prospering, had added to the mediaeval castle a
large and elegant wing in the new, fashionable style.

He was succeeded by his daughter Margaret who became
Countess of Wemyss in her own right after having first married a
cousin so as to preserve the family's name.   She was to follow in
her father's footsteps in both religion and politics and during the
persecution of the 1680s took under her protection an outlawed
Covenanting minister whose services she attended in the burgh at
great risk to herself.   She would have got into serious trouble had
not a relative pleaded her cause with Lord Tarbat, then a power in
Scottish affairs, begging him not to condemn her for 'preferring
the ministrations of a Presbyterian minister.'   Needless to say she
welcomed the 'Glorious Revolution' of 1688, and on hearing that
Claverhouse had been killed at Killiecrankie she wrote to her
daughter Lady Leven, whose Whig husband had come over with
William of Orange, 'I scarce believe [he is] dead, Lord grant I may
hear your good news confirmed.'

In 1697 the Countess' only son married Lady Anne Douglas, sister
of the 2nd Duke of Queensberry, who was to be one of the leading
politicians of the day and to become the chief author of the Union.
The engagement was celebrated at the Queensberry mansion in
Edinburgh amidst a great concourse of Scottish nobility.   Her other
daughter married Lord Northesk, a match which did not give her
the same satisfaction, the groom being suspected of Jacobite
leanings. But they were in love and she believed in love matches.
The Wemyss' were a close-knit family, Elcho and his sister Lady
Leven being particularly attached to each other.

Her son once married, Lady Wemyss retired to Elcho, the
impressive 16th century castle she possessed on the south bank of

the Tay. Three years later she married Lord Tarbat. This set
Edinburgh tongues awagging, there being thirty years difference
between these two grand-parents. Leven was opposed to the match
and threatened not to attend the wedding. He was an upright man
in whose eyes Tarbat was nothing but a trimmer ready to serve
whoever happened to be in power. However, he relented on seeing
how devoted the couple were to each other.   The elderly groom
was a real charmer and as such was greatly beloved in both London
and Edinburgh; he was also to prove an excellent stepfather. The
fact that he was an Episcopalian had endeared him to Queen Anne
who had created him Earl of Cromartie and placed him in charge of
Scottish affairs. This entailed the couple moving to London, where
Margaret died in 1705, leaving him broken-hearted. He had planned
a fine tomb to be erected in the Kirk at Wemyss where he would
be laid beside her when his time came. But so ornate a monument
would have shocked the Presbyterian worshippers and instead a
post of catechist was created and endowed in her memory.
Cromartie's wish to be buried beside her was not fulfilled; he died
in 1714 at a time when the Castle had fallen out with the Kirk over
politics.

The fourth Earl of Wemyss started by showing every sign of
wishing to follow in Earl David's footsteps. He developed the coal
trade, acted as spokesman for the owners who were endeavouring
to get their taxes reduced, and maintained close contacts with the
Kirk of which his wife was a fervent member.   Alas! she was soon
to come to a tragic end when her clothes caught fire, and she died
ten days later in agony, her last wish being that her two small sons
should be brought up as Presbyterians. Her bereaved husband could
not face living at Wemyss without her, so he entrusted the 'brats',
as he called them, to the care of his sister, Lady Leven, put the coal
and salt trades into the hands of his factor and moved to Edinburgh.

The capital was then seething with discontent, the projected
Union of the two Parliaments being extremely unpopular. He,
however was in favour of it believing that it would benefit the coal
trade, and having taken his seat in Parliament after the death of his

mother, he took on its defence. This led to his being sent to London in 1706 as one of the Commissioners of Union, whilst his services were rewarded with the post of Vice Admiral of Scotland. This was something of a sinecure, because the Scots navy was minute in size; but it was a lucrative sinecure as it entailed getting a share of the shipwrecks. On his return home in 1708, he found the Union now in force but wildly resented: 'People are not easy with the great change', he wrote to Lord Mar, then Secretary for Scotland; they were 'grumbling damnably.' The presence of French privateers in the Firth made life difficult as he was accused of not doing enough to get rid of them. So he got himself elected a representative peer and returned to London taking the 'brats' with him.

Life in the capital of England was much to his taste. He was handsome, liked fine clothes and must have cut quite a figure in London society where he frequented Swift amongst others. He would have liked to get a Government post and took to attending the Court in the hope of catching the Queen's eye. In the meantime he bought a house in Soho Square against the advice of his stepfather. Cromartie rightly feared that in so doing he would cut himself off from his Scottish roots. He married an English woman and was well on the way to becoming completely anglicised in both religion and politics, for he developed a taste for the Prayer Book and the Tory party, both being favoured by the Queen.

On the death of his second wife in 1708 the fourth Earl returned home, a very different man from what he had been before leaving Scotland, having shed the homely habits of his youth in favour of the more refined ways of the capital. The estate was now run by a 'chamberlain' instead of a factor, and although he did not as yet break openly with the Kirk, he no longer took an active part in its affairs. The bonds which had so long bound the burgh to the castle were loosening. It is difficult to know on what terms he lived with the Fife gentry which was then deeply divided on the subject of politics. He always remained very attached to the Whig Levens, but he also saw a great deal of his cousin and close neighbour, the Jacobite Lord Sinclair and his daughters. He was probably happiest in Edinburgh with the Earl of Cromartie and the Royal Company of Archers of whom the latter was Captain General.

These formed the sovereign's Scottish bodyguard, but had been suspected of Jacobitism during the reign of William and Mary. They had, however, taken on a new lease of life when Cromartie persuaded Queen Anne to allow them to function once more. They were little more than an archery club which met at regular intervals on the sands at Leith to compete for various trophies, including a bowl donated by Cromartie and Wemyss. The proceedings would end with a banquet held in a tavern to which Wemyss was in the habit of bringing the 'brats' of whom he was very fond. But they were disposed to be Jacobite to a man.

At the time, the last years of Queen Anne, David and James were about twelve and fourteen. They had returned to a home of which they had no recollection, being still very young at the time of their mother's tragic death. Scotland must had appeared a barbarous land in the eyes of boys brought up in an England where rank was held in high esteem. They probably did not even understand the language. They had had as a tutor Andrew Ramsay, known to posterity as the Chevalier Ramsay, whose influence may well have taken them further from their Presbyterian antecedents. Ramsay was the son of a Presbyterian baker and had been brought up by his fanatically Episcopalian mother to hate his father's faith. His books figure in the library at Wemyss.

The boys must have been frequent visitors at the Sinclairs' who lived at Dysart House, which is within easy reach of Wemyss. Here they would have found themselves in a purely Jacobite atmosphere. When the Master of Sinclair had returned home from Marlborough's armies, it had been his intention occasionally to attend kirk 'so as not to be odious to the people', the local population being staunchly Presbyterian. But he raised a storm at home, where he was accused of being a traitor and a renegade, and he had been obliged to abandon the plan. In the Rising of 1715 he was to command the Fife Squadron in the cavalry of the Earl of Mar's Jacobite army.

The fourth Earl had been willing to accept whoever Queen Anne might choose as successor. He still held the post of Vice Admiral of Scotland when George I came to the throne in 1714. However the new sovereign was not well informed about Scotland, and an enemy — possibly the Earl of Rothes, his Fife neighbour who coveted the post — made out that he was a Tory, a breed the King abhorred. Like all Jacobites Wemyss had expected that the failing Queen would nominate her half brother, young James now a pensioner at the French court, as her successor. So when he went south to swear allegiance to George, he was informed that the Admiralty had been awarded to his rival, Rothes. He returned home a convinced Jacobite though his close connection with his brother-in-law, Leven, prevented him from being admitted into the party's secrets at a time when the uprising was being plotted. Anyway, he had little to contribute, having no military experience, whilst his people were Whig to a man.

To get the Jacobite rising of 1715 going the Earl of Mar landed in the east of Fife. From there he proceeded to his Highland estates, where as a cover he had summoned the clans to a great hunt. The Royal Standard was raised, James was proclaimed King and the rebels marched on Perth which they entered. Here they were joined by forty Fife lairds led by a somewhat reluctant Master of Sinclair. Rothes proved worthy of the trust which the king had placed in him and called on the 'sensible men of the county' to assemble. Some fifteen hundred or so responded to the summons, but on hearing that the rebels had occupied Perth, melted away, remembering the terrible mauling their ancestors had suffered at the hands of Montrose's Highlanders. All Rothes was able to do was to maintain neighbouring Kinross under the Crown, and defend his own estates against Rob Roy and his MacGregors, now installed no great distance away at Falkland.

But the rebellion had been badly planned. The one successful operation was carried out by Sinclair, who seized in the port of Burntisland a shipload of arms destined to the loyal Earl of Sutherland. In November 1715 the battle of Sheriffmuir proved indecisive, and when King James arrived later, having been delayed by sickness, the rising was well on the way to collapse amidst a welter of recrimination.

The 4th Earl of Wemyss had taken no part in the proceedings. In addition his eldest son was dangerously ill. He was shortly to die and to be buried at Holyrood instead of in the Wemyss Kirk as had always been the case up to now, a sad proof of the worsening relation between the Earl and his people. This must have been largely due to the growing influence of the Hon Elizabeth Sinclair, one of the Master of Sinclair's Episcopalian sisters, whom Wemyss was soon to marry as his third wife. An Episcopalian chapel was now set up in the Castle. The couple were to have a son, who died in infancy, and two daughters, one of whom became the Countess of Sutherland and the other the Countess of Moray. But the 4th Earl had not long to live. He died in 1720.

Hardly had James become the 5th Earl in 1720 than he eloped with Janet, only child of the fabulously rich Colonel Francis Charteris. Charteris was a well known and very controversial figure. Grandson of a Dumfriesshire baronet, he had run away from school and had joined the army as a volunteer, where he acquired the barrackroom vocabulary, for which he became notorious, and developed an uncanny skill at cards. This, joined to a flair for finance, was to enable him to amass a very large fortune. His father bought him a commission and he became a Colonel in the English Guards.

It was common practice at the time for colonels to claim more men than actually figured on the rolls in order to pocket the pay. Charteris, who was nothing if not ingenious, improved on the practice by enrolling men in trouble with the authorities — soldiers could not be arrested — and making them pay a monthly fee under threat of being denounced. All went well until he enrolled an Irish gentleman who was an even greater rogue than himself. Whiggish Scot and Irish Jacobite were sure to clash, and the two men soon hated each other. As long as the Whigs were in power Charteris was able to torment his enemy with impunity; but with the return of the Tories in the closing years of Queen Anne's reign, the roles were reversed, and he found himself on his knees at the Bar of the House of Commons suing for pardon. The loss of his commission did him no great harm financially, gambling proving far more lucrative; nor seemingly did it harm him socially for he was a welcome guest in the great Whig houses. But he never forgave the humiliation and from now on he waged a constant war on the Jacobites, whom he systematically despoiled whilst at the same time holding them up to ridicule. They retorted by circulating distorted versions of his misdeeds which only made him and his friends laugh, for he was something of a wag.

All this did not prevent the Levens with their close family and neighbourly interest in the Wemyss' from approving the match when it took place in 1720. The girl came from good Scottish stock, the Charteris being well established in Dumfriesshire, whilst her mother was the daughter of a judge, and related to half the Edinburgh Bench. The Wemyss finances were in shambles; there were not even six horses in the stables to bring the newly married couple home in style, and the new Earl was already showing signs of become a spendthrift. What is more, his bride might well detach him from the Episcopalian Jacobitism his father had largely adopted out of pique, and which was so contrary to both the traditions and the interests of his House. True the Colonel was a profligate, but since Charles II's time profligacy was socially acceptable. The bridegroom was lent the horses he had asked for.

How little did the Levens know their nephew! Whilst the girl was infatuated, all he seems to have thought about was her father's money bags and how angry he would be at the thought that they would one day fall into Jacobite hands. The marriage got off to a bad start, she refusing to worship in the chapel he was decorating at great expense. Janet was a silly girl and was to become a sillier woman, but she was not lacking in spirit and she insisted on inviting her Whig friends and relations to stay at Wemyss, which must have pleased the Earl of Leven, who was a regular visitor.

The Colonel had made up his mind that his son-in-law would not benefit from his fortune. Following the birth of his eldest son,

David, Lord Elcho in 1721, the Earl of Wemyss had a growing family. The Colonel left the bulk to his second grandson, Francis, on condition he took the name and arms of Charteris; and should he inherit the earldom the money would go to the youngest boy, James, the next heir. The three girls were to receive ample dowries, whilst their mother would get an annuity sufficient to keep her in comfort, but not enough for her to pay her husband's debts. Elcho was left £12,000 which would allow these debts to be paid off on his accession to the earldom, and in the meantime he would get £500 a year for his education. Wishing to see his grandchildren grow up as loyal subjects of the Crown, he appointed the Whig Duke of Argyll to be their guardian. This must have reached their father's ears, for poor little Elcho was dragged away from the nursery and placed in the care of a nonjuror parson with strong Jacobite views. It must have been a painful wrench, for he was very fond of his brother and sister, both called Francis or Frances after their grandfather, although the girl was known as Fanny.

Unaware as yet of the other contents of his father-in-law's will, the Earl went on spending lavishly on furniture, jewels and ornaments for the chapel. The bills began to pour in and there was no money with which to pay them. The factors — for these were continually changing — received orders to produce more salt and coal at less expense, with the result that the salters took to rioting and found themselves in gaol.

Having for years cocked snooks at his Jacobite opponents, the Colonel finally fell victim to their machinations. In 1730 he was arrested on the charge of having raped a maidservant, and was imprisoned in Newgate where he languished for a very long time before being brought before the courts and sentenced to death. His principal tormentor was a fellow Scot, Dr John Arbuthnot, physician to the late Queen, and son of an Episcopalian parson who had been 'rabbled' at the time of the 'Glorious Revolution' of 1688. He worked in close collaboration with Swift and Pope, those masters of vituperative prose. Between them they ran a campaign of extraordinary virulence even by the standard of the day. The case was the talk of the town, but contemporaries were too well informed to take these libellous assertions at their face value, and not to realise that they were motivated by political spite rather than moral indignation. The whole business was ended by a pardon after some of his land had been confiscated. However, the Colonel was no longer young and what he had gone through proved too much even for his robust constitution. He died two years later, pursued even beyond the grave by his enemies.

The fifth Earl would no doubt have willingly thrown offal into his father-in-law's grave, for the will left him with no hope of ever being able to pay his debts. This proved to be the last straw which broke up what had been from the start an unhappy marriage. The following year Lady Wemyss returned to her mother taking with her all the children with the exception of Elcho, whilst her debt-ridden husband deserted Wemyss in favour of a place he bought in county Durham. It is not clear what prompted him to act in this way. Was he fleeing from his creditors, or from the hostility of his tenantry, or from the reprobation of his neighbours who may well have taken sides with his ill-treated wife? Did he wish to conceal dark Jacobite machinations, or more simply, the presence of a mistress? What is certain is that he never received visits from his children, not even from Elcho who on the whole remained on surprisingly good terms with him.

CHAPTER TWO

Young Elcho

Elcho was twelve when his parents parted in the year 1732. The breakup of his home cannot have affected him much having already been wrenched from it seven years before. By now he must have outgrown the pain caused by parting from his mother and siblings. The nonjuror parson to whom he had been confided was a kindly old man who took good care of his health, giving him white wine when he was ill. This cannot have occurred very often, for he was a robust and turbulent little boy — there are bills for windows 'broken by his Lordship'. His school was in Dunfermline, doubtless a small establishment run by an Episcopalian cleric and frequented by sons of Jacobite lairds.   Being in Scotland, he would have been fed on a diet of Latin grammar which would bring shudders to a present day sixth former. He was no scholar, and books were never to play much part in his life, but he wrote in a plain straightforward fashion which exactly conveys his meaning.

He was alert, observant, took a vivid interest in his surroundings, and enjoyed the company of his fellow creatures.   He must have inherited some of the Colonel's jovial ways for he was later noted as a wit. He had also inherited his ungovernable temper, and his opponents were always careful to remain out of reach of his fists when a boy, and his rapier when a man, for he became a redoubtable swordsman. Having been on his own from a very early age, he was self-sufficient, and had learnt how to conceal his feelings. When reading his *Journal* one is almost inclined to believe he had none, so factual is it, and it is only when reaching the account of his wife's death that one realises that beneath the polished and rather cynical man-of-the-world lurked a sensitive spirit starved of affection.

The fifth Earl was not a fond father. He seems to have relinquished without a tussle the guardianship of the younger children to the Duke of Argyll, and his behaviour towards Elcho betrays no affection. He had set his heart on the House of Wemyss remaining within the Jacobite fold. In 1737 there is in the Stuart papers a letter to King James at Rome from the Earl protesting his loyalty to the House of Stuart. He decided that his son and heir should grow up in England out of reach of the Whigs who surrounded him in Scotland.

The novelty of the journey must have been pure delight for an adventurous boy who may never as yet have been out of Fife, for England was then vastly different from Scotland. The language, the customs, the clothes, the food, as well as the landscape and the buildings were all new in his eyes; it was indeed a foreign country. On reaching London his father sent him to Winchester under the care of Dr Alexander Mackenzie, who was to be his tutor for the next seven years. Mackenzie is an enigmatic figure. He was no pedagogue, nor was he a disciplinarian for his charge clearly did exactly what he pleased; but he was an ardent supporter of the House of Stuart and in all probability an agent. For the time being his task was to keep Elcho safely within the Jacobite fold and prevent him from having any communication whatsoever with his mother. This Elcho must have foreseen for he was to remain in touch with her by means of his brother Francis, with whom he was allowed to correspond.

Elcho was fortunate in having had so tough a childhood, as he was able to stand up to the cruel baiting by his English school fellows, the Scots being then despised in England as poverty-stricken boors. 'Nothing is baser than the abuse the English are in the habit of pouring on the Scots, calling them beggars because they are poorer than they, and Scotland a wretched country because it produces less wheat' he recalled in the *Journal*.   It was to defend the land of his birth that he 'learnt to fight with his fists', as he puts it, for 'English schoolboys are as ready as their elders to insult the Scots.' Like so many expatriates he became an ardent patriot. Having thus established his position by means of his fists, he merged into the life of the school where his passage has left no trace in the records.

Winchester, he tells us, was made up of 'seventy scholars who were boarded and educated free of charge', and a hundred or so of 'young noblemen or sons of gentlemen who lodged in boarding houses and only went to the College for lessons.' Differences of rank were preserved: 'On Sundays peers and sons of peers wore blue, red or green robes adorned with gold lace to go to church; the knights-baronet wore black robes, whilst the untitled boys wore their ordinary clothes.' The school was divided between 'Jacobites' and 'Georgites'. So cordially did they hate each other that

> having to write a piece of verse of which I knew myself incapable, being no poet, I asked Mr Mundy, a master if he would do it for me. He at once asked "Are you a Jacobite or a Georgite?" I answered I was a Jacobite. "Well" said he, "I will do it, but should I ever see you frequenting so-and-so, or such a one who are Georgite knaves I will never help you again."

The young Elcho probably looked upon Jacobitism as a party rather than a Cause, and one in which he took very little interest. He never saw any reason why he should not be friends with Georgites, more especially when they were fellow Scots. This was more especially the case of Lord Drumlanrig, heir of the Duke of Queensberry, with whom he became friends. However Mackenzie does seem to have prevented him from frequenting his friend's home, which was unfortunate as it was one of the pleasantest houses in London.

Discipline was lax: 'We gambled, we went to public houses and we frequented prostitutes, which if discovered led to nothing more than a flogging.' 'In these sorts of schools,' he goes on, 'one does not learn as much Greek and Latin as with a private tutor, but one learns how to cope with the world and one makes friends who can prove useful if one keeps up the friendship.' He enjoyed social life, and the highlight of his year was 'the race week which attracted all the local aristocracy. They spend their mornings hunting foxes and hares with packs of forty or so hounds, and after dinner they congregate on the race course where the ladies sit in carriages, the day finishing with a ball. Both the King and the town give prizes of a hundred guineas, whilst private individuals race horses against each other for large sums of money.   So great a concourse of carriages, horsemen and people on foot is indeed a wonderful sight, and there are tents where food can be obtained.'

The summer holidays were spent touring the country with his tutor staying with Jacobite friends of his father, or visiting the great country houses which were of easy access to anyone of birth. In Bath he was presented to Lord Strafford, head of the Jacobite party in England and who, as he proudly noted, 'had been our ambassador at the Peace of Utrecht and was very amiable.' He must have made a good impression on the old man, for he was later invited to stay at Wentworth where he made friends with his son. The Christmas holidays were spent in London, either in lodgings or staying with school friends. He saw a good deal of the Hamiltons who were kind to him — the Duke was looked upon as head of the Scottish Jacobites.

It was two years before he received a visit from his father. 'He gave me a music teacher from whom I acquired a great taste for Italian music.' Not all his tastes were as commendable for he shared the prevailing love of cruel sports and violent displays.   He describes, not without relish, the 'gladiatorial fights when two men would fight with swords inflicting terrible wounds on each other so as to earn money. At Winchester I saw cock fights . . . also men fighting with staves for a hat or some such prize presented by the local squire at a village fair.' It was a violent society.

By 1737 his schooling was over and he spent the winter in London waiting for the funds needed to go abroad, where he was to finish his education. In March of the following year his tutor received orders to take him immediately to France. Such was the hurry that he did not even have time to tell Francis, who was now at Eton. They boarded a ship lying in the Thames and landed at Boulogne where they were greeted by the Scottish merchant Charles Smith, one of the most active of the Jacobite agents. The news of Elcho's arrival had evidently spread through the Jacobite diaspora. Several gentlemen who had been implicated in the '15, came to Boulogne to see him, amongst them John Cameron of Lochiel whose son was to play a key role in the '45. Much was expected of Elcho for he was rich, thanks to his maternal grandfather — and the Jacobites were perpetually short of funds.

The Grand Tour usually started in Paris, but Elcho was taken to the garrison towns where Scottish officers were serving with Irish regiments. In Bethune those from the *régiment de Roth* called upon him, among them being Captain Lord John Drummond who was to play an important part in his life. On the advice of Smith Rheims had been chosen as a suitable place to begin his 'education'.

To Elcho Rheims was little short of Paradise. He was introduced to all the distinguished families in the town.

> After dinner I would attend social gatherings where cards were played. and I was often invited to dine with the *Procureur du Roi* and many other people as well. There was also a troop of actors as well as public concerts. In summer gentlemen would take me to their country houses to shoot and, as was the custom of the country, I attached myself to Madame la Baronne de F . . . who took great care to teach me the French language and manners.

She probably also initiated him into the mysteries of the boudoir, which goes to explain why he was so popular with women. 'I was received with great courtesy in this town, and the obliging and easy-going manners of the French pleased me so much that I have remained very attached to this nation.'

Gambling nearly got Elcho into serious trouble. He was seeing the Old Year out in company of friends when he lost his pocket money. He dare not tell Mackenzie for fear of being reported to the Earl, his father, of whom he stood in awe, so he wrote to his mother. 'I am very much ashamed that such a subject should be the occasion of a letter from a son having quite neglected for five years past a

Mother to whom certainly all the love and respect is due. But as I fancy your ladyship knows my negligence in not writing is none of my fault being strictly forbidden so much as to mention your name in my letters.' Janet did understand all the more in that Elcho was in the habit of sending his 'love and duty' through Francis who knew where 'they were due'. This taught him a lesson and although he never ceased gambling, as was then the custom, he never again got into debt.

The twice-yearly passage of the regiments to and from their garrisons to camp was the highlight of the Rheims season. The officers were 'greatly feasted' in the houses he frequented and he was invited to all the parties given in their honour. He was very interested in all he saw, carefully noting the names of the regiments, their uniforms and who was in command. He was to retain these interests until the end. After nine months stay he regretfully left Rheims where he had acquired a sound knowledge of the language. It was no idle boast when he wrote 'I spoke French very well' and he was later able to pass himself off as a Frenchman. He had also learnt to fence and to dance and had acquired a taste for good food. The next stage was Angers where he was to attend an academy much frequented by the English. He left in Mackenzie's charge, and they stopped in Paris at the Hotel Imperial where they were greeted by Sir Hector Maclean, the landless chief of the Macleans of Mull and a veteran Jacobite conspirator; Sir Hector took Elcho to the Opera.

The pair now travelled on to the valley of the Loire, the very heart of France where the purest French is still spoken, sight-seeing on the way as was their custom. They safely reached Angers where they were greeted by the Director, M. de Pignerol, who turned up accompanied by all his pupils. His establishment might be described as a finishing school for well-born young 'heretics' for there were also some Germans. As such it had no legal status; since the Revocation of the Edict of Nantes in 1685 which turned Protestantism into a persecuted faith in France, education was a monopoly of the Catholic Church.

The curriculum was planned to produce well-mannered young officers, for, in France, as indeed all over the Continent, the nobility was liable to military service. 'In summer one attended the riding school at five in the morning, in winter at eight and one rode three horses, two for dressage and one for jumping. On leaving the riding school one went to the fencing hall, this being followed by lessons in mathematics, drawing and music; after dinner one went to the ballroom before dressing to attend social gatherings held in town, and one went shooting on the days when there were no lessons.' It was a way of life which would have suited him to perfection had not his English school fellows been so deeply divided. 'Since my departure from Winchester I had given no thought to politics, but wherever Englishmen are to be found parties must necessarily exist.'

Elcho went to board with M. de Pignerol 'where only French was spoken,' instead of living in lodgings with his tutor as did the other pupils. His host introduced him to 'all the houses where social gatherings were held and where there were concerts and theatricals, but no refreshments.' He was clearly regretting the delicious 'gouters' he had so enjoyed at Rheims. Seemingly he was the only pupil to avail himself of so splendid an opportunity to improve his French and get to know the local gentry. 'the English (then as now) being in the habit of entertaining one another.'

Elcho was fortunate in making the acquaintance of *la Belle France* when she was at her most alluring. She had thrown off the mantles of pomp and gloom in which she had been enveloped by the ageing Louis XIV, whilst retaining that refined way of life born at Versailles and now being imitated all over Europe. Cardinal Fleury's peaceful rule had enabled her to recover from the damage caused by the Marlborough wars, and lightness of touch was the order of the day. Elegant stone buildings, whose large windows let in the light, were rising all over the country; gracefully curved furniture wrought in precious woods was replacing the heavily gilded and uncomfortable seats of the previous reign; the men had discarded their ponderous periwigs whilst the women had exchanged the stiff brocades of their mothers' day for light flowered muslins. Conversation was

witty and not as yet subversive, and cuisine, raised to the status of
a fine art, was at its most luscious, chefs glorying in the delicious
new sauces they were inventing.

By March 1740 Elcho's formal education had come to an end.
He had mastered French, acquired those social skills which would
enable him to feel at his ease in any society, as well as enough
military science to serve with distinction in any army, a profession
towards which he felt more and more attracted. The time had come
for him to join the ranks of what the Italians contemptuously called
the *golden asses*, those well-heeled young aristocrats who travelled
under the care of a tutor in search of culture.

They set off at a leisurely pace for Avignon visiting Toulouse,
Narbonne, Nimes, where Elcho saw his first Roman remains,
Marseilles with its sinister départment des galères where galley
slaves, many of them innocent Huguenots, were condemned to row
his Christian Majesty's men o' war, Toulon 'where the King stations
the greater part of his fleet', finally reaching their destination in
May. Elcho had greatly enjoyed this his first long trip abroad. 'We
enjoyed good company at the tables d'hotes where we met many
officers on their way to Corsica to rejoin their regiments.' Elcho
had discovered, greatly to his satisfaction 'that the French prefer
the Scots.'

Avignon had been a Jacobite stronghold ever since 1717 when,
debarred from France by the Treaty of Utrecht and expelled from
Lorraine under English pressure, the Chevalier de Saint-George
whom Jacobites recognised as King James III and his enemies knew
as the Pretender had briefly found refuge in this Papal State. He
had been joined by some four hundred refugees from the '15. They
were well-received both by the papal authorities and the local
population. However, the former had been dismayed on discovering
that about half of them were heretics, as they had been under the
impression that Jacobites were Catholic victims of Protestant
intolerance. Stringent regulations had been laid down so that the
local population should not be contaminated. The worthy prelates
need have had no fear; Calvinism, as practised by the Huguenots

across the Rhone, was as abhorrent to the Episcopalian Jacobites as it was to themselves. All the refugees thought of was having a good time, and Carnival had been particularly uproarious the year of their arrival. Since then they had greatly contributed to the amenities of the place being, amongst other things, responsible for the building of a theatre.

The Pretender had soon been obliged to leave Avignon when the English threatened to bombard Civita Vecchia in the Papal States, and after having roamed round Italy he had finally settled in Rome, in the gloomy Palazzo Muti loaned by the Pope. But the Duke of Ormonde, looked upon as the head of the English Jacobites, had made his home at Avignon, as had many other Stuart supporters attracted by the pleasant easy-going way of life. Lady Mary Wortley Montagu, prominent in London society, was to find it greatly to her liking, despite her being a well-known supporter of the Hanoverian Crown: 'This is perhaps the town in the whole world where politics are the least talked of', a trait which cannot but have delighted Elcho. In the absence of the Duke of Ormonde, now in Spain on Jacobite business, Lord and Lady Inverness were acting as heads of the community. Colonel John Hay, as he originally was, had been amongst those who had joined the Pretender after the '15 and had remained with him until Queen Clementina's jealousy of his wife, a forceful woman, had obliged the couple to leave Rome. They settled in Avignon as Earl and Countess of Inverness, a title conferred upon him by a grateful Pretender over whom he still exercised a good deal of influence. Indeed he took second place after Ormonde in the Jacobite hierarchy. They immediately took Elcho under their wing, introducing him to 'the Papal Legate and to all the more prominent members of Avignonais society, including the Marquise de Vaucluse, said to be the Duke of Ormonde's mistress, and at whose house I supped in company of the most distinguished of Avignon's denizens — and no provincial town has better. The belle of the town was the Marquise de Villeneuve with whose charms I was greatly taken.' Life was much the same as in the French provinces, and if Lady Mary is to be believed there were 'assemblies every night which conclude with a great supper.' There were also 'comedies tolerably well acted.' Elcho must have felt all the more at his ease that ' the people of Quality all affect the French manner of living.' Echoes of his stay must have reached the Palazzo Muti; this was indeed a promising young man who could contribute a great deal to the Cause.   Avignon marks a turning point in Elcho's life for it is here that he shed the last remnants of boyhood.   Mackenzie is relegated to the background and henceforth he takes charge of his own affairs: he had become a man.

The next port of call was Lyon where arrangements were made to cross Mont Cenis, a route much favoured by English tourists. It was both safer and cheaper to travel in a group.   He chose his companions from amongst the Jacobites and joined forces with three Englishmen, Messrs Pitt, Castleton and Dashwood, who were also on the Grand Tour. 'Mr Pitt had a tutor called Oldsworth, an ardent Jacobite, so we all belonged to the same political party. We hired four chaises to take us to Milan at a sequin per head per day, the Italian drivers paying all the expenses at the inns including the servants.'

All this took some time to arrange, and while he was waiting for the departure Elcho made the acquaintance of a man who was to exercise more influence over his life than anyone else. Sir James Steuart of Goodtrees — the family estate near Edinburgh — was short and ugly, and already at the age of twenty-seven showing signs of becoming potbellied. But what was lacking in looks was amply compensated by a quite exceptional charm allied to a brilliant brain. Lady Mary Wortley Montagu was to be completely bowled over by him.   Had he not got involved in the '45 he would have taken his place amongst that cohort of Scotsmen, the David Humes, Adam Smiths, Principal Robertsons who were to earn for Edinburgh the title of 'Athens of the North'. As it was, his *Principles of Political Economy* of 1761 preceded and has often been compared to Adam Smith's *Wealth of Nations*.

All this still lay in the future; for the time being Sir James was just back from Rome where he had been converted not to Catholicism but to Jacobitism. His background was Presbyterian and Whig. He was descended from one of the great Covenanting preachers and his immediate forebears had distinguished themselves at the Edinburgh Bar. He had already lost both his parents by the time he had gone to Leyden to pursue his studies, and being free to do as he pleased he had decided to tour the Continent before settling in Edinburgh as a lawyer. This took him to Avignon where he fell in with the Duke of Ormonde. Ormonde was too experienced a politician not to realise what an asset Steuart would be. So he took him to Madrid as his secretary, where he had gone in the hope of inveigling the Spaniards into invading Britain. It is not clear if Sir James acted on his own initiative or on instructions from Avignon, or even from the Palazzo Muti; what is clear is that Elcho was completely dazzled: 'Sir James is a man of great intelligence who in my eyes surpassed all the Englishmen or Scotsmen I had ever met. We became great friends.'

The negotiations with the Italian drivers having been brought to a satisfactory conclusion, the party started off. 'On reaching the foot of the Mont Cenis our vehicles were taken to pieces and loaded on mules and we were given mules to ride to the top of the mountain, where we found sedan chairs in which we were carried down to the other side.' They then reached Turin where, being the only titled member of the party, Elcho received a call from the British Minister. 'This honour is paid to a peer or the eldest son of a peer by every diplomatist under the rank of ambassador.' Here they also received a visit from Lord Lincoln, and met amongst others Elcho's old schoolfellow Lord Quarendon. They were just back from Rome where, however, they had not worshipped at the Stuart shrine, being loyal subjects of King George.

By the time they reached Milan the weather was too hot to travel in comfort, so they hired a house and a cook. 'The mornings were spent taking lessons in music and Italian; after dinner we would walk round to look at the sights or listen to music in the churches

— we gave three very good concerts in our house — whilst the evenings were spent at the Comédie Italienne. Shortly before the start of the play, fashionable Milan would roll up in its carriages and eat ices in front of the cafés which stand round the great square. One day we saw a criminal hanged here. He arrived escorted by a hundred members of a religious brotherhood, all of them nobles and all of them masked. One of them parted from the group to act as hangman. They had started by meeting at the prison already masked, and had drawn lots as to who would act as executioner, no one knowing his identity.'

He now received the disturbing news that his Paris banker had gone bankrupt. This obliged him to part from his companions, whose luxurious way of travelling he could no longer afford. But they remained friends, and were to see a good deal of each other during the rest of the tour. Elcho now left more modestly by mail coach for Florence.

CHAPTER THREE

Companion to the Princes

It was an October day in 1740 when the Florence mail coach disgorged Elcho with his tutor and servant on to the Piazza d'Espagna in Rome from where they went to the neighbouring inn. They did not have to wait long before being escorted by someone from the Palazzo Muti to lodgings which had been rented for them. On the following day Elcho received a delegation of no less than seven senior members of the Chevalier's household, amongst whom figured the Earls of Winton and Dunbar, as well as Edgar, the erstwhile Angus laird and James' devoted Secretary. 'Lord Winton, who had take part in the '15 affair and had lost an estate worth 120,000 *livres* a year, was in disgrace for having slapped a member of the household in the Chevalier's presence. He now lived in town on a small pension given him by the latter. Lord Dunbar was the Prince's Governor, and there was an Anglican Chaplain for the Protestants. Sir Thomas Sheridan, the Prince's tutor, was a zealous Catholic . . All these gentlemen lived at Court receiving small pensions which were regularly paid.' So flattering a welcome extended to so young a man shows the importance which was being attached to this Lowland Scot, most of whose relations — his father excepted — were Whigs.

> I was now told by my tutor that I must be presented to the Chevalier, and a request for an audience was made through Mr Hay. He came to fetch me at about seven o'clock in the evening, and we soon found ourselves in a small street besides the Palazzo Muti, which we entered through a little door leading into the cellars. Before saying goodbye, Mr Hay pointed out the staircase which I must go up. Having followed his instructions, I found myself in

the presence of Mr Edgar, as the secret stairs or ladder led into his room. He opened a door, showed me a suite of rooms and told me I would find the Chevalier in the fourth. I duly found him there, and after having kissed hands he made me sit close to him before the fire. He was a tall spare man with large features, and he resembled the pictures of his father, James II, and his uncle, Charles II. He told me that he knew that my father was very attached to him, and that this would be taken into consideration should he ever come to the throne. He asked me many questions about my travels and my connections, and he seemed well acquainted with Scotland and Scottish families, more especially with those raised to the peerage since 1688 when his father lost his crown, and whom he described as 'Mr' and not 'my Lord'.

'He now rang a small bell and the Princes came in from the next room. I kissed hands and called them 'Your Highness' just as I had called their father 'Your Majesty'. The Chevalier made me stand back to back with the elder, Prince Charles, who was a year older than I and much taller. He now bid me farewell after having showered civilities upon me, and I returned to Mr Edgar's room where I had supper tete-a-tete with him. He told me that of all the British visitors, the Duke of Beaufort was the one who most often climbed that ladder. It was illegal for British subjects to visit the Palazzo Muti, hence all the secrecy.'

In fact, no one was ever arrested on their return home, although everyone's moves were well known, Rome being riddled with spies.

The flattering treatment which had proved so successful with Sir James Steuart, was now applied to Elcho. 'We were given great dinner parties by the Earls of Winton, Nithsdale and Dunbar, and by Messrs Hay and Irvine; but the food and wine were provided by the Chevalier and brought over by his cooks.' On one occasion Elcho was taken shooting by Hay at Ostia 'where we were entertained on the instructions and at the expense of the Chevalier.' Most flattering of all was an invitation to sit in a 'gallery especially constructed in the church for the Chevalier during the great religious festivals, and where the French ambassador was always in attendance . All these attentions, added to the education I had received from my father, made me very attached to his House.'

The afternoons were spent in the company of the two Princes in the gardens of the Villa Borghese, 'where they were wont to take their exercise. Prince Charles did not have much to say to those who came to pay him court, and would spend all his time shooting blackbirds and thrushes, or playing the Scottish game of 'golf'. The Duke of York, on the contrary, loved conversation and seemed to want to learn all he could about English affairs, and in general, showed more promise than his brother. On leaving the garden Lord Dunbar would occasionally take me to a *conversazione* at one of the palazzos belonging to the Roman nobility'. According to a French source these gatherings must have been incredibly dull: 'each lady would arrive with her *cicisbeo*, with whom she would sit for a time, no one daring to interrupt their conversation. The rest of the evening was taken up with cards. The refreshments, when they existed, were of a most frugal nature'.

However, having to dance attendance on the Prince had its compensations, and Elcho thoroughly enjoyed the shoot given in Charles Edward's honour by the Prince of Caserta. 'All the peasants were mobilised to act as beaters. On the first day we drove out in carriages to shoot snipe, of which we bagged two hundred and fifty; we dined in the woods in tents erected for the purpose, and on our return were regaled with a good concert and a sumptuous supper. On the second day we went big game shooting and brought back twenty-five head of hind, doe, wild boar and roebuck. On the third our host took us to a lake where a great wooden pavilion had been erected with a large dining-room and bedrooms at the back. We embarked, each sportsman in his own boat, and in a short time killed no less than six hundred wild duck. During all this time the Prince received every possible mark of attention and respect.'

This outing must have been a welcome change for the Prince from the tedium of the Palazzo Muti, where life was regulated with clockwork precision. The Chevalier 'went every day to mass and it was on his leaving the church that people paid him homage. After dinner he would make his devotions at the church of the Porta dei Popoli, leaving it in a carriage from which he would alight to take an hour's-long walk. In winter he would go every evening to the Opera where supper was served in his box during the performance. The French ambassador never failed to pay him a visit.'

Fortunately Elcho's time was not wholly taken up with dancing attendance on the Princes: he frequented the café on the Piazza d'Espagna, where the English were in the habit of foregathering to play billiards, and he also went to the *conversazione* Lady Pomfret and Lady Mary Wortley Montagu held every week, for those ladies were spending the winter in Rome. 'When abroad the English only frequent each other and seldom make the acquaintance of the local inhabitants. One of them would give a dinner party every day. When they go to a *conversazione* they would arrive in a bunch, talk to each other and have little to say to people from other countries it may well be said that they travel to see objects of interest, not to discover how people live. They are popular in Italy being easily duped and are made to pay twice as much as other visitors.'

By now Elcho had taken charge of his own affairs, Mackenzie having disappeared from the horizon. (Was he gone on some secret mission?) He would spend the mornings exploring the city under the guidance of a professional guide. On his return home there were lessons in music and Italian, his teachers being abbés.

Unlike his fellow countrymen, Elcho wanted to discover 'how people lived'. He did not think much of the nobility whose love of display went hand in hand with sordid parsimony.

This same love of display was to be found at the Vatican. 'On his daily visit to one of the churches, the pope drives in a carriage drawn by eight white horses, preceded by a priest on horseback carrying a cross as a warning for all to fall on their knees at his approach. He is followed by several six-horse-drawn carriages carrying the priests of his household, and is surrounded by twenty-four cuirassiers, twenty-four light horsemen and twenty-four Swiss foot guards. He blesses the people with the sign of the cross as he drives by. There are monks and nuns of every possible order, amongst them Franciscan friars who live on alms, and one sees nothing but abbés, for beside the genuine ecclesiastics many married men have adopted this dress which is now all the fashion.'

However all this display could not conceal economic decline and abject poverty:

> The city has shrunk to an extraordinary degree; the outer walls would make it larger than Paris, but half the ground within them consists of gardens, fields and vineyards. The convents are so isolated that they might be in the depths of the country. The population is reckoned at fifteen thousand souls, and is largely made up of the poor who sleep in the streets or under church porches. Many convents hand out soup at midday which only encourages their natural idleness, for they are lazy and dislike work. There are a great number of prostitutes who are relegated to *rues barricadées*. They stand before their doors and are obliged to receive any passer-by willing to give them a *tetone*, some of which goes to the Government.

With Carnival this somewhat drab society came to life. 'The balls given by the nobility are magnificent. It is the foreigners who lead the dances, Prince Charles and the Duke of York always leading the minuets. These are always followed by English quadrilles which are directed by Mr Roy Stewart who belongs to the Prince's household.'

No grand tour was complete without a visit to Naples, and Elcho set off in company of young Lord Strafford, son of the kindly old peer who had been so nice to him when he was still at Winchester. The stay followed much the same pattern as in Turin and elsewhere. The two friends went to have a look at the King and Queen, 'who were in the habit of visiting the Carmelite church after dinner. However, we were not presented, there being no English representative, only a consul. The King proved very attentive and we sat every evening in his box at the Opera. The music is better here than anywhere else, and most of the composers are Neapolitans'.

Elcho threw an amused glance at a 'numerous nobility who live very frugally at home in order to be able to make an ostentatious display when abroad.' Here too he was struck by the contrast which existed between the relatively rich and the abysmally poor. 'There are thirty thousand men called *lazzaroni* who have no fixed abode and earn their living by doing commissions of every sort and kind. But having earned five sols they refuse to do any more work that day, having earned all they need to live on. There are also thirty thousand prostitutes who pay tax to the Government; they are dressed in yellow with red facings whilst in Rome they are dressed in white with red facings.'

Having returned to Rome, Holy Week was to afford Elcho another opportunity for studying aspects of Roman life, and he made a point of being present at the ceremonies in which the Pope took part. 'On Maundy Thursday he blesses the people from the steps of St Peters, and throwing a lighted torch onto the Piazza, excommunicates heretics. He then washes the feet of twelve paupers, seats them for a meal at his own table and serves them himself from dishes presented by his attendants. The Holy Week processions present a curious feature in that men are seen flogging their chests and backs 'til the blood runs.'

It is probably the music that he enjoyed most. 'On feast days great music is performed in all the churches both in the morning and in the evening. In the larger ones it is produced by orchestras normally made up of fifty to sixty players, and because there are so many of these there is work for a great number of musicians.'

With the arrival of spring the climate became unhealthy and the Italians — or at least those who were able to afford it — retired to Tivoli, whilst the English migrated to Venice so as to witness the great festival of the Ascension, when the Doge throws a ring into the sea as a token of the city's marriage with the sea. Elcho put in a request for a farewell audience. 'The same precautions were taken as on my previous visit. I was received in the same courteous fashion and made to sit next to the Chevalier, who entrusted me with messages for my father.' He also told Elcho that in the case of a rebellion taking place in Scotland he would be put in command of the Body Guard, which it would be his duty to both raise and train. He was delighted and spontaneously promised the Chevalier to serve him all his life. The strategy had worked; Elcho had fallen into a trap from which he was never to extricate himself.

He left Rome extremely grateful for the good time he had enjoyed. It was probably the happiest period of his life. 'The Chevalier seems to me to be a most affable, well-informed and sensible Prince. He is good at managing his affairs and the pensions he grants are regularly paid... but his great weakness is his bigotry.' As to Charles Edward, six months of daily contact had left Elcho with a poor opinion of him. His appalling lack of education as shown by his spelling, and his ignorance of a country over which he hoped one day to reign, augured ill for the future. 'He appears to have no other interests but shooting and music [the latent antipathy between Elcho and the Prince, to erupt so memorably at Culloden, already showing]. The Duke of York has far better manners and is more popular. Lord Dunbar is a man of the world and should have been able to give him a better education, which he is accused of having neglected; Sir Thomas Sheridan is an ardent Papist with no knowledge of how England is governed, and who holds the loftiest notions about the divine right of kings and absolute power.'

The Royal family having left for its summer quarters at Albano, the time had come for Elcho to continue the grand tour. Having in his words 'learnt from the French how to be economical' he could now afford to travel by *vitorino*, and he left for Venice in company of a French man with whom he had made friends, where he rejoined Horace Walpole, Lord Lincoln, the Pomfrets and their pretty daughters, as well as Pitt and Dashwood. They hired a gondola from which they were able to follow the progress of the *Bucentaure* 'a magnificently carved and gilded vessel the size of a twenty-one gun ship' through the harbour and out to sea where 'the Doge carried out the ceremony of marrying Venice to the sea.'

As was then the custom, Elcho had arrived with letters of introduction to Irish officers in Venetian service, who helped him to track down a distant relative, the Comte de Wemyss, whose ancestor had entered Imperial service. Elcho was to meet the last survivor, 'a very decent sort of man and very attached to the family. He told me that his father and two of his brothers had been generals; that they had owned land in the Morea which they had lost in 1715, when it had been conquered by the Turks, and that although he possessed a small place in the country, he was by no means rich. We dined together every day.'

The friends now separated and Elcho headed for Paris by way of the Tyrol and Bavaria. Up to now he seems to have been unaware of what was happening in the world of politics. He was therefore only vaguely aware that the death of the Emperor Charles VI, which had occurred whilst he was travelling to Rome from Florence had put Europe into a state of turmoil.

The Emperor had died with an easy mind in the belief that he had ensured the succession of his daughter, Maria Theresa. However the ambitious young king of Prussia, Frederick II, now seized Silesia by means of a whirlwind campaign. As if this were not enough, the Elector of Bavaria, backed by the French who saw in him a useful tool in their centuries-old rivalry with the House of Hapsburg, laid claim to the Imperial Crown which the late Emperor had destined for Maria Theresa's husband, Charles of Lorraine. As Elector of Hanover, King George would inevitably play his part in the coming election and would side with Maria Theresa, thus putting England at odds with France.

Jacobite hopes rose as a restoration could only be achieved with the help of a foreign Power. Ormonde and Marischal's failure in 1739 to induce the Spaniards to attempt an invasion of Britain had been a bitter disappointment. But France would be a far better ally. So while Elcho had been busily exploring Rome, the Palazzo Muti had been abuzz with plans and intrigues of which, however, he remained completely unaware, and it was only on entering Austrian territory that he became dimly conscious that something untoward was happening. In Nymphenburg he noted that Maréchal de Belleisle was walking in the garden with the Elector of Bavaria, evidently discussing the war they were planning to wage.

It was June 1741 when Elcho reached Paris, where he took up his quarters in an hotel, and started leading the life 'of all Englishmen. I had a hackney coach, and masters came in the morning to teach me music, dancing and mathematics. My dancing master was no other than the celebrated Marseille, who charged six francs per lesson and arrived in a carriage with two lackeys behind. Not only did he teach one how to dance, but also how to walk, to bow, to enter a drawing room, to sit down and to serve meals. All French gentlemen receive this training which explains that ease of manner which distinguishes them from members of other nations.'

As was his wont Elcho went to see all the sights, attended the *Comédie Française*, the *Comédie Italienne* and the Opera. He went to Versailles 'to have a look at the Dauphin and the other members of the Royal Family.' However, he was not presented, there being no British Representative in Paris at the time. Paris society paid little attention to young foreigners, however well born and well heeled they might be, and he was reduced to the company of the friends he had made in Italy, the Pomfrets, Lord Lincoln and Horace Walpole. He makes no mention of prominent Jacobites although he must have met some at the house of his banker, Aeneas Macdonald, younger brother of a Highland laird, a fervent supporter of the Stuart Cause and one who was to accompany Charles Edward to Scotland four years later. 'Like many other young gentlemen, I had a mistress, an actress from the Opera. She was kept by an old Lieutenant General who gave her fifty louis d'or a month, so all I had to pay for were the suppers we had together, and the trips we took to visit the royal palaces of St Germain, Marly, Meudon, etc.'

He had been four months in Paris when he was summoned home by his father under pretext that a rich marriage was in the offing. 'My mistress had become so attached to me that I had all the trouble in the world to get away, she being bent on following me to London. On the day of my departure I was about to step into my post-chaise when she arrived before my hotel and created such an uproar with her tears and her cries, that a crowd gathered in the streets and I had to leave by another door and betake myself to the house of Mr Macdonald, where the post-chaise was brought by my tutor. We were about to set off by the St Denis road when my servant, whom I had sent on to secure post horses, came to warn me that the young lady was waiting for me at the barrier. So I gave orders to the postillion to take another route, and we arrived safely at Calais where we embarked for Dover.'

CHAPTER FOUR

The Making of a Jacobite

'I posted from Dover to London, and as I was wearing my hair French fashion, high boots, my hair in a plait, a Parisian whip and a Parisian cocked hat I was taken for a Frenchman; and as I rode through Rochester the people cried "French dog" and threw stones at me all along the street. Clapping spurs to my horse, I was able to rid myself of the mob without getting hurt.' Elcho felt bewildered: 'I have seen Englishmen walking in the streets of Paris in the dress of their country — and very strange it seemed in French eyes — as unmolested as the French themselves. At the worst someone might say "what an odd way of dressing" '. It was enough to bemuse a young man just back form the Grand Tour, when his time had been taken up with sightseeing and listening to music in company of friends.

On his arrival in London he fell in with his brother James, who had recently joined the navy as a midshipman, and was on his way to join his ship. They must have met as strangers, for James was not even born when Elcho had been sent away from Wemyss. 'I now discovered that the reason for my father recalling me was that he was in serious financial straits, having contracted debts of £50,000 [multiply by eighty to get the present-day value] since his father's death.' The prospect of a rich marriage was nothing but a bait to lure him home. He must have found some comfort in the thought that the colonel's legacy must be safe.

Britain was then in the throes of an acute attack of election fever and an Opposition made up of disgruntled Whigs and Hanoverian Tories, as well as Jacobites, was straining every nerve to turn Walpole out. No pamphlet was too libellous, no rumour too slanderous, no caricature too outrageous to serve their purpose, whilst the war with Spain was providing them with yet another stick with which to beat him: every success being attributed to the admirals, every reverse to the meanness of a Government which had allowed the ships to fall into disrepair.

The War of Jenkins' Ear of 1739, which had raised Jacobite hopes, had not lived up to their expectations. Though Ormonde and Marischal had failed to entice the Spaniards into attempting a new invasion, up to now things had gone well for the British. However, the tide seemed to be turning. 'News had reached the capital of the raising of the siege of Carthagena, and the death of Lord Cathcart who commanded the troops.' But the fighting was taking place in South America, too far away to have much impact on what was happening at home. The situation seemed more threatening on the Continent where 'the French had crossed the Rhine on the way to Bavaria.' Hanover might soon get involved. As it was, the public affected to be outraged at the way the French were treating the Queen of Hungary, as Maria Theresa was then called; hence Elcho's adventures at Rochester. It looked as if England would soon be at war with France, which was the necessary precondition for a Jacobite restoration.

Having run short of money Elcho left by post for Edinburgh. 'I was met by my father, as well as by my brother Mr Charteris and my four sisters, Frances (known as Fanny), Walpole, Anne and Helen who were then in an Edinburgh boarding school.' It must have all been somewhat embarrassing, for with the exception of his father, who had paid him but one visit all the time he was at Winchester, and Frances with whom he had remained in correspondence, he had had no contacts with his family since he had come to England eight years before. 'I then left with my father for Wemyss Castle, visiting the Earl and Countess of Moray opposite to Edinburgh on the Fife shore at Donibristle. I was acquainted with the deplorable state of my father's affairs, which was attributed to his residence in England, and the way he had neglected his Scottish estate.' The situation was even worse than depicted in the *Journal*, for Lord Wemyss had lain hands on the silver his mother-in-law, Mrs Charteris, had left to his wife with a proviso that it should go to Elcho, or whichever of her grandchildren might need it. What was still worse from Elcho's point of view, was that his father had found a way of laying hands on the Colonel's legacy, to which he was helping himself in a large way. The stay at Wemyss cannot have passed off peacefully. On parting his father gave him a paltry £100 with the advice to get himself a rich wife.

The Earl of Sutherland, who had married Lady Elisabeth Wemyss, Lady Moray's sister, now took pity on his unfortunate nephew. The Earl of Sutherland was an important personage indeed, combining, as he did, the roles of chieftain of a large and powerful clan and prominent member of the Hanoverian establishment. His ancestor had taken sides with Dutch William, whilst he had finished his education in Hanover instead of the more habitual Italy, after the usual stop in France to learn the language. He was a representative peer, one of the handful of Scottish peers who took their seats in the House of Lords, and as he was about to leave for London to take his seat in the new Parliament, he invited Elcho, Fanny and Francis to come with him.

As we have seen, the Jacobites had great hopes of Elcho, and they cannot but have been perturbed at the way he was being taken in charge by this great Whig magnate. Sir James Steuart of Goodtrees was sent to the rescue and renewed the friendship started at Lyon. 'Whilst in Scotland I had seen Sir James,' wrote Elcho, 'He was amongst the most ardent of the Scottish Jacobites,' and such were his powers of persuasion that it was as a keen Jacobite that Elcho travelled down to London. In the view of a Scottish lady who knew him well, Sir James was 'a Jacobite with Whig principles.' That about sums him up.

> We arrived on St Andrew's Day 1741. I took rooms with my brother in Pall Mall Street. He was about to start on his travels and I induced him to take my old tutor Mr Mackenzie, despite the opposition of the Duke of Argyll, who was his guardian, and who wanted him to be in the care of a man attached to the Hanoverian cause. On my arrival in London I received the visit of the Earl of Lincoln, who

was a gentleman-in-waiting, and who offered to present me to the
King and the Court, and of Mr Walpole who offered to recommend
me to his father, the Prime Minister, with a view of my getting a
civilian or military appointment. Knowing my father's feelings on
the subject, I refused the obliging offers made by these gentlemen
and frequented the Coco Tree where the Jacobites were in the habit
of gathering.

Elcho continued to take a vivid interest in his surroundings:

> It was the first session of the new Parliament, so I went to the
> House of Lords on the first day, and being the eldest son of a peer,
> I took my stand behind the throne. The King entered with his crown
> on his head, dressed in his royal robes, the sceptre in his right hand
> and the globe in his left. he took his seat upon the throne with the
> Prince of Wales on his right hand the Duke of Cumberland on his
> left. Then came the archbishops, dukes, marquises, earls, viscounts,
> barons and bishops to the right and left, ranged according to their
> rank, all clothed in their scarlet robes lined with ermine. The King
> now summoned the House of Commons, which arrived headed by
> the Speaker, Mr Onslow, and remained standing whilst the peers
> remained seated. . ... The ceremony was very impressive.

> During my stay in London Lord Stafford (an Irish peer) arrived
> from Paris that winter and I went to see him. He was a great admirer
> of France and French manners. He invited me to dine, and as his
> hotel was quite close to the park, we went there for a walk before
> dinner. He had a French muff and carried his hat under his arm,
> which led people to make insulting remarks about his clothes, he
> being taken for a Frenchman. After dinner he suggested taking me
> to a play, and we found ourselves in a box in Drury Lane. As soon
> as we were seen by the pit and the gallery, they started shouting, '
> French dog, down with the muff!' and other foolish things. Seeing
> that we paid no attention, they took to spitting on us from above
> and throwing apples and candles from below until we were obliged
> to leave the theatre. Lord Stafford has never since lived in London,
> but always in Paris.

Elcho longed to join Francis in France. So he asked his mother
for a loan 'under any terms'. She was now living in Taplow on the

Thames, where she was building herself a house, and could not, or would not oblige. By January 1742 he had spent most of the £100 his father had given him, and there being no rich heiress in the offing, he sought refuge at Hornby, a Lancashire estate the Colonel had won gambling and which now belonged to his younger brother, Francis. He therefore did not witness the wild enthusiasm with which the fall of Sir Robert Walpole was greeted in London. However, life in the country was never much to his taste, and as soon as the condition of his finances permitted, he returned to Wemyss where he was made welcome by 'many relations who took an interest in the welfare of our house, and more especially Lord Sinclair [the Master of Sinclair] and the Earl of Leven.'

The Earl of Leven had remained true to his family's traditions in both religion and politics, being a dedicated Presbyterian and a loyal supporter of the Protestant Succession. He had, however, exchanged the sword for the pen and was a senator of the College of Justice and a Chamberlain to King George, as well as a leading member of Scottish society with a fine house near Edinburgh. Both Leven and his son, Lord Balgonie, tried to wean him away from Jacobitism, as they rightly feared that it would get him into serious trouble. But it was the arguments of his neighbour at Dysart House, the Master of Sinclair, which were to carry most weight. 'Lord Sinclair had spent a long time in exile [for his part in the '15]. He owed his pardon to his brother, General Sinclair, to whom he had made over his property before going into exile. He knew I had been brought up a Jacobite by my father, a cause whose strength and weaknesses he well understood. He told me that the Stuarts were ungrateful; that they looked upon everything done for them as a mere discharge of duty; that they preferred winning over those who served the House of Hanover [a dig at Sir James Steuart then staying at Wemyss]rather than conciliating those who were ready to sacrifice their all for their sakes; in short it would be madness to risk life and fortune for such people and he strongly advised me to abandon and enter English service, all of which I have since verified for myself. I was greatly tempted to follow his advice, but was prevented from doing so by Sir James.'

It is probably at this stage that Elcho was let into the Jacobite secrets as a means of attaching him firmly to the Cause, for after a long period of quiescence the Jacobites were again active. Elcho was still at Angers when the veteran Aberdeenshire laird called Gordon of Glenbucket (Glenbuchat on the upper Don) had gone to Rome averring that twenty thousand Highlanders were ready to rise if they were furnished with arms. The suggestion was turned down by the Chevalier who rightly judged it to be unrealistic. But he did despatch an agent to Scotland who recruited seven devoted Jacobites who formed themselves into the 'Association' with a view of keeping in close touch with the Palazzo Muti, and carrying out the Chevalier's instructions.

The 'Associators', as they came to be called, were not an impressive lot. The highest in rank was the young Duke of Perth, dubbed a 'horse-loving boy' by Horace Walpole. This was unfair: his was a very gallant spirit encased in a fragile body, and he was to take an active part in the Rising despite being continually ill. However, what singled him out was his Catholicism and his blind obedience to the will of his master. With him was his uncle who ostensibly led a retired life in Perthshire. Another Catholic was the Earl of Traquair whose seat was in the Borders. He had close links with his co-religionists in the South and acted as liaison officer with the English Jacobites. Another Associator was that old reprobate Simon Fraser, Lord Lovat, who had started his career by forcibly bedding the widow of one of his relatives, after which he had retired to France where he placed himself at the disposal of Louis XIV, and turned Catholic to win the support of that all powerful bigot, Madame de Maintenon. He was to pursue throughout his life a devious course, and no one quite knew where his loyalties lay. But he was very powerful as he could rely on the blind obedience of the numerous clan of Fraser. Lochiel, the acting Chief of the Camerons (his father still lived in exile) was an Episcopalian and Associator. He was short of money having kept the clan ruinously at full strength, far in excess of what the hills of

Lochaber could sustain. Finally there was Lochiel's father-in-law, Sir John Campbell of Auchenbreck, on the verge of bankruptcy. Murray of Broughton was later added to the group. He had studied at Leyden, after which he had gone to Rome. He was later described by Louis XV's delegate as 'the only Jacobite I have met with a good head on his shoulders.' He might had added that he was devoured by ambition and according to Elcho, was chronically short of money.

The Associators had as their foreign delegate William Drummond (or MacGregor) of Balhaldie, a first cousin to Lochiel, and like Lochiel, short of cash. His orders were to work in close collaboration with the Jacobite peer, Lord Sempill. Sempill was in all but in name a Frenchman and was generally believed to be in French pay. In March 1741 — Elcho still being in Rome at the time — Balhaldie returned to Scotland with the news that it was King Louis' intention to send money and Irish troops to Scotland, and that they were due to arrive in the autumn of 1742, or at the latest the following spring.

The Jacobites now sprang into action: instructions were issued to recruit as many adherents as it was sage to do and to raise funds. The former proved easier than the latter, there being a great deal of merely sentimental Jacobitism lying about. Sir James Steuart proved particularly successful over the former, according to his son 'he converted more people to Jacobitism than anyone else.'

Elcho now left Wemyss Castle and went to Edinburgh in company with Sir James. He had been invited to the General Assembly of the Church of Scotland where Lord Leven was High Commissioner that year. He had been brought up to despise Presbyterians. In an effort to counter the 'pernicious' influence of the Kirk, the Jacobites now held the annual parade of the Royal Company of Archers. That year it was led through the streets of Leith by the Earl of Wemyss in his capacity of Lieutenant General, for the Captain General, the ever prudent Duke of Hamilton, had remained at home. Elcho tells us that 'they were on their way to shoot at a white target after which they dined together, the day ended with a ball given for the Edinburgh young ladies. I was assistant major.' The banquet was traditional, as it afforded yet another opportunity for drinking the king's health over the finger bowls, but the ball was a new departure for which he may well have been responsible, for he dearly loved a party. Handsome, and dressed in the striking uniform lovingly designed by his grandfather, he must have caused many a damsel's heart to flutter!

The Earls of Sutherland and Leven took the opportunity of the spendthrift Earl of Wemyss being in Scotland to challenge the way he was running the estate to the detriment of his heir's interests. The confrontation took place at Wemyss 'where the Earl was presented with a list of his debts by Lords Leven and Sutherland who were worried by the poor state of his finances. As this was largely due to his continual residence in England, I suggested we should live together at Wemyss, and added that I was willing to forego my claim to the £10,000 left me by my grandfather, Mr Charteris, and which he had taken to pay his debts. He refused my offer but suggested I should take over the estate and pay him an annual sum which would enable him to go on living in England. I was, however, unable to accept this offer, the sum he demanded being too large. So he returned to England and I went to Edinburgh to see my relative Mr Fletcher of Milton (then the Lord Advocate) who advised me to take out a mortgage for my £10,000 on the Wemyss estate, which I did.' This proved to be but a palliative, and Elcho was never able to prevent his father from helping himself to the Colonel's legacy.

Finding himself at a loose end, Elcho accepted the Sutherland's invitation to accompany them home to Dunrobin, visiting friends and relations on the way. With them went Lady Fanny who had finished her schooling in Edinburgh, and had nowhere else to go. Politics were no barrier and both Whigs and Jacobites figure amongst their hosts, one of these being Duncan Forbes of Culloden, the influential Lord President of the Court of Session who lived on the friendliest of terms with his Highland neighbours, many of whom were Jacobites.

At Dunrobin, 'the Earl lived the life of a monarch; his castle was guarded by his people; the fare was sumptuous; the wine came straight from Dunkirk without paying duty and the whole of Sutherlandshire was his except the part of the country of the Mackays which belonged to Lord Reay.' Elcho might have added that both chieftains were staunch supporters of the Protestant succession. 'It is a good country for game there being stag in abundance and white partridges.' However, even the 'sumptuous fare' could not reconcile Elcho with life in the country, and he was delighted to accept Lord Sutherland's invitation to accompany him to Edinburgh. He no doubt hoped to get news of the French expedition which was due to arrive very soon but he discovered that during his absence the Associators had received a discouraging letter from Balhaldie which had led them to send Murray of Broughton to Paris to find out how things stood.

As Murray of Broughton was not yet back from France, Elcho returned to Dunrobin taking with him Sir James Steuart of Goodtrees, who had asked 'the permission to pay court to my sister. Not only did I give my consent, but I promised to take him myself to Dunrobin. In the meantime I introduced him to the Earl of Sutherland with whom we left for Dunrobin on New Year's Day 1743. The Highlands were deep in snow, and I saw Highlanders who had been overtaken by the night get up from the snow in which they had slept and continue their journey as if they had just got up from a good bed.' At first the path of true love proved somewhat stony, and Sir James 'endured the pleasures and pains of courtship ... for love was for some time withheld, whilst her father's prudence had to be satisfied'. (However the obstacles were duly overcome and the marriage was celebrated at Dunrobin in October 1743. It proved to be a great success.)

In the meantime the two friends returned to Edinburgh, possibly in the hope of hearing Murray of Broughton's report on what he had seen in Paris. He had been greeted on his arrival in the French capital with the news that Cardinal Fleury was dead, but had been assured by Sempill and Balhaldie that nothing had changed. However it soon became clear that the promised expedition would not happen. An audience with Cardinal de Tencin, reputed to be the Chevalier's champion, proved equally unrewarding as it had only lasted a few minutes, whilst the new Foreign Secretary, Amelot, professed he had never even heard of the business!

The Jacobites did not lose heart and started bombarding Louis XV with pleas to come to their rescue. Conditions were beginning to look more favourable. The war which started well for the French, had faltered when Frederick of Prussia pulled out, he having achieved his goal which was to annex Silesia. This had so weakened the French that they were now in full retreat. The thought began to arise that the way out of their difficulties was to stage an English diversion.

Shortage of funds had again obliged Elcho to seek refuge at Hornby, a property of the Charteris grandfather near Lancaster, from where he emerged in June 1743. He first went to Wentworth to stay with his friend, Lord Strafford, 'where I was very well received and then on to London where I heard that the Allies, under the command of the King of England, had defeated the French under the command of Maréchal de Noailles at Dettingen.' The country had gone mad with joy; the King was ceasing to be unpopular.

This did not detract Elcho from having a good time, he being on pleasure bent. 'I returned to my lodgings in Suffolk Street, and would spend the afternoons at Ranelagh and Fox Hall [Vauxhall]". It was in the leafy groves of these pleasure gardens that he seems to have lost his heart for the first time. He had inherited many of the Colonel's traits, amongst them something of his amorous disposition, and as we have seen, he had started frequenting brothels when still at school. But his heart remained untouched. 'I now had the honour of making the acquaintance of Lady Caroline Fitzroy, daughter of the Duke of Grafton and one of the most amiable ladies in England.' It is the only time one finds even a hint of romance in the pages of the *Journal*, although there are plenty of references to affairs. Events were to nip the romance in the bud, if romance it was.

In September 1743 Elcho was instructed to go to Paris and stay on the way with the Earl Marischal at Boulogne. George Keith, 10th Earl Marischal, was about fifty at this time. He had been serving in Marlborough's armies when he learnt in 1715 that the Royal Standard had been unfurled, which led him to leave his regiment. The rising having collapsed, he sought refuge in Spain in the company of his brother, to whom he was very attached. In 1719 he was placed in charge of a small Spanish contingent which landed in Scotland, where he met up with the Marquis of Tullibardine, the Jacobite son of the staunchly Whig Duke of Atholl, who had been placed by the Chevalier at the head of the very few clansmen who had rallied to his call. Tullibardine had also united his regiment to take part in the '15 in company of a younger brother, Lord George Murray. But here the resemblance ended. Marischal was extremely intelligent, exceptionally well read, and very independently-minded, whilst poor loyal Tullibardine is continually referred to as a "poppinjay". A clash was inevitable, and it proved so bitter that they had to pitch their respective camps at some distance from each other, thus weakening what had been from the start a pretty hopeless venture.

Marischal entered Spanish service, but as a volunteer, his refusal to convert to Catholicism precluding him from holding a commission. He loved Spain: the people, the climate the food, but not the priests. In Elcho's *Journal* he appears as kindly and uncensorious, but unforgiving when crossed. Elcho found him 'living with Mademoiselle Emetee, a Turkish girl his brother had captured at the siege of Otchakoff. (In fact the relationship was platonic at her request). He had two servants, a Turk called Ibrahim and a Tartar, Stepan by name.' Such was the strange household in which Elcho now found himself, and with which he was to become very familiar as time went by. The two men took to each other, each supplying what was lacking in the life of the other: the company of a greatly beloved younger brother now far away in Russia, and the father figure which had never as yet existed.

Elcho now left for Paris, where he stayed at the Hotel d'Orléans at his brother's expense. 'He paid for my food and lodging as well as for a hackney coach.' But it was no longer the Paris of yore, with its glamorous lessons in deportment and its sightseeing expeditions in company of his adoring little mistress. Daniel O'Brien — later Lord Lismore — who was the Chevalier's official representative at the Court of Versailles, put his trust in Cardinal de Tencin. But it was Sempill and Balhaldie who had the upper hand, having the ear of Amelot, the foreign secretary. Marischal looked on from afar. He did not conceal the contempt he felt for their machinations, with the result that they loathed him.

Elcho made the acquaintance of the two conspirators at the house of his banker friend, Aeneas MacDonald. He was later to tell Murray of Broughton that they, Sempill and Balhaldie, were looked upon as being 'low-life fellows void of truth. . . [They] had had dealings with Lord Marischal, who had found them so false that he positively refused to have any more to do with them; that they had tried all methods to get him to give credit to their negotiations, but that his Lordship had laughed at their attempts, and said 'til they could give him security for their speaking the truth he would have nothing to do with them.'

Another welcome caller was Lord John Drummond, brother of the Duke of Perth, who was in French service. Elcho had met him at the time of his first arrival in France, when Drummond was a captain in an Irish regiment, as were most Scotsmen in French pay. But this made recruiting in Scotland difficult, there being a congenital dislike of serving under the Irish, and recruits tended to join the Dutch regiments. This with the possibility of a descent on Scotland had led to the formation of the *Royal Ecossais*; the plan being to 'confer captaincies on those Highland Chiefs known to be loyal to the House of Stuart.'

The arrival at the Hotel d'Orléans of Elcho's old schoolfellow, Lord Drumlanrig, must have been like a breath of fresh air in this over-heated and fetid atmosphere of intrigue and recrimination. France and England were not yet at war (France was supposedly supporting the Bavarian Emperor and England his Hapsburg rival,

Maria Theresa) and Drumlanrig had come to Paris to have a last
fling before joining his regiment in Flanders. Did he, like Leven,
Sinclair, Duncan Forbes the Lord President and his other wellwishers, endeavour to wean Elcho from the Jacobite cause? 'The
King of England was then at Worms with his army, and I was so
dissatisfied by the way I was being treated by my father, who never
repaid me any of the money he owed me, and was most irregular in
paying the interest, that I felt a great desire to go to Worms to seek
employment. I was dissuaded by my old tutor, Mr Mackenzie, who
assured me that my brother, whom he had turned into a Jacobite,
intended to give me £40,000 at his majority.' At this particularly
critical moment Elcho's defection from the Jacobite cause would
have given the lie to the Jacobite assertion that the regime was
universally hated, whilst the Stuarts were greatly beloved.

In order to get Elcho safely out of temptations's way Mackenzie
suggested he should take his brother to Rome. The brothers had
started off, but had got no further than Fontainebleau, where the
Court was in residence. But the prospect of having to cross the
Alps in winter was too awful even to contemplate. So they went
instead to Angers, where they were made very welcome by Elcho's
old headmaster, M. de Pignerol, who was so pleased to see him
again that 'he refused to take any money for our board and lodging'.

Back in Paris, they plunged into the social life of the capital.
'We went to the play and to public balls, and we frequented the
house of the Countess of Sandwich, where the French were wont
to foregather. We also saw all the English and Scots, as well as the
Baron d'Anstruth, whose ancestor had settled in Burgundy three
hundred years ago, having originally come from Fife.' It was
probably through Drumlanrig, to whom she was related, that the
brothers got an *entrée* into Lady Sandwich's *salon*. Although she
was in her seventies, she had lost none of the 'fire and vivacity' she
had inherited form her father, the 2nd Lord Rochester. She had
settled in Paris after the death of her very dull Tory husband,
averring that she would only return to London when a Stuart was
again on the throne. But her Jacobitism was sentimental rather

than political, and she opened her doors to all who found grace in her eyes, regardless of their political affiliations. Clearly Elcho made himself agreeable, his expensive lessons in deportment having allowed him to mix freely in any society however exclusive it might be.

It must have been some French friend of Lady Sandwich's who procured for the brothers invitations to the marriage of the Duc d'Orléans. It was fortunate that Francis had plenty of money, for the 'magnificent clothes' he had made for himself and his penurious brother must have cost a fortune.

> On the day of the wedding the Court presented a brilliant sight. The King and the Princes were dressed in gold and silver embroidered with diamonds, the nobles had embroidery on the seams of their coats and the ladies' dresses were also embroidered in gold and silver. In the morning we attended the ceremony which took place in the chapel at Versailles, and in the evening we watched the King play Lansquenet. He was seated in the company of several Princes and ambassadors, whilst the spectators, who stood round the table, could stake money on their hands. I lost twenty-five *louis d'or.*

Elcho also frequented less reputable circles.

> I was fortunate in escaping from a terrible accident in which several of my acquaintances were killed. I had arranged a supper-party with several courtesans, a Hanoverian baron and a few Swedes and Danes which, however, I was prevented from attending through the inflammation of my bowels, which kept me at home for a long time. The house caught fire whilst the guests were at supper, the floor collapsed, and the whole party, which was thinking of nothing but pleasure, was precipitated into the flames and was burnt to death, some fourteen or fifteen of them. I later went to see the ruins of the house.

King George's victory at Dettingen was not a great battle in military terms, but it was to have far-reaching political repercussions. The French, who had been frightened out of their wits, now started looking round for ways of dealing with the threat to their military superiority, and the usefulness of the Jacobites came to their mind. At best an invasion of England might lead to a hostile German monarch being replaced by one whose forebears had been subservient to the French Crown; at worst, it would oblige the British to withdraw their troops from Flanders.

However, before embarking on what would be a major operation, it was thought prudent to find out more about English Jacobitism. The first informant to be summoned to Versailles was a Boulogne merchant, a friend of Smith, the Jacobite agent who had greeted Elcho on his first arrival. He had serious reservations as to the wisdom of the enterprise, and believed that those in Elcho's words 'might well be living under delusions. Many so-called Jacobites were merely malcontents and even should it succeed, James might well have to conform to the will of Parliament, as Queen Anne had been obliged to do. Nor could one rely on the whole-hearted support of the Catholics. Many were well content with the freedom they now enjoyed, and there was always the fear of rousing the dreaded cry of 'no popery'. Above all, the nation would never accept a monarch imposed upon it by a foreign Power, and above all not by France.'

By some means best known to himself, Sempill must have managed to discredit this all too truthful document, and get the canny merchant replaced by a naive young equerry of Irish extraction called James Butler. The whole thing was superbly stage-managed by Balhaldie, who never left the envoy's side. They crossed the Channel under pretext of buying horses, and on their arrival Butler was presented with the names of seventy peers who, he was told, were ready to lend their support. The fact that no signatures were appended to the document went unnoticed — some so-called signatories might well have been surprised to find themselves on the list! He was also given the names of aldermen pledged to return the city of London to its rightful sovereign, and he was widely entertained by Tory squires, whose enthusiasm for the cause increased with the number of their libations, the whole thing being crowned by a great banquet held during the Lichfield races, when only one of the hundred or so guests refused to drink the health of the 'King over the water.' When Butler asked how it was that so unpopular a regime should still be in power, he was told that the Elector of Hanover had placed 'fanatical mercenaries at the head of the armed forces, and that the country was riddled with spies'.

The matter was finally clinched on 15th November 1743, when Britain, Austria, Saxony and Sardinia signed a treaty of alliance. Preparations for the counter-stroke of a French invasion now went ahead as secretly as possible, for Britain and France were still at peace, and it was hoped to spring a surprise. The plan was to land a force at Maldon on the Essex coast which would march on London, where it would hopefully be acclaimed as liberators. This would be followed by the landing in Scotland of the Irish regiment promised. They would be joined by the twenty thousand clansmen reported by Glenbucket as being ready to rise, the Scottish operation being under the command of the Earl Marischal, whilst that in England was, at least nominally, to be under that of the Duke of Ormonde, the Maréchal de Saxe being really in charge. That King Louis should appoint this prestigious soldier, already looked upon as the greatest commander of his day, shows the importance he attached to the operation.

Elcho was in the habit of frequenting the house of his banker friend, Aeneas Macdonald, and in December 1743, he noticed the absence of the confidential clerk, Duncan Buchanan. On enquiring where he was,

> I was told in confidence that he had left for Rome in company of Mr Macgregor of Balhaldie, and that I would soon learn the purpose of the journey. Sure enough, these gentlemen, who had travelled by way of Switzerland, had gone to Rome which they left in the company of Prince Charles. They had embarked at Genoa on a *filulque*, had safely sailed through the British fleet commanded by Admiral Matthews and had landed at [Antibes] from where they had come to Paris where the Prince lodged at the house of Lord Sempill.

There had been a certain amount of speculation about the Prince's escapade, of which Elcho gives a fairly accurate account. What is clear is that it was the work of Sempill and Balhaldie, either at the instigation, or more probably with the connivance of Amelot, whom Sempill seems to have had under his thumb. What is not clear is King Louis' attitude. Charles believed himself to be in Paris at Louis' invitation, but he may well have been deliberately misinformed by the two conspirators. His arrival had certainly placed Louis in a dilemma: on the one hand his presence with the expedition gave a certain air of respectability to what was, in fact, an unwarrantable act of aggression in time of peace; on the other, the presence of a Stuart prince on French soil was in flagrant breach of the Treaty of Utrecht, and as such much resented by the German allies. Hence the secrecy surrounding Charles Edward's stay in the capital.

What the pair had evidently not anticipated was his bringing commissions for Marischal and Elcho. They had whittled down the Scottish part of the plan to a mere token force of six hundred men, and had deliberately dropped Marischal from their calculations, even omitting to keep him informed of what was happening, whilst Ormonde was treated in the same cavalier fashion.   However, it was difficult to disregard entirely a man appointed by the Chevalier to command an operation destined to put him back on the throne. All that could be done was to raise as many obstacles as possible in his way.

> After a fortnight, Lord Sempill brought Lord Marischal to see the Prince, and a fortnight later it was my turn. I found him drinking tea. He opened and shut the door himself, and seemed very keen that his presence in Paris should not be known. He told me that he had been sent for by the King of France, who had promised to send him to England at the head of a force ten thousand strong which would be under the command of the Maréchal de Saxe.   It was assembled at Dunkirk and was ready to sail; and he handed me in his father's name a commission of colonel of Dragoons. He had told the same tale to Lord Marischal, whom he appointed, always

in his father's name, head of the force which was to invade Scotland, and we were both ordered to go to Dunkirk at the end of February [1744], Lord Marischal, who had not been consulted, and who was unaware of what was going on, felt embarrassed as he did not possess the money needed to go to Dunkirk in the guise of a general, so I induced my brother to lend him seven hundred *louis d'or*.

Francis also gave Elcho three hundred gold coins which he was later able to return. 'Some time later the Prince went to Gravelines in company with Mr MacGregor of Balhaldie, where he remained incognito all the time of his stay, whilst Lord Marischal went to Dunkirk with Lord Lewis Gordon, Mr MacDonald of Glengarry and M. de la Guerches who were to act as his aides-de-camp'

The expedition had originally been billed to sail on January 9th. But the departure had been delayed, possibly in order to await the Prince's arrival. Further delays had been caused by the remissness of the English Jacobites. Lord Caryll, who acted as liaison officer, was constantly bringing over messages to the effect that winter was not the proper time to start an invasion; that the landing should only take place after the break-up of Parliament, as the mass departure of the Jacobite MPs would betray its existence— a foolish argument at a time when the English papers were full of nothing else. Worse still, the promised pilot never turned up, and Saxe had to go as far as Bordeaux to find one familiar with these waters. The great man was getting understandably impatient with people so reluctant to be freed from the intolerable yoke of the German tyrant. He was beginning to have serious doubts as to the accuracy of the Jacobite reports, those of his own agents giving a very different picture of the situation: in the coastal towns the inhabitants were furbishing their arms so as to repel the invaders, whilst pledges of loyalty were streaming into St James' Palace. Nor were matters better at sea. M. de Roquefeuille, whose task it was to protect the convoys, had been defeated by Admiral Norris and had died shortly after of a stroke, whilst many of the transports had been scattered and sunk during two terrible gales, when many men had been drowned. These disasters provided the French Government with a useful pretext for shelving an operation they had already decided to abandon.

It was 11th March before Elcho reached Dunkirk in the midst of the last of these gales. He must have found the Earl Marischal as angry and frustrated as was Saxe, for Sempill was using his influence with Amelot to make things as difficult as possible for the Scottish expedition. The promised three thousand men turned out to be a paltry six hundred; not a penny was forthcoming towards his expenses, and worst of all, his repeated demands for instructions remained unanswered. At the start Saxe had not even deigned to receive him, although by the end he was declaring him to be the only Jacobite possessing any sense at all. 'Lord Marischal often went to see him so as to find out if any instructions had come for him. He was told that he would go to Scotland with an Irish regiment, but that he would only leave after the departure of the expedition destined for the Thames'.

It fell to the Earl Marischal to apprise Charles Edward that the expedition was being abandoned. The Prince was in despair and suggested they should hire a ship and go it alone. 'This Lord Marischal refused to do. The Prince was very ignorant of what was happening in the United Kingdom, and he had been persuaded by his tutor . . . 'that the House of Hanover was detested and that the whole country would rally to his standard on his appearance and desert the reigning monarch.' The expedition being now over, Elcho went to Boulogne in search of a ship for Scotland. He was acting against the advice of the Earl Marischal who had grown very fond of him. 'He feared I should be arrested on arrival and he wanted me to go to Sweden where his brother, Marshal Keith, was ambassador.' But Elcho relied on the protection of his powerful kinsman, the Lord Advocate. 'I embarked on a Scottish ship, landed on the East Lothian coast and went to the house of my brother-in-law, Sir James Steuart. The next day I went to Edinburgh to call on Lord Milton, who asked me many questions about my trip abroad and the Dunkirk affair. I answered that I had spent the winter in Paris and had then gone to the coast in search of a ship to bring me back to

my native land, but on my arrival I discovered that an embargo had
been placed on all shipping, and that as soon as it was raised I had
taken the first available ship to quit a country about to declare war
on Great Britain, and I described Dunkirk as if it were an accident.
He received me very politely and invited me to supper', which Elcho
must have enjoyed, for Milton had a well-established reputation
for being a *gourmet*. It can be assumed that this astute statesman
did not believe a word of the cock-and-bull story of what he had
been up to; but he was fond of his foolish young relative, whom he
hoped would soon see reason and join the British army.

CHAPTER FIVE

The Rising

The news that the French were preparing to invade had led the British Government to prorogue habeas corpus and clap Lord Barrymore and Colonel Cecil into the Tower. This sent the Associators into hiding, from which, however, Murray of Broughton emerged on hearing that Elcho was back from France, from where no news had as yet come. He found him at Goodtrees near Edinburgh in company with Sir James and Lady Fanny, Francis Charteris, and the three unmarried Wemyss girls, whose school fees the Earl said he could no longer afford.

They were united in their impatience to know what had happened to the Prince. Where was he, and what were his plans? As in 1742, Murray of Broughton was sent to Paris to find out where things stood. But England was now at war with France and he could no longer just step on to the Dover packet and proceed openly to the French capital. He must go by way of Flanders, and in order to hide his tracks, he decided to visit the Scottish camp of the British army on the way. This was common practice for those who had friends amongst the higher-ranking officers. But this was not his case; it was, however, that of Elcho who was related to half the Scottish nobility.

At first Elcho demurred: he had never as yet sailed under false colours; having always proclaimed himself to be a Jacobite, and if he went to the camp it would be supposed that he had come in search of a commission. Finally boredom got the better of his scruples. He was living a homeless, aimless and purposeless life, dividing his time between Wemyss, where his father was endeavouring to put some order into his affairs at last, Goodtrees,

Amisfield, the Colonel's place which now belonged to Francis, and Donibristle, seat of the Earl of Moray, who was married to his half-aunt, sister of Lady Sutherland. On arriving in London he found Murray infuriated by the careless ways of the English Jacobites. Had he not found the cyphers just pushed under a bench in a room open to all?

'After having spent a month in London,' Elcho says 'where I received much attention from General Dalziel and other Scotsmen, I proceeded with Mr Broughton [Murray of Broughton] to Dover where we embarked for Ostend where there was an English garrison, and which we reached on 21st August 1744. We spent the night at Bruges', from where they went on by way of Ghent, Oudenard and Tournay, reaching 'the Allied armies encamped on the plain round Lille on the 26th'. The combined forces amounted to 70,000 men. The Maréchal de Saxe was encamped at Courtrai on the Escaut. The allied generals did not get on with each other, and as they did not have the cannon needed to besiege Lille, nothing was being done.'

'On reaching the camp Colonel Campbell, who commanded the Scots Greys, sent me two horses and a groom, and on the 27th I took part in a foraging expedition on the right of the force commanded by General Wentworth. The Duke of Argyll invited me to his tent, and on my return to the camp I dined with General Campbell, who had his nephew, Lord Loudon, with him as well as many other Scottish officers.' The next day Elcho dined with General Sinclair, brother to the Master of Sinclair who had given him so much good advice, and where he met yet more Scottish officers. On the following day he dined with Lord Crawford when they were forty to sit down to dinner. Finally he dined with Mr Barrington and the officers of the 3rd regiment of Foot Guards. 'Mr Stuart, brother of Lord Moray and a cavalry captain in the regiment of Ligonier was kind enough to lend me a tent. There were very few contacts between the Scots and the English.' By the time he left Elcho must have met every Scottish officer serving in Flanders. Unfortunately for him, his visit was not forgotten, and did him irrevocable harm as he came to be seen as a Jacobite agent. Although this was true of Murray of Broughton, whose intention it was to recruit officers for the future Jacobite army, Elcho was not one to pursue such a course: which he would have thought of as being unworthy of a gentleman. But he had allowed himself to be compromised, and this was not forgotten.

The two men now moved on to Brussels where they parted, and in order to while away the time, Elcho indulged in a little trip round Holland. Elcho had lost none of his zest for sightseeing. He started by Amsterdam where he visited the 'Town Hall, the Stock Exchange and the harbour and the canal which leads to Utrecht'. At Leyden he met the 'famous Comte de St Germain. No one knows where he comes from, and he passes himself off as being able to make gold and possessing the secret for prolonging life. All I know about him is that he is a very good violinist.' After having visited the Hague he went to Rotterdam where he had a rendez-vous with Murray of Broughton.

Having remained longer in camp than he had anticipated, the latter had missed his rendez-vous with Balhaldie, who had left on an arms-buying expedition. When they did meet, he was upbraided for having dared keep waiting so important a personage as the Prince's minister, and was then told that there was no way he could get to Paris. At this Broughton stuck his toes in the ground, and said he would travel in the guise of Balhaldie's servant; and it was in this menial capacity that he made his entry into the French capital in the Prince's luxurious carriage Balhaldie had borrowed for the journey. He was now introduced to the Prince at the house of Aeneas Macdonald the banker, and delivered documents amongst which figured a letter from Elcho. He then managed to outwit Sempill and Balhadie, who were endeavouring to prevent him from meeting the Prince in private. It was a frustrated young man that Murray met on the following day behind the Tuilleries stables. Charles Edward, who still seemed to believe that he had come at the invitation of the King of France, had been kept incognito until the expedition had been called off; he had then expected to be received with full honours at Versailles, instead of which he was told that he must remain incognito! The fact was that his presence was embarrassing; already the German princes were protesting at this flagrant breach of the Treaty of Utrecht. Nothing could be done that year, the campaigning season being practically over, but if the French did nothing next year, he would come over, as he said 'with a single footman if necessary'. Murray was later to claim that he had discouraged so rash an enterprise; but Elcho was to have his doubts, and he came to believe that far from discouraging the Prince, he had egged him on.

Back in Holland Murray and Elcho met at Rotterdam as had been arranged. The former 'showed me the letters and commissions he had been charged to deliver in Scotland. Fearing that we might be searched on our arrival, we agreed to buy two pistols, fill them with powder, cram the documents into the barrels and shoot them off should any effort be made to search us.' However, they safely reached London where they parted, Murray returning to Scotland, after having been warned that he had become suspect. Elcho now met up with Francis who wanted to discuss family business. He was courting Lady Catherine Gordon, sister of the Duke of that name. But before proposing he wanted Elcho to get married, for 'our maternal grandfather had left him all his property on condition he should assume his name and arms of Charteris; and there was a clause in the will by which should he ever become Earl of Wemyss, the property would pass to his younger brother, Mr Wemyss. He now proposed to give me 50,000 francs should I get married. I accepted his offer and proposed to go to Scotland in search of a wife'. During this stay in London Elcho made a point of frequenting his Whig friends including Lords Pomfret and Lincoln. He was beginning to adopt the devious ways of a conspirator.

He now returned to Edinburgh to redeem his promise, and arrived at Goodtrees only to discover that Sir James was at Coltness, his place in Lanarkshire, endeavouring to rally to the Cause Elcho's old school friend, the new Duke of Hamilton. His family were traditionally looked upon as heads of the Scottish Jacobites. (The

Duke of Perth's title was only titular having been conferred by James VII when in exile). Argyll was a pillar of the Hanoverian establishment and Atholl a Whig by religious conviction; Roxburgh was also a Whig; Montrose was to support the Government during the '45, and even Gordon, whose Catholic father had been arrested for having fought at Sheriffmuir, was to remain prudently on the sidelines until Cumberland reached Aberdeenshire, when he openly espoused the Hanoverian cause. Amongst the papers the conspirators had stuffed into their pistols was a letter the Prince had written to Hamilton and had confided to Elcho in the knowledge that they had been at Winchester together. He discovered that the Duke 'was very zealous for the Stuart cause. I now returned to Edinburgh where I spent the winter.'

His arrival must have caused no end of a flutter, all the more that it was assuredly known that he was in search of a wife. It is easy to picture the whispering and headshaking which took place round the tea tables where the 'leddies' were wont to foregather, and all the caps which must have been set at him. 'That winter I frequented a public assembly where there was dancing once a week, Lady Glenorchy's assemblies and the theatre. We also gave balls for the Edinburgh young ladies who are very pretty. I had not forgotten my brother's promise to give me £20,000 should I get married, and I asked for the hand of Miss Graham of Airth and was accepted. I went to see my father at Wemyss to tell him of my engagement. He signed a deed in the presence of Lord Leven, Lord Balmerino and my brother-in-law, Sir James, by which he declared me heir to all his estates, divesting himself of the power to make any other dispositions, or to contract debts of over £2,000.'

All this time Murray of Broughton had been preparing for the arrival of the Prince, which he secretly planned for the following summer. He hit on the notion of founding a club where all 'the well affected could meet.' Elcho was enthusiastic, it being very much in his line. It would be a way of recruiting more adherents, getting them to know each other, and in Murray's words, 'draw them to make public declarations of their principles and thereby leave them no pretext to excuse their non-appearance when things came to an open rupture.' Soon the Buck Club was meeting once a week for supper. As admission was by the unanimous vote of all the members, secrecy was ensured, and Murray was able to inform them that he had been to Paris where the Prince had told him of his intention of coming to Scotland in the summer of 1745, 'when he would throw himself into the arms of his Scottish friends, and he asked what should be done under the circumstances? The majority of those present, which included the Earl of Buchan, Sir Alexander MacDonald of Sleat, Sir James Steuart of Coltness and Lord Lovat, were of the opinion that a message should be sent to the Prince that if he were able to come with six thousand regular troops, arms for ten thousand more, and thirty thousand *louis d'or* all his supporters would join him. But should this not be possible he was strongly advised not to come, as his presence would cause his own ruin, as well as that of the Cause and of all those who embarked on so dangerous an adventure.'

'Mr Murray, who had been entrusted with the task of preparing the despatches, was suspected of not having dissuaded the Prince from coming, as the Club had recommended. He was heavily in debt and sought to keep the situation on the boil. In the Club he aimed at getting everyone to promise to join the Prince even should he come alone. Quite a number did so, including the Duke of Hamilton. However, when it came to the crunch quite a few fell off, including the Duke; but only two, Sir Alexander MacDonald of Sleat and Mr MacDonald of MacDonald [a slip of memory here for the apostate was Macleod of MacLeod] took arms against him after having taken part in all the plots hatched by his friends.' Elcho's position was clear: without French support the rising would be a failure, and he saw no reason why he should risk his whole future on behalf of a foolish young prince.

This was followed by another long silence. By March 1745 the conspirators were getting desperate, none more so than Lochiel. There was no news from Paris; the culprit being the Prince. Some step must be taken. Elcho offered to go to Paris, but it was too dangerous for him to go, he being now singled out as an active Jacobite, and all he could do was to stress the fact that he 'was desired to tell Your Royal Highness that it will be absolutely necessary to send someone over soon to this country . . . so that, your friends here, who are as yet altogether unprepared, may have time to put themselves in order,' The weeks went by and there was still no answer.

In the meantime Francis was having difficulty in raising the £20,000 Elcho needed to get married, for 'although he had an income of £30,000, he failed to raise it in Scotland as his property was entailed, and he could neither mortgage nor sell, so he suggested we should go to London. They arrived in the capital just three days before the Duke of Cumberland's departure for Flanders, where he was soon to suffer a defeat at Fontenoy. With Paris after Fontenoy no longer at risk Louis had little incentive to waste men and money on so hazardous a venture as an invasion of England.

Francis was not more successful in London than he had been in Edinburgh, and he finally gave Elcho a deed by which he bound himself to give him either £10,000 or £500 a year during his lifetime, or until he could raise the promised sum, after which Elcho had to 'marry at his request'. His mother gave him £1,000 out of Mrs Charteris' bequest. 'I now found myself rich having an income of 22000 *livres* and 2200 *livres* in ready money.' It was the end — or so he believed — of his financial troubles.

It took a couple of months to reach this settlement during which time the brothers went into society: 'We frequented the house of the Duke of Montrose and attended the levees of the Duke of Argyll, who was the Secretary for Scotland', [another slip of Elcho's pen, for the Duke was not the Secretary of Scotland, though its effective ruler] and they dined at a tavern frequented by other Scots, for the most part supporters of the Government. There were however, exceptions, one being the Hon. John Stuart, brother of the Earl of Moray whose house, Donibristle in Fife, Elcho was, as has been said, in the habit of frequenting. At this time Stuart was an ardent Jacobite, indeed so much so that he told Elcho 'that should Prince

Charles Edward land in great Britain and find that another had
joined before him he would cut his throat.' He was to think better
of it. 'A few days after the Prince's landing he entered English service
as a captain . . .I took him prisoner at the battle of Preston and
reminded him of our conversation. By way of an excuse he said he
had done his best to desert and join us, but had failed in his attempt.
He gave his word he would never bear arms against the Prince, but
he broke it, and we found him at Culloden with the Duke of
Cumberland.' He was probably not alone to be torn between two
loyalties.

With money again in his pocket, Elcho in London was able to
return to the gambling tables. He was not a compulsive gambler,
nor was he a brilliant one as his grandfather the Colonel, had been,
but he liked cards, a pleasure from which he had long been deprived.
'I went every day to the play and to Vauxhall and Ranelagh and on
one occasion to a masked ball which was held in the latter place.
Here I played roulette and having five guineas in my pocket I won
in a short time eighty. The next day I returned with three hundred,
expecting to have the same luck and win more by increasing my
stakes, but I lost my three hundred guineas! Some gentlemen were
staking a thousand guineas on the result of one throw.'

His time was not solely spent in so frivolous a fashion. He had
made friends with Archibald Stuart, the Lord Provost of Edinburgh,
who also sat in the House as an MP and who introduced him to Mr
Onslow, the Speaker, thanks to which he now spent his mornings
at the House of Commons. The House was investigating the
conduct of Admirals Matthews and Lestock during the battle of
Toulon: 'Had they worked in closer union, the combined fleets of
France and Spain would not have done so well', and Charles Edward
might not have reached Paris.

The brothers left London after two months spent amongst many
objects of interest and amusement, and went off to stay at Hornby
in Lancashire, of which Francis had not as yet taken possession.
Elcho's arrival roused a good deal of interest; the Town Council of
Lancaster, which had previously sent two Councillors to Scotland

to invite him to become their MP, now gave a banquet in his honour. However, being on the verge of getting married, he had no wish to go into politics, at least for the time being. So, after having duly thanked them, he asked them to choose his brother in his stead. 'This they promised to do . . . and I was immediately presented with the freedom of the city. A few days later we left for Edinburgh, and on his arrival my brother proposed to the sister of the Duke of Gordon and was accepted.'

Elcho found the Edinburgh Jacobites extremely perturbed by the recent arrest of Sir Hector Maclean, the kindly old Jacobite who had taken him to the Opera on his first visit to Paris. He had been sent by the Prince to 'rouse the clans' preparatory to his own arrival, and had been carrying the long awaited answer to Elcho's letter. But he had foolishly lingered on in Edinburgh so as to have a shoe fitted, for he was lame, and he was now a prisoner in the Castle. Fortunately he had been able to save the Prince's answer: 'I should have been glad to see you, and discussed matters more fully with you, but am sensible to the strength of your reasons for not venturing it,' Charles Edward had written, but 'I have now taken my final resolution, or rather I am on the point of executing that which I had taken and given my word six months ago . . .' So the Prince was coming. But was he coming alone? Now the prospect of a Jacobite Rising was a horrid reality.

On August 2nd Elcho was brought a letter from Murray of Broughton 'in which he gave me to understand that the Prince had landed at Lochaber. I met Mr Murray who was about to set off to join the Prince, and I entreated him to beg the Prince to return to France should he have not brought the backing in arms and men we had asked for. He promised me to do so. However, this promise was not kept for he and the Duke of Perth and some others were pressing the Prince to come over whatever might happen . . . I decided to remain quiet, watch for further developments and only join the Prince should he come close to Edinburgh, so I went to Fife to be within better reach of news. I spent my time with my father, to whom I confided what was going on, and with my aunt, Lady Moray.'

He had met Forbes of Culloden on the boat bringing him across
the Firth, who had told him ' as a piece of news that the Prince had
landed in Scotland. He was on his way North to prevent as far as
he could the Chieftains from joining him. But he had little hope of
success, knowing their zeal for the Stuart cause. For this he was
truly sorry, for the Prince could kindle a fire which would be quickly
put out by General Cope and which would end by the ruin of many
honourable gentlemen whose fate he deplored. He referred amongst
others to the Duke of Perth and Mr Cameron Lochiel. I did not tell
him I had already heard the news.' Forbes was obviously making
one last effort to save the grandson of his old friend, the Colonel,
from what he rightly saw as his inevitable ruin.

> I was staying with my father at Wemyss when the Prince arrived
> at Perth and sent a servant with a letter to secretary Murray
> [Murray of Broughton] begging him as a friend to inform me as to
> the state of the Prince's army, and the officers he had brought from
> France.   He replied that it consisted of 6,000 men, that he was
> expecting more who were on their way from France, and that he
> had with him a Spanish General Macdonald [he was only a captain]
> and the French General O'Sullivan [who was also no more than a
> captain].
>
> It was with lies such as these that Secretary Murray deceived
> everyone in order to embark them in the enterprise. He gave the
> same answer to Lord Kenmure, who had, like myself asked for
> information; however when he joined the Prince he discovered he
> had been misled, and returned home.

Elcho was always to regret that he had not followed his example.
    Reassured by this answer, for at this time he still trusted Murray
of Broughton with whom he had been working all these months,
Elcho left for Edinburgh, after having told his father that he was
going to join the Prince, 'a decision of which he greatly approved. .
he told me to present his respect to the Prince who could rely on
his attachment to the Royal House of Stuart.' He had been greatly
honoured when Elcho had told him that the Chevalier had
appointed him Lord Lieutenant of Fife. (Fortunately for him he was

never called upon to take up his duties).

'On my arrival in Edinburgh I was informed that the Town Council had decided to defend the city. The citizens had been enrolled into regiments and cannons had been placed on the town walls.' Up to then the citizens had had no reason to believe that the Lord Provost was anything but loyal to the Crown, but he was in Elcho's opinion a Jacobite, and 'being a man of Spirit and courage and a zealous supporter of the Prince, seeing that he could not prevent the magistrates and citizens from taking arms, he decided that these arms should fall into the hands of the Prince's army, it being in great need of them, it being only half armed. As the Prince's army drew nearer the citizens held meetings where the Lord Provost appeared to be little disturbed at what was going on. This led the more violent amongst them to suspect his attachment to the Prince, so they proposed he should place himself at their head and lead them into battle. He immediately accepted this suggestion, and when he later saw their courage failing, he ordered them to lay down their arms, accusing them of not being worthy of carrying them. Thus it was that on his arrival in Edinburgh the Prince found enough arms for 1500 men.'

Elcho spent the next three days at Preston Hall in Midlothian, home of the dowager Duchess of Gordon where his brother's wedding was to take place. The marriage was a grand affair, and the procession taking the newly married couple to Amisfield was so long that it created something of a panic, it being mistaken for the vanguard of the Prince's army! 'On the 15th (September) I bid my brother farewell and told him I was off to join the Prince's army. Whereupon he took a key out of his pocket, and bid me go to his place at Newmills [near Haddington] and take all the money I could find in his writing table. So I spent the night there and took £1500. I had besides £1000 of my own.' This was to be Francis's last gesture in favour of the Jacobite cause. No doubt at the behest of his wife, or in deference to the wishes of his mother-in-law, a Protestant Englishwoman who was in receipt of a £1000 pension to bring her children up as Protestants, he henceforth kept out of politics, and concentrated his efforts on freemasonry.

On the following day in the gathering dusk of a September evening, Elcho joined Charles Edward at Gray's Mill on the western outskirts of Edinburgh. 'It was dark, and the Prince, whom I had known in Rome and Paris, received me with the greatest cordiality and appointed me his first aide-de-camp. We talked for a long time and he told me, amongst other things, to be on my guard with Lord George Murray whom he knew had joined him with the intention of betraying him.' Elcho must have been taken aback, for Lord George, with whom he was probably acquainted, had the reputation of being a very honourable man indeed. But knowing that Charles Edward 'was extremely credulous and was ready to believe whatever those in whom he had confidence told him' he did not attach much importance to these accusations.

'The Prince now confessed . . . that he was in the greatest financial distress, not having the wherewithal to pay the army . . . I asked his Highness of how much he stood in need, and he said £1500. I at once drew out my purse and counted them, saying that I was delighted to find myself in a position to advance the money [Francis' gift] as I still had a thousand to go on with. The Prince took them and thanked me very much.' Clearly Elcho looked upon this as a loan, not as a gift. His father's habit of collaring his money had made him careful, more especially at a time when he was contemplating matrimony. But either he did not make the point clear or Charles Edward wilfully misunderstood him, and he was never to get the money back.

Elcho and the Prince were still talking when 'Mr Coute [Coutts, former Lord Provost of Edinburgh] arrived with a delegation to negotiate the capitulation of the city.' But the Prince with a sureness of touch would not hear of it, and he sent Elcho to tell him that he would accept nothing but a complete capitulation, and despatched Lochiel with eight hundred picked men who, taking advantage of the gates being opened to let in the negotiators' carriage, took over the city without firing a shot.

It was about eleven when the main force of the Prince's army approached the city from the South, thus avoiding going within range of the Castle's guns, for that citadel was still in Government hands, and was to remain so. The Procession was headed by Lord Strathallan 'marching first at the head of the horse, the Prince next on horseback with the Duke of Perth on his right and Lord Elcho on his left, then Lord George Murray on foot at the head of the column of infantry.' The plan had been that the Duke of Hamilton should ride on the right and the Duke of Perth on the left, but Hamilton had remained at home, and Elcho was acting as a stopgap. 'When the army came near the town it was met by vast multitudes of people, who by their repeated shouts and huzzas expressed a great deal of joy to see the Prince. When they came into the suburbs the crowd was prodigious and all wishing the Prince prosperity; in short nobody doubted that he would be joined by 10,000 men at Edinburgh (this being the number of those who had volunteered to served in the King's army) if he could arm them.' The Prince 'dismounted in the inner court [of Holyrood House] went upstairs into the gallery and from thence in the Duke of Hamilton's apartment. The crowd in the King's Park, now thronging the forecourt at Holyrood had seen a slender young man, not quite six foot in height, reddish hair, brown-eyed, princely features, clad in tartan, a blue sash over his shoulder, breeches of red velvet, a green velvet bonnet with gold lace round it and bearing a white cockade. And it felt as if the whole of Edinburgh had been gripped by the high emotion of the moment, the return of a Stuart Prince to Holyrood. But within the Palace, the Great Apartment, built three-quarters of a century past for King Charles II (who never came) wore the sad aspect of neglect; hence the recourse to that of the Duke of Hamilton, the Palace's hereditary Keeper. On entering the Palace, awaiting him were only the unimpressive Earl of Kellie from Fife; two veterans of the Fifteen, Arthur Elphinstone and James Hepburn of Keith; from Tweeddale the sixteen-year-old nephew of Murray of Broughton; from Stirlingshire Lord Elcho's prospective brother-in-law, the heir to Graham of Airth; and 'Willie' Hamilton of Bangour, much given to versifying in high-flown augustan metres.

To give something of a much-needed flourish to the occasion
Hepburn of Keith stepped forward, drew his sword and preceded
the Prince into the Palace. This was a morning for the casting off of
inhibition.

'Charles Edward's first orders were to cause his father to be
proclaimed and his manifestos to be read.' Patrick Crichton, a
saddler in the Grassmarket, who described himself as belonging to
the 'honest party', (by which he meant the Government supporters')
went to Parliament Square where the proclamations were to be
made. He found, to his indignation, at the Bristo Port, 'a boy
standing with a rusty drawn sword . . . catching the vermin lurking
about his plaids and throwing them away. I said to the minister of
Liberton, 'Are these who surprised Edinburgh by treachery?'   He
answered, ' I had rather seen it in the hands of Frenchmen, but the
devil and the deep are both bad.' Parliament Square was crowded,
it being where the manifestos were going to be read, and it was
from a window that he was able to witness what he called 'this
comic farce or tragic comedy.' Lochiel's Camerons marched up,
bagpipes playing and formed a circle within which officers' 'special
favourites and one lady in dress' [Mrs Murray of Broughton].   He
was not impressed by the rank and file, the unkempt men and boys
bearing weapons of every kind and period, but having seen the
officers, grudgingly conceded that here was 'the most daring and
best militia in Europe.'

Another who watched was Miss Magdalen Pringle, daughter of
a staunchly Whig Berwickshire laird. 'Dear Tib,' she wrote to her
younger sister at Green Knowe Tower back in the Merse, 'A little
before twelve o'clock seven hundred or thereabouts of the
Highlanders that had taken possession of the town surrounded the
Cross and at one o'clock five heralds and a Trumpet with some
gentlemen, amongst them Jamie Hepburn, ascended the cross and
read two manifestos in the name of James the Eight King of Great
Britain, etc. And, at the end of that, everyone threw up their hats
and huzza'd in which acclamation of joy they were join'd by all the
crowd which was so great I incline almost to call it the whole Town.

The windows were full of Ladys who threw up their handkerchiefs and clap'd their hands and show'd great loyalty to the Bonny Prince'.

In this (the first recorded reference anywhere to 'Bonny' Prince Charles Edward) Magdalen Pringle added, as if by way of a postscript perhaps for the eyes of her staunchly Whig father back in Berwickshire. 'Don't imagine I was one of these Ladies. I assure you I was not.' But then, a little wistfully she wrote 'All the Ladies are to Kiss the Prince's hand. I've an inclination to do so, but I can't be introduced'.

King James duly proclaimed, the Highlanders sauntering in the High Street were 'quiet as lambs, civil to everybody and takes nothing but what they pay for'. The only danger they offered was from carelessness was with firearms: Mady Nairne was looking over Lady Keith's window along with Katie Hepburn. On the other side of the street there was a Highland man and a boy standing with a gun in his hand which gun went off and shot in at the window and went in at Mady Nairne's head. Mr Rattray [surgeon] took out the ball and sow'd up her wound. The Prince has sent several messages to inquire after her which has help'd not a little to support her spirits under the pain of her sore wound'

The familiarity with which Miss Pringle here referred to 'Mady' Nairne and 'Katie' Hepburn, both from staunchly Jacobite families, suggests what many other sources attest — the absence at this stage in the conflict of any rancour between gentry families with deep-felt allegiance to the Stuart King, and those like the Pringles of Stichill who stood for King George.

Two days later the Jacobite army was again on the march, the news having reached the Prince that General Cope, who had been unsuccessfully pursuing him through the Highlands, had landed at Dunbar. The Highlanders took up their position on a ridge at Prestonpans, where they remained all day within sight of the enemy who had taken its position on the lower ground. We are told that Charles Edward lay down on the stubble of a newly harvested field of peas wrapped in his plaid with a sheaf in guise of a pillow just as Elcho had seen Lord Sutherland's vassals do when on his way to the north. We do not know how he slept; probably not a wink.

On the following day the Jacobites set off before dawn on a path through the bog shown them by a local sympathiser, and fell upon the enemy with blood-curdling cries, the pipes droning away all the while. The sight of these wild-looking savages brandishing broadswords, who had a well-established reputation for killing prisoners, proved too much for them. They panicked and fled with the Highlanders in hot pursuit. The most frightened of all were the dragoons, who were Irish and already suspected of a proneness to treachery. To add to the horror, the MacGregors, short of arms, had picked up scythes, and according to the Chevalier Johnstone who was there at the time, 'cut the legs of the horses in two, and their riders the middle of their bodies.' The carnage was appalling. 'The field of battle presented a spectacle of horror being covered with heads, legs, and arms and mutilated bodies.' The Jacobite officers did their best to calm the bloodthirsty ardour of their men, making a point of protecting their Hanoverian counterparts. The whole ghastly proceedings were over in a quarter of an hour. The losses being computed at ten to one in favour of the Rebels.

This was not the sort of warfare taught at Angers and practised on the fields of Flanders; the rising was turning out to be a very different affair from the *guerre en dentelles* [war with the conventions of politeness] Elcho had been looking forward to waging. His appearance immediately after the battle was such as to frighten out of his wits young Alexander Carlyle who had come to offer what help he could to the wounded. Elcho had distinguished himself on the field of battle, had been publicly congratulated by the Prince who appointed him colonel of his as yet non-existent bodyguard. Now he demanded to know of young Carlyle where the nearest inn was. The explanation for his aspect which so terrified young Carlyle however may have been a humanitarian one; his anxiety to find a tavern may have been not to assuage his own thirst but, as was normal in the aftermath of an 18th-century battlefield, to find ale to sustain the wounded.

Prestonpans left the Government forces angry, ashamed and thoroughly disoriented, whilst their unfortunate commander, General Cope, unjustly became a general laughing stock. Accusations of cowardice were bandied about and suspicion of treachery became general. For the Jacobites it was a great victory indeed whose echoes were to resound all round Europe. It gave credibility to what had been looked upon up to then as the rash escapade of a frustrated young Prince; and Jacobitism re-entered the domain of international politics from which it had long been banished. It was to have two results which more than anything else were to shape the character of the Rebellion. In the first place it led Charles Edward to believe that the Highlanders were invincible and that the success of the rebellion was a foregone conclusion which made him turn a deaf ear to those who preached caution. But in the end it brought forth a terrible retribution. The blood-soaked field of Prestonpans became the seedbed of Culloden.

CHAPTER SIX

The False Crest

Prestonpans left the Jacobites in a state of euphoria. What many of his supporters had seen at first as the rash escapade of an impatient and ill-advised young man had succeeded beyond their wildest dreams. Edinburgh had fallen into their lap like an over-ripe plum and the usurper's highly professional army lay defeated at their feet. Scotland was theirs and Westminster now loomed large on the horizon. They saw themselves as liberators from the still reviled Union.

What part the Lord Provost had played in the fall of Edinburgh has never been established. It was computed that one third of the Edinburgh male population was Jacobite, the numbers being reversed when it came to women, who were to provide the Prince with his most devoted followers. The Prince's adherents in the Lowlands came from the 'big hoose' rather than the cottage — it was otherwise in the Episcopalian north-east — and they had little influence where the Kirk held sway. The Highland army was distinctly outlandish. The Highlanders' dress, language, customs and moral values were totally different from those of the local population. Their loyalty lay with their chieftains, who had absolute power over them, and were (some of them) more at home in Paris and Madrid than in London or even Edinburgh.

They enjoyed their brief triumph, and Charles Edward set up his court at Holyrood. 'The prince lived in Edinburgh with great splendour and magnificence, had every morning a numerous court of his officers. After he had had Council he dined with his principal officers in public, where there was always a crowd of all sorts of people to see him dine. After dinner he rode out attended by Elcho and his Life Guards and reviewed his army, when there was always a great number of spectators in coaches and on horseback. After the review he came to the Abbey [of Holyrood] where he received the ladies of fashion who came to his drawing room. Then he supped in public and generally there was music at supper and a ball afterwards.' The 'ladies of fashion' to use Elcho's expression, must have thought themselves back in the good old days when a king still lived at Holyrood.

Freed from the presence of sceptics and scoffers — most of the 'honest party', as those loyal to the Crown called themselves, had either left the city or were lying low — the Jacobites indulged unchecked in an orgy of hero worship. 'Medallions, ribbons, poems and pamphlets' were the order of the day and the Prince lived in an atmosphere of perpetual adulation: 'Hail glorious Youth! The Wonder of the Age!' and many suchlike encomiums being lavished upon him. The women became positively hysterical. It must be said that he walked straight out of fairy tale: a real live Prince, tall, handsome, aloof, with that melancholy air so attractive to the fair sex, and with a throne to recover; it was enough to make every woman and girl lose her head.

Unfortunately Charles Edward received the same, fervent admiration from the Irish, although perhaps not for the same motives. With the exception of the aged and doting Sir Thomas Sheridan they were suspected by the Scots of being out to better themselves. For the time being they were only three: Sheridan, John William O'Sullivan who was appointed Quartermaster General, and the papistical Sir John Macdonald who became 'Inspector General of the Cavalry' on the strength of his having served as captain in the Spanish army. Of the three, O'Sullivan was the one who had had most military experience although this, unlike his portly person, was thin enough, he having acted as aide-de-camp to Marshal Maillebois in Corsica after having been his children's tutor.

The Prince now set up a Council which 'met every morning in his rooms in Holyrood. The gentlemen that he called were the Duke of Perth, Lord Lewis Gordon, Lord George Murray, Lord Elcho, Lord Ogilvy, Lord Pitsligo, Lord Nairn, Lochiel, Keppoch, Clanranald, Glencoe, Lochgarry, Ardshiel, Sir Thomas Sheridan, Coll, O'Sullivan, Glenbucket and Secretary Murray.' It is to be noted that amongst all these only Elcho and Murray of Broughton were Lowlanders, and only Elcho had any real knowledge of England which they were hoping to conquer.

At first great hopes were entertained about the Prince. In Elcho's words 'he had born himself well at the head of the second line at Prestonpans and had shown great moderation at the time of his victory', forbidding any form of celebrations, the defeated being also his father's subjects, whilst the wounded and the prisoners had been treated with humanity. However, disillusionment soon set in when it was 'perceived in the Council that he was extraordinarily ignorant, having no knowledge of the country's history, government or geography. He was unable to tolerate any advice which did not coincide with his own views and was firmly convinced that the whole country and its inhabitants were his slaves'. In *The Affairs of Scotland*, Elcho puts this down to the influence of his tutor, Sir Thomas Sheridan, a zealous Irish Catholic who filled him with these notions.

> There was one third of the Council whose principles were that Kings and Princes cannot act or think wrong, so in consequence they always confirmed whatever the Prince said. The other two thirds, who thought that Kings and Princes sometimes thought like other men and were not altogether infallible, and that this Prince was no more so than others, begged leave to differ from him when they could give sufficient reasons for their differences of opinion, which very often was no hard thing to do, for as the Prince and his old Governor ... were much for the doctrine of absolute monarchy they would very often, had they not been prevented, have fallen into blunders which might have hurt the Cause.

It must have been during these Council meetings that Elcho and Lord George got to know and appreciate each other. They had a good deal in common. Both were cut out to be soldiers; had Lord

George remained in the regiment which he deserted in 1715, he would no doubt have figured amongst the best of the British commanders of his day; whilst had Elcho listened to his wellwishers he would have been at the start of what might well have turned out to be a brilliant military career; both had friends amongst the Whigs. But both had been thoroughly indoctrinated in their early youth, and both felt grateful to the Chevalier who had paid Lord George's youthful debts and had given Elcho so good a time in Rome.

Lord George was the fourth son of the first Duke of Atholl. After having dabbled in Jacobite plotting in 1708, his father had become a fervent supporter of the Protestant succession seemingly on religious grounds, for he was a devout Presbyterian. Austerity is seldom attractive to the young, more especially when it is practised by a stern parent, and three out of his four sons succumbed to the charm of their aunt, Lady Nairne, one of those passionately Jacobite women who found in the Cause an outlet for their pent up romanticism. In 1715 he joined Mar in company of his eldest brother, Lord Tullibardine and both took part in the '19, after which Tullibardine was attainted, and lived obscurely in Paris until he embarked for Scotland with Charles Edward. It was he who raised the Royal Standard at Glenfinnan. Lord George, who seems to have served in the ranks of some European army, got himself into youthful scrapes before returning home with the blessing of the Pretender, who generously paid his debts. His father managed to procure him a pardon, and he married a widow, an admirable woman to whom he was rightly devoted and who continued to support him even though she had begged him not to get himself involved in the Rising.

As far as one can tell he had settled quite happily in Scotland, where he got on well with his brother, the 2nd Duke, who like their father, was loyal to the Crown. As time went on he came to play an ever-increasing part in the running of the Atholl estate. Duke James as the 2nd Duke came to be known in Jacobite circles to differentiate him from 'Duke William', Tullibardine to the rest of the world, only having daughters, it was arranged that Lord

George's eldest boy, who was in the direct line of succession, should marry Duke James' daughter so as to keep the estate together. In the meantime young Murray, who had been educated at Eton at his uncle's expense, had recently joined the British army. Lord George, who had in secrecy dallied with Jacobitism when approached by the Duke of Perth, surprised everyone when he unexpectedly joined the Prince at Perth. It is clear from the letter he wrote to his Whig brother that he did so with a heavy heart, believing it was his duty to God and King. His joining the Rising was indeed fortunate for the Cause as it provided it with a disinterested leader who possessed a real understanding of Scottish affairs, a certain experience of London life, a good grasp of business and an inborn flair for Highland warfare. He already exerted a great deal of influence over the men of Atholl, who were to furnish the Prince's army with its largest contingent. But his arrival upset Murray of Broughton who was planning to gather all the reins of power into his own hands, and who started instilling into the Prince's ever suspicious mind doubts as to Lord George's loyalty. Hence Charles Edward's warning to Elcho at their very first meeting in Scotland. However Elcho, who had a low opinion of Charles Edward's judgement, did not allow himself to be influenced.

It is surprising that so independent-minded and self-assured an individual as Elcho should have attached himself so whole-heartedly to Lord George, described by the Chevalier Johnstone, who had acted as his aide-de-camp and admired his qualities, as being 'proud, blunt and imperious [and who] wished to have the exclusive disposal of everything'. The fact is that they had certain traits in common which differentiated them from their companions. Lord George certainly spoke some Gaelic, but it was not his mother tongue, which was Lowland Scots, as Elcho's had been until he had gone to Winchester. Both had had their initial grounding in a Scottish school, Elcho at Dunfermline and Lord George in Perth; both knew London, where they had frequented their fellow countrymen, most of whom were Whigs; both had good friends in this party, such as the Lord President and the Lord Advocate; both felt loyal to the Old Pretender rather than to his son, and neither were fanatics. They belonged to the English-speaking world.

One of the problems which must have often been discussed by the Council was that posed by Edinburgh Castle, where the Governor, General Guest, was holding out under pressure from the eighty-two year old veteran, General Preston. Preston, whose place, Valleyfield, lay just across the water in West Fife, had come over with William of Orange. He had lost none of his fighting spirit and had himself wheeled round at two hour intervals in order to see that everyone was on the alert. The Jacobites did not possess the heavy guns needed for a siege, which was all the more frustrating since within the Castle's walls lay not only the money deposited by the banks, but also a large quantity of arms. Their one hope of seizing this booty lay in reducing the garrison by hunger. (So it seemed until the Chief Cashier of the Royal Bank of Scotland succeeded in wheedling out of Generals Guest and Preston the money he had deposited there. He was a clandestine Jacobite, nephew of an elderly Earl of Breadalbane, who had been involved in the '15. He promptly handed over the money to the Prince's Secretary). 'The Prince, having had information that provisions were scarce in the Castle, and that they were daily supplied from the town, issued out a proclamation that it would be death to anybody to carry provisions into them, and on 29th September ordered it to be blocked up with orders to fire on everybody seen going in or out. Upon which General Preston sent word to the city that if they did not send up provisions as usual he had orders from the Court to fire upon the town.' The unfortunate citizens begged Charles Edward to lift the blockade, but he turned down their request. 'On 1st October the Castle fired their great guns on The Weigh house and whenever they saw any of the Prince's soldiers. Some of the townspeople were killed and some houses damaged.' This was followed by a series of attacks, a 'terrible fire from the Castle' and a sortie when more townspeople lost their lives. 'The whole town was in such consternation that people began to abandon their effects and run out of it.' The Prince now sent a message to the

General that if he did not stop firing on the town he would burn his house in Fife. The answer came that the *Fox* man o' war had orders to burn Wemyss Castle in retaliation. Elcho was indignant, 'as Lord Wemyss was not with the Prince it was an odd sort of reprisal'. He evidently forgot that being a Fifer, Preston would be fully aware of the Earl's Jacobitism. Finally, the Prince having realised that 'he could not think of getting possession of the Castle without having cannon and bombs' raised the blockade. The firing now ceased, although 'the appearance of one of the Prince's soldiers would still draw a volley or two'.

A much more pressing problem was that of funds (apart from the moneys exacted from the Royal Bank) and supplies. The Prince's very first move after his triumphal entry into Edinburgh had been to send 'Lord Elcho to the Magistrates who were assembled at Provost Stuart's to demand under pain of military execution (if not complied with) 1000 tents, 2000 targets, 6000 pairs of shoes and 6000 canteens'. 'Under pain of military execution' was to become Elcho's watchword although he never seems to have put the threat into execution. After Prestonpans the levying became much more systematic, and a committee was set up to procure forage for the army. 'It was composed of Lord Elcho President' and five other Lowlanders who 'issued out orders in the Prince's name to all the Gentlemen who had employment under the Government to send in certain quantities of hay, straw and corn under the penalty of military execution if not complied with, but their orders were very punctually obeyed'. Thanks largely to the Chief Cashier of the Royal Bank of Scotland, the Highland army mostly paid its way, for the time being at least, for what it took, and first call was made on the forfeited estates of the Jacobite Earl of Winton, but Elcho was not a good choice for this kind of work, for having grown up away from home, he had no notion what could be demanded without reducing the population to starvation. Yet, the exactions were done generally with an air of civility, as at Redbraes Castle in the Merse of Berwickshire, the home of the ultra Whig Earl of Marchmont which ended with the officers of the

Glengarry Regiment being entertained round a warm fire by the daughters of the house.   The levying of money extended to all occupied Scotland, which was soon overrun by bands of Highlanders whose task it was to lay hands on all the money they could find.   Public funds were confiscated, and heavy penalties were imposed on towns notorious for their Whiggery; amongst these figured Kirkcaldy and Dysart where Elcho was well known. Nor were individuals spared, and one wonders what Elcho's feelings were on learning that Lady Leven had been held to ransom under threat of her home being burnt before her eyes. Lord Stair's place at Newliston was ransacked, as was that of Colonel Gardiner, a universally respected soldier who had lost his life at Prestonpans. It is easy to picture the wrath of the victims. Years later, when the '45 was largely forgotten and he had long been mixing freely with his fellow countrymen of all parties visiting the Continent, Elcho was insulted in public by the Lothian peer Lord Hopetoun, an incident which must have created something of a sensation in Venice where it took place. Lothian suffered most from this incessant levying and marauding — it is difficult to distinguish between them — carried out by the Highlanders encamped at Duddingston, and it was only to cease with their departure.

Since the departure of the Whig nobility, gentry and above all the judiciary, now impatiently waiting in Berwick for Cope to recapture the capital, 'the honest party' was without leadership. It fell to the Kirk to fill the void. Ever since the Reformation it had been more or less at odds with the Stuarts whose claim to divine right of kings was seen as unscriptural. The Chevalier's manifesto, written in Rome in 1743 for the benefit of the English whom Saxe was preparing to invade, only reinforced its hostility. Memories of Charles II and his success in introducing bishops; and of the 'killing times' under James VII began to haunt the minds of the faithful. Unlike their Episcopalian rivals, the ministers could not rely on broadswords. On the Sabbath following the Jacobite occupation the Edinburgh pulpits remained vacant, the clergy being resolved not to pray for King James; nor would they resort to the ubiquitous formulas used by their Episcopalian counterparts. Now Edinburgh was church-going, and the empty pulpits brought home the seriousness of the situation. Although the ministers seem to have acted spontaneously, they received the unanimous backing of the Presbytery, which went on meeting as usual. Violent sermons were discouraged, yet some were preached in those country parishes where Jacobite rule was bitterly resented. 'The Prince's only enemies are the Presbyterians', the Marquis d'Eguilles shortly to arrive as an emissary from Versailles, reported to King Louis. 'They fear that the Prince will put the Episcopalians in their place. Their ministers have refused to take services and pray for James III. Fortunately', he added with the contempt the French aristocracy felt for the lower orders, 'their flocks are made up of bourgeois, artisans or Lowland peasants who are timid, lazy, and avaricious, and in consequence lacking in initiative; they are therefore not greatly to be feared'. Like all his kind he underestimated the influence of public opinion, whilst overestimating the power of the aristocracy, which he wrongly believed was entirely 'Catholic or Episcopalian', and wholly committed to the Cause. Better informed, Charles Edward did all in his power to get the clergy to return to their pulpits; but in vain. Promises of immunity fell for the most part on deaf ears, or when taken up produced sermons so violently opposed to Jacobitism that he must have regretted his leniency. Although the Kirk's resistance was not particularly heroic, it provided a sheet anchor to which the bewildered faithful could cling.

In the meantime recruits had started arriving in Edinburgh. There were some additional clan regiments but there was also a goodly number of gentlemen on their own accompanied by retainers. The bulk came from Aberdeenshire, Banff and Angus, their numbers gradually diminishing the further south one went and practically disappearing on reaching the Borders. With the exception of North and East Fife, where there was a good sprinkling of Jacobite lairds, Elcho must have had few acquaintances amongst the newcomers with, however, one notable exception. Arthur

Elphinstone, 6th Lord Balmerino, as he was soon to become, was not only a close relative — he was his father's first cousin — but also a man with whom he had been familiar since his early childhood, for unlike the other relations such as the Levens, Balmerino fully shared Lord Wemyss' Jacobitism. Exiled after the '15, he had obtained a pardon and had set up as a lawyer in Edinburgh, in which capacity he was being continually consulted by the Earl. It was also he who had drawn up the deeds for Elcho's projected marriage to Miss Graham, a marriage which was never to take place.

'The Prince formed such as did not belong to other corps into two troops, one of seventy, which he gave the command of to Lord Elcho, whom he made Colonel of the Guards upon the field of battle at Prestonpans . . . the other he gave first to Lord Kenmure, and upon his not joining at Carlisle [as had been expected] then to Lord Balmerino. They formed a squadron of 150 horse including their servants . . . the squadron being under Lord Elcho's orders.' Elcho was now in his element, the many hours he had spent in the riding school at Angers having turned him into a first-class cavalryman, and Edinburgh was treated to the sight of him drilling his squadron according to the principles laid down by the French. Months of intense activity lay ahead, for the Life Guards were to take an active part in all the battles and most of the skirmishes which occurred during the Rising. For the time being, however, their principal duty was to escort the Prince. Indeed Elcho became so associated with the latter in the mind of the public that he is depicted in a 1747-8 propaganda leaflet as sitting by Charles Edward's side in the carriage taking him to Versailles and the flattering reception he is supposed to have received on his return to France. (Elcho was in Italy at the time, where he had had to seek refuge from the Prince's malevolence!). The news of Prestonpans, which was to reach France in a greatly exaggerated version, was received there with much satisfaction. In Elcho's words, 'The French Court decided to make the most of it so they despatched four or five ships, which disembarked at Montrose, some Irish officers, arms and guns and about 120,000 livres in silver, as well as M. du Boyer, Marquis d'Eguilles, son of the President of the Parlement of Aix-en-Provence, who described himself as being the King of France's minister come to reside with the Prince. He was an intelligent man who had been sent to find out how things really stood in Scotland which would enable the French to make the most of the situation.' He had arrived to a rough reception, the Montrose authorities refusing to meet him whilst the mob proved hostile. It was only after the appearance of two hundred Highlanders that the magistrates changed their tune and became obsequious.

It took a week for this French *aristo* to reach Edinburgh, probably because the Firth was then patrolled by HMS *Fox*, whose captain would only allow those holding a pass signed by General Preston to cross the Forth. He was, however, 'vastly well received by the Prince and treated by everybody with a great deal of respect. The Prince gave out that he brought letters to him from the King of France wherein the King promised him assistance, but the Prince never showed these letters to his Council. The Prince told likewise that the King had sent M Du Boyer to reside with him as minister, he gave out publicly everywhere that the French were to send over to England the Duke of York who had arrived in Paris at the head of a number of troops. The news gave the Prince's army great spirits as they expected to hear of a French landing daily.' The Life Guards were now entrusted with their first military mission, for Rear Admiral Byng with his Royal Navy squadron 'came into the Firth and cast anchor at Leith roads. Ever after a party of Lord Elcho's troop was ordered to patrol at nights betwixt Cramond and Musselburgh. 'The men o' war fired often ashore but never killed anybody.'

Charles Edward now suggested that Elcho should go to Versailles as his representative. The offer was turned down, for Elcho saw himself as a soldier, not as a diplomat, a role for which he felt himself to be in no ways qualified; but he put forward the name of his brother-in-law as a suitable candidate. It is difficult to assess the strength of Sir James' Jacobitism now that the threat of rebellion had turned into actuality. He feigned reluctance to kiss the Prince's hand, but then is credited with writing the Prince's manifesto of October which gave a much more lucid statement of the Jacobite cause. As to his despatch to the Continent Sir James gave out that he had been under arrest at Holyrood, from where his departure was organised with the same aim in view: he being arrested in the middle of the town by a group of Highlanders who marched him off loudly protesting. He then made his way secretly to Wemyss and then on to Stonehaven, where the same charade was enacted, he being seemingly embarked by force on a French vessel. However, the excellent terms with which he was seen to be with his so-called captors gave this elaborate piece of deception away.

With the arrival of the French envoy, the question arose as to what next should be done. D'Eguilles wanted the Prince to tarry a little longer in Edinburgh, which would allow reinforcements to arrive from the Highlands, and the French to land in the South of England as they seemed to be planning to do. But there was the problem of supplies: 'If all the clans come up as is talk, they will eat up this poor place if they continue long here,' wailed Patrick Crichton. By now the excellent discipline which had reigned at the start showed signs of breaking down. No horse was safe. These were now driven into the hills at the slightest alarm, but often not fast enough to escape from the predatory Jacobites. The 'banditti', as they were now called by their 'nonfriends', could plead exigencies of war. When one who had suffered at their hands complained to Lord George, about the way his animals were stolen, he was told that it was regrettable but that nothing could be done about it. The hardly pressed inhabitants were beginning to react, though in the main the Highland Army, as has been said, paid its way: on one occasion marauding Highlanders were fiercely attacked by a group of miners from the Hopetoun Estate. All this was potentially damaging to the reputation of those who prided themselves on being liberators. It was high time to leave. But in which direction should one go?

Opinions were divided. The chieftains favoured returning to the

Highlands there to await the promised French support, none more so than Cameron of Lochiel. They had been seduced by the prospect of an independent Scotland which D' Eguilles was dangling before their eyes on orders from his King. But the Prince would not hear of it. He had set his heart on reigning in all three kingdoms and would have liked to have challenged Field-Marshal Wade, now in Newcastle preparing to recapture Edinburgh with an army twice the size of the Prince's. It had taken a great deal of persuasion to deflect Charles Edward towards Carlisle, whose great castle towered over the landscape, veritable symbol of royal power. His hands had been greatly strengthened by the presence of the newly arrived Irish officers, whom he had promptly promoted and who now sat on the Council. So when it came to the vote his choice prevailed, but only by two voices, those of the ever subservient Perth, and of Elcho! It must have been the only time the latter differed from Lord George. He was probably thinking of Jacobite Lancaster whose freedom he had been so recently awarded and of Hornby. Significantly neither in the *Affairs* version or the *Journal* does he make clear that his was the vote that swung the decision.

The 1st of November was chosen as the day of departure, and the Jacobites had had the humiliating experience of seeing the Castle celebrate King George's birthday by a cannonade taken up from the Firth by the guns of Rear Admiral Byng's squadron. It was celebrated in many other places in Scotland even in occupied Perth and Dundee, where the populace drove the Jacobites out of their Town Houses. It took quite a large force of Highlanders to get them reinstated. So impatient was the Prince to get away that he refused to wait for the expected reinforcements and his army now only numbered 5,000. In order to conceal its weakness the departure was fixed for six in the evening when it was already dark, a policy which was pursued during the whole of the ensuing campaign. But it was to lead to a dangerous over-estimation of its strength, with the result that the French seemed not to hurry to come to its aid. The Prince was sanguine as to his prospects, as he was absolutely persuaded that 'a great body [of English] would join him on his entering their country. . . that everybody in London was for him and would receive him as they had already done in Edinburgh.'

'We are happily delivered from the Highland host' wrote the Whiggish *Evening Courant*, which went on to apologise to its readers 'for what has been published . . . these several weeks past; [it] has been solely by authority.' As was to be foreseen, there was a backlash, which would have been far worse had not two Whig gentlemen asserted their authority. As it was, 'the people from the Castle insulted and abused everybody that had appeared to be the Prince's friend and it was said they used some wounded men the Prince had left behind very inhumanely.' Paradoxically, amongst the victims figured the daughters of the Whig Duke of Atholl, whose father had asked his brother, Lord George, to take them to safety before knowing that he intended to defect. The poor girls were to have a bad time: all the window panes in the house in which they were then living got broken during the bombardments, and the occupation once over, they were insulted in the street, their tartan dresses having led people to believe that they were Jacobites. The ministers were the first to resume their duties and on the Sabbath following the Prince's departure the streets were again empty during 'sermon time', while the Commission of the General Assembly denounced in no uncertain terms 'the wicked and desperate rebellion . . against our rightful and lawful King George'. The magistrates proved less prompt. This was greatly deplored by the citizens who were hankering after 'a revival of civil government'. So when Lord Milton 'entered the city in procession attended by the Sheriffs of East Lothian and the Merse as well as a good many gentlemen', the huzzahs did not have to be orchestrated. These were repeated on the following day with the arrival of two regiments, forerunners of Field-Marshal Wade's army now under the command of General Hawley, an officer renowned for his brutality.

'To write of the transactions of the latter part of this year 1745 is to write of wonderful things. A poor Italian Prince, C Stuart . . .

with an ill-armed mob of Highlanders and a bankrupt Tweeddale laird as secretary and bagpipes surprising Edinburgh and overrunning Scotland . . .defeating a Royal army, penetrating into the heart of England, seizing garrison towns, proclaiming a King in spite of a mighty King with some six million in hand with powerful armies and fleets and many generals and the Parliament of Great Britain now sitting to support all. Yet this Prince landing so obscurely with seven persons was able to make such a figure show as want of intelligence and conduct in the administration and must stand as a blot in the British history to latest posterity', wrote an indignant yet relieved Patrick Crichton, thus aptly summing up what were, effectively, 'wonderful things'.

But the last word about the Jacobite occupation of Edinburgh has to be d'Eguilles reporting from Edinburgh to d'Argenson, the Foreign Minister. The march on London was the only course open. 'I have had to put up with the insolent and suspicious ways of the people among whom I live,' he continued, 'their divisions among themselves, their short-comings and above all their indolence, the main weakness of their army. But happily, I can console myself by relying on their courage, their pride and the terror they inspire in their enemies.'

CHAPTER SEVEN

To England

It was as a proud young colonel that Elcho rode out of Edinburgh at the head of the Life Guards at six in the evening of November 1st 1745. This low-key, almost surreptitious, departure was in strong contrast to the triumphal entry only six weeks before, when he had ridden in on the left of the Prince through cheering crowds. In that short time he had grown from being a pleasure-loving man of fashion to a competent staff-officer enjoying the full confidence of his commander, Lord George Murray, who was not a man to be easily pleased. His first task had been to levy food, forage and goods; he had then taken part in his first battle when he had been named colonel of the bodyguard on the battlefield by the Prince. From then on his time was taken up with training, disciplining and equipping his men, and acting as royal escort, which brought him into close contact with Charles Edward. As we have seen, he also had his seat on the Council. He had therefore been at the very heart of the rising which had given him a great deal of authority, probably too much for his own good. But he had not alienated his fellow Scots engaged in the Rising with whom he was always to remain popular.

This well-drilled and smartly turned out body of horsemen opened the march and was followed by other cavalry units and by the Highlanders divided into clan regiments commanded by their chiefs and officered by his kinsmen. At the rear were the women, herds of black cattle, and according to Patrick Crichton '150 carts with provisions, ammunition and baggage and all the General Cope's wagons they had taken at the field of Preston.' There were also three carriages, that of the Prince which he had lent to the gallant old Aberdeenshire laird, Lord Pitsligo, and those of the elegant young Mrs Murray of Broughton, whose habit of wearing of the tartan uniform of her husband's regiment of Hussars was the cause of much ribald laughter in Whig circles, and the charming Lady Ogilvy who was to remain with her husband throughout the campaign. Elcho and the Ogilvies were to become friends.

The country was indifferent if not hostile. There may have been some sympathy for the Cause lurking in certain 'big hooses', at least amongst the women folk, but not enough to induce the men to take arms. The Catholic Earl of Traquair, one of the Associators of 1741, had not stirred. Only one Border laird set out to join the Prince, and he got lost on the way! Of recruits there were none whilst desertions were numerous. By the time the army reached Carlisle, it had lost a thousand men by desertion and was reduced to a mere 4,500; concealing its true numbers had become a matter of urgency. As we have seen, Charles Edward had wanted to march to Newcastle in order to confront Wade, but on it being pointed out that it would be folly to engage a force double the size of his own on a terrain probably unsuited to Highland tactics, he had accepted to undertake the siege of Carlisle instead. However, on hearing that Wade was in pursuit he turned back leaving the siege in the hands of the Duke of Perth backed by Murray of Broughton. He was soon back, the Field Marshal having got bogged down in the snow. The capture of this great citadel, symbol of royal power, did not present an insuperable problem but it was a dangerous error to confide the negotiations for surrender to a Catholic peer at a time when the Government was whipping up anti-papist feeling. Lord George was all the more dismayed that he was familiar with the area and could guess what the feelings of the inhabitants would be. Although he was supposed to share the command with Perth, he was never consulted, and he therefore refused to bear the responsibility for so monumental a blunder. So he wrote to the Prince relinquishing his command which he passed on to Elcho. In the future he would serve in the ranks as a volunteer. Charles Edward was delighted to get rid of this abrupt and outspoken man who never resorted to flattery, and whom he still suspected of treachery. What is more, he had been nettled at the way Lord George had stressed that his loyalty lay with the Chevalier rather than himself. So the resignation was accepted in none too gracious a manner. This infuriated the Scots who threatened to go home. They had always been opposed to going to England, and they now refused to serve under Perth, whom they liked and respected as a man, but of whose military capacities they had the lowest opinion. Generous as ever, the Duke resigned his command and returned to his regiment to act as its colonel, leaving the Prince sore and frustrated. The rift between Charles Edward and Lord George was becoming a chasm.

The Prince held a Council wherein he proposed going straight to London. 'The answer that was made was that the army came up to join his English friends or a French landing, but could not pretend putting him in possession of the crown without either, and that it would be better to wait in Carlisle for reinforcements .. The Prince said he was sure all his friends would join him in Lancashire. M du Boyer assured everybody of a French landing daily . . . and Mr Murray said that it was impossible to stop in Carlisle for want of money]. A march forward was ordered. Lord George, who was now in sole command, divided the army into three: the vanguard, commanded by Elcho, would prepare the way and would be followed twenty-four hours later by himself at the head of the Atholl brigade, the Ogilvy and Glenbucket regiments and the small Edinburgh contingent under Roy Stewart, whilst the Prince would bring up the rest after another twenty-four hours interval. The march would start before dawn and end after dark which would help conceal the lack of numbers and prevent that marauding which had lost the Jacobites some popularity in Scotland. It fell to Elcho to have the Chevalier proclaimed king in every town and village through which he passed; seize all public moneys; demand that those who had contributed towards the war should pay in the same sum to Jacobite funds, and arrange for quarters and provisions for 10,000 men — another way of concealing the size of the force. The men were fed and lodged at the expense of the communities whilst the officers paid for themselves, and were to complain about the exorbitant prices they were being charged. Bells must be rung, bonfires lit and windows lighted with candles, all this under threat of 'military execution. Which word,' a Government officer was later to write, 'I used as freely as Lord Elcho did in England.'

Elcho was now on familiar ground, having first travelled this way at the age of twelve on his way to Winchester, and more recently up and down from Hornby. Both his title and his appearance — he was tall and good looking — made him a conspicuous figure, and in the old days he would have been met at the various coaching inns with a respectful doff of the cap followed by a friendly exchange of greetings. Now it was sullen hostility. This change of attitude made a deep impression upon him, and he continually refers to it in the *Narrative*. Doubts were beginning to creep into his mind as to the feasibility of the venture. This first occurred at Burton in Kendal, where it came to his ears 'that the people at Lancaster intended to hold out the castle'. The people of Lancaster who had so recently made him a freeman, and who had invited him to become their MP! He could not believe it. He wrote to his friend the Mayor of Lancaster 'informing him that part of the army would be there the next day, and told him if there was no resistance made, no harm would be done to the town.'

His next stop was Hornby where he went to pick up food and fodder and gather information. It was here that he learnt that the Catholics, in whose company he had drunk many a toast to the 'King over the water', were lying low on instructions from their priests, who feared a revival of the old recusancy laws which had long been in abeyance. This was indeed bad news and the draconian measures imposed on the town of Lancaster may well reflect the disappointment he felt. He spent that night in the company of Lord George mulling over a situation which was indeed disturbing. Things looked up a bit at Preston 'where the people showed more joy on seeing the Prince than they had done anywhere else and there were for the first time in England several huzzas.' The Prince was now joined by two Welsh gentlemen, 'the first men of any consequence to do so'; however the Scots were beginning to share Elcho's doubts 'of being joined, and to say they had marched far enough' but upon the Prince assuring them they would be joined by all his English friends at Manchester' and Eguilles that 'the French were either landed or would land in a week, these doubts were laid aside.'

The occupation of Manchester was to follow the usual pattern of proclaiming James King, seizing public funds, and ordering bonfires, and bell-ringing; but here these orders were carried out less reluctantly than elsewhere. A few of the wealthier citizens came to kiss hands, as did two or three non-juror clergymen, one of whom attached himself to the army and would say prayers for the Chevalier in every church he encountered. But the Prince's 'English friends' turned out to be a mere two hundred or so unemployed men who did not conceal the fact that it had been their intention to join whichever army they encountered first, to whom must be added one or two gentlemen and a handful of craftsmen. They were all enrolled as the Manchester Regiment and put under the command of Francis Townley, a Catholic Lancastrian who had served in the French army. 'The Prince was so far deluded by these proceedings at Manchester of bonfires and ringing of bells, which they used to own themselves they did out of fear of being ill-used, that he thought himself sure of success, and his conversation that night at table was in what manner he should enter London on horseback or on foot, and in what dress. The reasons he thought himself so sure of success was that he himself knew nothing of the country, or the strength that was against him, and as he could not bear to hear that the Government had any friends. His favourites, who were mostly Irish and who were French officers, knew that at the worst they would be out for a month or two imprisonment' egged him on.

The Scots felt far less confident. Wade was marching south probably to Lancashire; the Duke of Cumberland, who had just taken over the command from Sir John Ligonier, stood between them and London, whilst troops were assembling at Finchley to repel an expected invasion by the French. Being so far from home, a defeat in this overwhelmingly hostile country would be nothing short of disaster. 'The principal officers of the army . . . met at Manchester and were of the opinion that now they had marched far enough into England, and as they had received not the least encouragement from any person of distinction, the French not landed, and only joined by 200 vagabonds, they had done their part and as they did not pretend to put a king on the throne of England without their [the English] consent it was time to represent to the Prince to go back to Scotland. But after talking a great deal about it, it was determined to march to Derby so that neither the French nor the English might have it to say, the army had not marched far enough into England to give the one encouragement to land and the other encouragement to join.' But not a word that the decisive voice in the decision to invade England had been Elcho's!

It would seem that the decision to go on to Derby was taken during a banquet Elcho gave in honour of St Andrew's Day. When drinking to absent friends one wonders to whom he silently lifted his glass? Francis and his bride, now safely in Government territory? The Levens? Lord Leven was now at Alnwick laid low by asthma, whilst his wife was having to get over the humiliation of having been browbeaten into delivering up £100 to the invaders. The Sutherlands? The Earl was holding his county for the Government whilst the Countess was proclaiming her admiration for the Prince. The Morays at Donibristle? They had once been Jacobites, but the Earl, now a representative peer, was also taking sides with the Government, although less decidedly than his Sutherland brother-in-law. The Master of Sinclair who had warned him against getting entangled with the Stuarts and whose brother was now a general in the British army? Only his sister Fanny might not look upon him as a misguided fool. Civil war plays havoc in families.

We are in possession of an eye-witness account of the occupation of Derby which in all probability did not differ greatly from what had happened in other towns:

Wednesday 4th December 1745 about eleven o'clock in the forenoon two of the rebel vanguard rode into the town of Derby, and their entry into it gave a specimen of what was to be expected from such a set of villains by seizing a good horse belonging to young Mr Stamford . . .after which they enquired for the Mayor's house and demanding billets for 9,000 men or more. In a short time after their whole vanguard came in, consisting of about 30 men (beside the officers and their servants); they wore gold laced hats with white cockades, were clothed in blue faced with red, had on scarlet waistcoats trimmed with gold lace, and most of them being likely young men made a handsome appearance. They were drawn up in the market place and sat there near three hours during which they ordered the bells to be rung and bonfires to be made, which was done accordingly to prevent any mischief which might ensue on a refusal.

About three Lord Elcho with the Life Guards and many of the chiefs also arrived on horseback to the number of about 150, most of them clothed as above. These made a fine show being the flower of the army. Soon after their main body also marched into the town in tolerable order, six or eight abreast with about eight standards; most of them were white flags with red crosses. They had several bagpipers who played as they marched along and in general answered the description given of them viz. a crew of shabby, lousy pitiful-look fellows mixed up with old men and boys, dressed in dirty plaids, and dirty shoes, without breeches and wore their stockings made of plaid not much above half way up their legs; some without shoes, or next to none and with their plaids thrown over their shoulders. Divested of their arms, they appeared more like a parcel of chimney sweeps than soldiers.

On the following morning Charles Edward was in the act of adjusting his blue bonnet over his perruque preparatory to going out, when he was told that Lord George and all the commanders wanted to wait upon him. Upon which Lord George told him in his usual brusque manner 'that it was the opinion of everybody present that the Scots had done all that could be expected of them. That they had marched into the heart of England ready to join any party that would declare for him, that none had and that the counties which the Army had passed through seemed more enemies than friends to his Cause, [and] that there was no French landed in England . . . but if he could produce any letter of distinction in which there was an invitation for the army to go to London, or any other part of England that they were ready to go . . . and it was in their opinion that they should go back and join their friends in Scotland, and live and die with them '. . . After Lord George spoke he desired all the gentlemen present to speak their sentiment and they all agreed with Lord George except two, the Duke of Perth and Sir William Gordon, who were for going to Wales.

The Prince heard all these arguments with the greatest impatience, fell into a passion and gave most of the gentlemen that had spoke very abusive language and said that they had a mind to betray him. The case was he knew nothing about the country nor had the smallest idea of the force that was against him, nor where they were situated. His Irish favourites had always diminished much all the force that was against him and he himself believed firmly that the soldiers of the regulars would never dare fight against him as he was their true prince . . .and he always believed he should enter St James' with as little difficulty as he had done Holyrood House . . . and continued all that day, positive he would march to London', to which Elcho dryly pointed out that he would be in Newgate within a fortnight. Unlike the others he had an intimate knowledge of London, a place with which he had been familiar since his Winchester days.

He was right. Even if by some miracle the Jacobites had first defeated Cumberland, then the forces assembling at Finchley — in both cases on terrain unsuited to Highland tactics — they would still have had to face a violently anti-Catholic populace which nearly lynched the (Jacobite) north of England peer, Lord Derwentwater while on his way to the Tower after his capture at sea by the Royal Navy.

The Prince spent the whole of that day endeavouring to persuade the Scots to fall in with his wishes. But in vain; they were adamant. So when night came he 'sent for them and told them he consented to go to Scotland. And at the same time he told them that for the future he would have not more Councils, for he would neither ask nor take their advice; that he was accountable to nobody but his father; and he was as good as his word for after he never advised (sic) with anybody but the Irish officers, Murray and Hay [of Restalig] and never summoned a Council'. Charles Edward Stuart had at last come face to face with reality. The shock proved too great and he collapsed. 'He could not walk or hardly stand, which was always the case when he was cruelly used'. He who had proudly marched at the head of his Highlanders from Carlisle to Derby was now to travel either on horseback or in his carriage. In Elcho's words 'his body was well fitted for war but his character did not match up with his constitution: he only liked those who flattered him as did the Irish, could not accept any opinion contrary to his own and was extremely ignorant, not having received a proper education.' He would get up late, thus retarding the departure of the army at a time when Cumberland was at its heels, and the orders he gave were soon to be followed by counter orders. In other words he had become a spoilt child.

But the decision to abandon the march to London appeared otherwise to the chiefs and to Lord George Murray. Intelligence was received at Derby that the *Royal Ecossais* under Lord John Drummond had arrived at Montrose. This was interpreted as meaning that the entire Irish Brigade would follow.

The Jacobite army left Derby on December 6th, as usual before dawn. The Highlanders were looking forward to the battle they thought they were soon to wage, and for which they had spent the previous day having their claymores and dirks sharpened by the local cutlers. However, with daylight they realised they were heading North. Discipline, exemplary up to then, now broke down. Two or three Highlanders could be seen riding bareback the same unfortunate horse with a straw bridle which they may well have stolen from one of their own people. There was some pillaging and in turn savage attacks by the infuriated country people. Some clansmen ended up in ditches with slit throats. They now encountered nothing but hostility. Even Manchester, reputed to be the most Jacobite town in the country, had turned against them. 'The quartermasters were sent before with a party of horse to prepare quarters . . . But as the whole town was in uproar and showed an inclination to attack them, they were obliged to return to the army, and there were two battalions and two squadrons ordered to support them, upon which the mob dispersed.' By way of a punishment the Prince demanded £5,000, a huge sum at this time; but he had to content himself with only half.

The retreat must have been a nightmare for Elcho who was now in command of the rearguard. Continually on the alert — enemy horsemen could be seen on the surrounding hills — he must have always been wondering what Charles Edward's next order might well be. After Preston he had a brush with a detachment of General Oglethorpe's troop in which he had the upper hand. The Highlanders were so speedy that they had outstripped Cumberland by the time they reached Lancaster leaving him behind. 'It was a shame', thought the Prince, 'to go so fast in front of the son of the Usurper,' and he decided to stay and give battle. This seemed reasonable in the eyes of the 'principal officers' who were not adverse to fighting on condition it was on a suitable terrain. So Lord George left to reconnoitre in company of O'Sullivan, now the Prince's sole military advisor. Needless to say the two men did not agree, the latter insisting on a place to conform to the rules laid down in military textbooks, but totally unsuited to the Highlanders' type of warfare. Whereupon the Prince changed his mind and the army marched on.

Lord George's progress was delayed by the locals who had rendered the road well nigh impassable. Whereupon he captured two of Cumberland's footmen through whom he learnt that their chief was close to hand. He 'had just time to march to a village called Clifton in a hollow when the Duke appeared and drew up his horse in battle on a hill half a cannon shot above the village.' Lord George sent an aide-de-damp to the Prince to tell him that this was a good opportunity to do battle as the numbers were about equal and the terrain suitable for infantry. 'Charles Edward, however, thought otherwise and only sent a detachment to succour Lord George [which was to arrive after the affair was over] and marched off the rest of the army to Carlisle and left orders for Lord George to follow.' As Elcho sarcastically noted, 'there was formerly a contradiction to make the army halt when it was necessary to march, so now there was one to march and shun fighting when there could never be got a better opportunity got for it.' In the ensuing encounter, known as the 'skirmish of Clifton', Lord George again made good use of the Highlanders own way of fighting, and attacking, sword in hand, drove the Dragoons first into the hedgerows, then back to the main body stationed on the hill, before making his retreat to Penrith after having killed forty or fifty of them; and then to Carlisle without being molested, the Duke not wishing to press on with men tired after long marches through the snow. The English saw Elcho as 'the joint author' with Lord George of the stand at Clifton. But Elcho was now notorious (the credit for the Jacobite success was more properly ascribed to Cluny Macpherson and to his clansmen). It was also put about that the Highlanders were being heard to clamour for the right to kill their prisoners.

The next move was to Scotland. The Prince now insisted, against unanimous advice, on leaving the Manchester regiment and some of the Irish piquets to hold the ancient castle of Carlisle in the name of King James. He could not bear having to relinquish the last of his English possessions, and gave as an excuse that the Castle was impregnable without siege cannon and that the road from the south was impossible for such. But Cumberland had siege cannon brought by sea to the nearby post of Whitehaven and in a very short time the unfortunate garrison was hanging out the white flag. All they could extract from the Duke was the promise not to 'put them to the sword', leaving it to his father to take the final decisions. King George was in no mood to be lenient. Although he never thought his crown to be in jeopardy — in which he showed more sense than his ministers — he was very angry at the way he had been obliged to withdraw his troops from the Continent, thus weakening the war against France. So the Irish, who were in French pay, were looked upon as prisoners-of-war, whilst the unfortunate English were to be treated as rebels, (as was to be the case for all prisoners, English or Scottish of the Forty-Five). He was acting strictly within the law. Charles Edward was blamed for having wantonly sent these unfortunate men of the Carlisle garrison to their death; but by now he was past caring.

Crossing an Esk in full spate was a remarkable feat which only Highlanders could have performed. They linked arms thus breaking the force of the torrent and the army crossed without loss of life with the exception of some poor woman who got carried away. On reaching the other bank the bagpipes began to play and the men began to dance, an excellent way of getting dry and keeping warm. They were soon in Scotland but the country was more hostile than anything they had encountered in England. It was the land of the Covenanters where the 'killing times' and the 'Highland Host' were still within living memory, and among the first things they came across were the still glowing embers of bonfires lit to celebrate their wrongly-reported defeat in Lancashire. Such behaviour demanded retribution, all the more that the inhabitants of Dumfries had pillaged their baggage during the siege of Carlisle. It fell to Elcho to exact it. The Jacobites 'behaved very rudely, stripped everybody almost to their shoes, obliged the town to give them £1,000 and a considerable quantity of shoes and carried away Provost Crosbie and Mr Walter Riddle merchant as hostages for £1,000 which was yesterday sent the to relive (sic) these gentlemen,' wrote the Duke of Queensbury's distraught factor. He had received 'orders to kill a great number of black cattle and sheep and to produce a great quantity of meal', it being the Prince's intention to bivouac at Drumlanrig Castle, property of the Duke.It must have been here that Elcho rejoined the bulk of the army.

Its behaviour was shocking. 'They laid straw in the whole rooms for the private men to lie on except Your Grace's chamber, where the Prince lay, and a few rooms more', wailed the distraught factor.

'They killed about forty sheep . . . most of them in the vestibule and the foot of the principal stairs which they left in a sad pickle as they did the whole house. Under the gallery they kept several of their horses which they made a shift to get up the stairs. They have destroyed all the spirits and most of the wine . . . They have broken every chair and table, melted down a good deal of pewter by setting it on fire and carried away a good deal of linen and other things . . . I found the house worse than I could imagine before I saw it [but] they would have done much more mischief had not the Duke of Perth stayed 'til most of them were gone.' One wonders what Elcho's feelings can well have been. Drumlanrig had been his grandmother's home, and was that of his old school friend with whom he had shared the delights of Paris only two short years ago.

It was the 27th December 1745 that Charles Edward made his entry into Glasgow 'the prettiest and most Whiggish town in all Scotland' and marched through the town 'dressed in the French dress attended by his guard', before reviewing the 'whole army that had been to England'. He 'noted with satisfaction that the losses have been inconsiderable.' Financially, too, the venture had not proved a disaster, as he had returned a little better off than when he had left. He evidently hoped to win over the Glaswegians, or at least their womenfolk, for never had he taken so much trouble over his appearance. But if he expected a repetition of his Holyrood successes he was doomed to disappointment, 'the very ladies would not accept a ball at his court, or go near it, and were even so loyal as to pronounce him as far from being good looking', although other sources do say that some of the younger ones allowed themselves to be tempted. According to Elcho the 'Prince supped every night in public and there was always a great deal of company come to look at him.' The coolness of his reception made him feel even more vengeful, and he ordered the town to produce 1,200 shirts and 6,000 bonnets, pairs of shoes, pairs of stockings and waistcoats 'mounting to near £1,000 and took hostage for the payment of it'. The Provost complained that 'the authority of the rebels was worse than a French and could only compare with a Turkish despotism.' Yet

the legend persists that Lochiel, the Prince residing with his
Campbell aunt at Shawfield House, saved Whiggish Glasgow from
being sacked by vengeful Highlanders.

Charles Edward had set his heart on capturing Stirling, and
Lord John Drummond was ordered to meet him there with the
cannon. From a strategic point of view the possession of this great
stronghold presented few advantages now that Edinburgh was in
the hands of the Government. It had been strengthened in previous
decades to contain the Highlanders; but these were now occupying
a large part of the Lowlands. However eighty years of fighting in
Flanders, where the aim was to secure or defend the great frontier
strongholds, had conditioned military thinking. Investing a fortress
was the hallmark of success and a source of prestige. Now the
Prince had failed to capture Edinburgh Castle and had just lost
Carlisle. So he set his heart on getting Stirling, and marched his
army off in two columns, which took up its quarters round Stirling.
Charles Edward made Bannockburn House his headquarters,
whilst Lord George chose Falkirk, possibly in order to avoid the
Irish, who now surrounded the Prince almost to the exclusion of
the Scots.

Bringing the cannon from Fife to the south side of the Forth
presented a problem. In the normal case of things it would have
been moved up the Firth on barges. But all the shipping was safely
on the south bank on Government territory thanks to the tireless
efforts of Walter Grosset, a Customs Officer and one of Lord
Milton's most active agents. So they had to be laboriously lugged
to Elphinstone over bad roads made worse by abominable weather
conditions where they would be transferred to flat bottomed boats
brought down from the Highland lochs for the purpose. This was
to take place under the protection of a battery of which Elcho was
placed in charge. In the words of the *Journal* 'It was about this
time that I just escaped being made prisoner. I was in command of
a battery on the shores of the Forth so as to protect the arrival by
sea of the guns and ammunition needed for the siege. I was living
in a house called Kersie, belonging to a gentleman called Wright,

which stood just above the battery which was at Elphinston. One night the enemy sailed passed the battery and searched Kersie. As luck would have it I was that night at the battery which opened fire on the boats as they returned, killing some men on board them. A few days later they returned in nine men-o-war but were repulsed.'

At first Stirling held out, but a few well directed cannon balls led the citizens to hang out the white flag. But General Blakeney who was in command of the Castle, was made of sterner stuff and the siege did not succeed. Digging trenches proved both difficult and dangerous, for there was solid rock under the thin layer of soil and the unfortunate Lowlanders and Irish to whom the task fell were always within range of snipers. No Highlander would demean himself by using pick and shovel.

Elcho was now in Falkirk with Lord George. One wonders on what terms he was with the Prince? Hardly cordial ones given what had happened at Derby. But it was difficult for Charles Edward to openly fall out with a man who had sacrificed his all to his cause and who had been his companion in Rome. With the exception of Sheridan, Elcho was the only man in Scotland holding that position. However, what is sure is that he frequented Bannockburn House, for it was here that he made what proved to be a lifelong relationship with Clementina Walkinshaw. Elcho avers that she immediately became the Prince's mistress. In this he is perhaps mistaken although she may well have told him so taking her dreams for reality. But at this time the Prince was still under a vow of chastity which he seems only to have broken on his return to France.

During this time Lord George had not remained idle, and on hearing that provisions were being poured into Linlithgow in preparation for the arrival of General Hawley, he decided to capture them for the Jacobites. On reaching the town he placed patrols on the Edinburgh road with instruction to inform him should the enemy come into sight. At about noon a message arrived saying that a party of dragoons had been seen. Elcho was sent in pursuit, a pursuit which he carried on even after they had received reinforcements and which he only abandoned when confronted with a very large body of horse. The enemy was on the march. Lord George now called a council of war where it was decided to wait 'til the enemy arrived close to the town and then retreat in good order' for as their numbers were not known it was not thought proper to engage them, especially as a general battle was expected.' All went according to plan 'til they were caught up whilst crossing a bridge. 'Very abusive language passed between both sides, but Lord George's rear made so good an appearance, and retreated in such good order that the dragoons never offered to attack them, nor did any of them pass the bridge that night'. The *Journal* becomes lyrical about the way Lord George 'made an admirable retreat right under the nose of the enemy without the loss of a single man', whilst the Chevalier Johnstone gives most of the credit to Elcho.

They now rejoined the bulk of the Jacobite army which was preparing to do battle. They seized the hill to the south of Falkirk. Fighting only started at four o'clock, with a disastrous attempt by Hawley's cavalry in the gathering gloom of a winter's day to dislodge them, followed by a melée which put the government left wing and centre to flight. Elcho lost track of the Prince whom he was escorting. At one time both armies believed they had been defeated, and it was only when the Jacobites discovered that the enemy had retreated to Edinburgh after setting fire to their camp that they realised they had won another victory. The Highlanders were soon streaming home with their loot, as was their wont.

Although pressed to recapture his capital, Charles Edward chose to return to Stirling. In the meantime Cumberland had arrived in Edinburgh to a tumultuous welcome. As soon as Hawley's defeat became known 'four Whig gentlemen' had been sent to London to beg the King to send up his son. This the monarch was all the more willing to do now that the threat of a French invasion was over.

William, Duke of Cumberland, was the very antithesis of his cousin, Charles Edward. All they had in common was their age, being both close to twenty-five. Large and very fat, he was not the heir to the throne, and therefore did not take much interest in politics. His whole life was dedicated to soldiering. He spent a great deal of his time studying the art of war and was always ready to seek the advice of men older and more experienced than himself. He was a strict disciplinarian, as was always the case in the days when armies were made of mercenaries recruited amongst the unemployed of many lands. But he had the welfare of his men at heart and was popular with them. He would no doubt have gone down as a competent, if not a brilliant commander had he not had the misfortune of always being pitted against Saxe, who was a genius in this field.

It did not take him long to re-establish the badly shaken confidence of the men, and the many deserters were soon returning to the colours; they had probably fled as much from the wrath of the notoriously brutal Hawley, as from the Highlanders. A fortnight later he was marching on Stirling, his army strengthened by new regiments, two of which came from the Scottish Lowlands and were therefore perhaps strongly motivated. 'Upon intelligence from Edinburgh that the Duke of Cumberland was to march west at the head of his army ... Lord George Murray and all the Chiefs of the clans held a Council and drew up a paper which they all signed and sent to the Prince, the purport of which was that vast numbers to their men had gone home . . and that they were no way in condition to face the Duke's army. They concluded by advising the Prince to march his army north to Inverness, to destroy Lord Loudon's army and all his enemies in that country, to take and demolish all the forts in the north . . and they assured him . . they would by next spring put him at the head of eight or ten thousand Highlanders to follow him wherever he pleased.'

The Prince was in bed at the time the message arrived and it was only delivered the following morning by old Sir Thomas Sheridan. 'When Charles read the paper he struck his head against the wall til he staggered, and exclaimed most violently against Lord George Murray. His words were "Good God! Have I lived to see this!"' There was, however, nothing to be done and 'he and Lord George Murray concerted that on the first of February all the army should . . . cross the Forth at the Frews, that all the heavy cannon should be nailed, and all the ammunition which could not be carried along should be destroyed and that Lord George should have 1200 chosen foot and Lord Elcho's troop with which he undertook to wait a great while after the army and make the arriere guard and prevent the Duke's horse from following.'

The plan was that the Prince should review the whole army at ten next morning, this being a way of checking the number of the deserters, after which it would retreat in good order to Dunkeld and then on to Crieff and Perth.   However, the whole plan was changed on the advice of the Prince's Irish favourites, who were systematically counteracting every move of Lord George's, who was not even told of the change.   When orders were issued to go to Dunblane 'everybody was struck with amazement for everybody . . . expected a battle, and it appeared strange to run away form the very army that had been beat only a fortnight before. Never was there a retreat [which] resembled so much a flight. . . for there was nowhere 1000 men together and the whole army passed the river in small bodies and in great confusion leaving carts and cannon on the road behind them. . . Elcho's orders were to remain on the bridge of Carron until ordered to leave.   But he never was told, either through negligence or by malice — his attachment to Lord George had made him many enemies — and he was very nearly captured by men from the Castle. He was livid, for although willing to die fighting for the Cause he drew the line at being 'hung drawn and quartered' by the common hangman.' His rage had not abated when he attended the council-of-war forced on the Prince by the Scots at Crieff, where according to Maxwell of Kirkconnel, 'there never had been such heats and animosities as this meeting;'   however, after a great deal of wrangling it was decided 'that the horse and low country regiments should march towards Inverness along the coast while the Prince with the clans took the Highland road thither.'

CHAPTER EIGHT

Retreat and Defeat

Lord George now assembled his troops at Perth from where he despatched them to different places: Lord Ogilvy and his men to their native Angus with the task of raising more recruits; Lord Pitsligo to Peterhead, where he was to secure the arms and money deposited by a Spanish ship, whilst Elcho was assigned Montrose which, however, he had soon to quit when the town was taken over by a boarding party from one of Rear-Admiral Byng's ships now cruising off the coast. He then rejoined Lord George Murray and Lord John Drummond who were now at Aberdeen. Lord George then rejoined the Prince at Culloden House after having placed troops at strategic points, Elcho's Life Guards being stationed at Forres. The whole operation had gone off smoothly, the local population being either friendly or battered into submission by Lord Lewis Gordon, whose country this was. The Jacobites had suffered more from the weather than from the enemy, it having been atrocious. 'At the end of this long march, Lord Kilmarnock, Lord Pitsligo and Lord Balmerino's troops went to nothing, the length of the march had destroyed all their horses.' Balmerino was made governor of Nairn and Kilmarnock colonel of an infantry regiment made up of the men from his own troop. The Life Guards, however, remained mounted, they being the elite cavalry corps.

Charles Edward had had an easier time. After a short stay at Blair Castle, home of the Dukes of Atholl, he went on to Moy, having captured on the way the fort of Ruthven, whose tiny garrison had held out against him on his way to Perth. At Moy the Chieftain of the Mackintoshes was absent, being with Lord Loudon, but Charles

Edward was welcomed by his wife, a fervent Jacobite who came to be known as Colonel Anne, she having raised the clan for the Cause. There then followed Lord Loudon's unsuccessful attempt to capture him from Inverness, foiled by Colonel Anne with the help of the local blacksmith, and Lord Loudon's retreat with the MacLeod militia into Ross-shire.

The Prince took up his quarters at Culloden House, home of the Lord President, from where he directed operations. The clan regiments were sent to their homes to visit their families, raise more men and besiege Fort William and Fort Augustus.

It seemed as if things were going reasonably well for the Cause. Loudon was no longer a threat, and the country north of the Tay was largely in Jacobite hands. Morale was therefore high when the Prince received a letter from a Captain Shee informing him that three troops of the Franco-Irish Cavalry regiment Fitzjames with horse furniture and funds had landed at Aberdeen towards the end of February. They were intended to be the forerunners of an invasion force some 800 strong. These succours were considerable in themselves and were looked upon as a proof that the Court of France was determined to support the Prince — a thing people had begun to doubt. Euphoria now reigned in Jacobite ranks; it really did look as if the luck had turned.

On hearing that the French were planning to send reinforcements to Scotland, Cumberland left Perth, where he had intended to spend the winter, and marched up to Aberdeen where three squadrons of the Franco-Irish Cavalry with red uniforms turned up with blue had successfully disembarked. But the main reinforcement was deterred from landing by the presence in Aberdeen of Cumberland's troops. As Cumberland was being supplied by sea he was not obliged to make inroads on the local provisions, which made his occupation far more acceptable. Once settled in Aberdeen he set about to systematically destroy the Episcopalian places of worship, which 'our soldiers burnt but with good husbandry and good frugality, not consuming the pile at once, as was often the case, the wood being industriously preserved to heat our bakers' ovens', wrote the volunteer Rae. This was no wild act of blind fanaticism but an effort to stamp out a church seen, not without some reason, as the source of Jacobite ideology. Nor did he neglect social life; he gave many balls and made himself so pleasant that despite his girth many a young lady switched her allegiance from one cousin to the other. But his main preoccupation was preparing his men to meet that Highland furia which had led to their defeat both at Prestonpans and at Falkirk. He had worked out a method by which this could be achieved by holding the bayonets at a slant so that they transfixed the left hand assailant under his right arm raised to strike. It was to prove effective at Culloden, the only place where it was every put into practice, but it demanded a great deal of drill.

The ship carrying Shee was soon followed by another bringing funds which had to be remitted to the French ambassador in person. So d'Eguilles left for Peterhead in company of Lord John who wanted to check on the disposition of his troops. They were met on the way with the news that Aberdeen was now in the hands of Cumberland whose men were systematically clearing the country of Jacobites.

This led the Prince to move to Elgin where he fell ill, but not before he had awarded 'superior commissions' to the newly arrived Irish officers, 'mounting 70 of Fitzjames' on horseback', and this at a time when two Scottish cavalry regiments had just been dismounted for lack of mounts. Such partiality was greatly resented. He also mendaciously gave out that 'he had received letters from France . . . that the French were equipping a squadron of men of war at Brest and Rochefort in order to send over his brother the Duke of York. It was necessary to give out such pieces in order to keep up his men's spirits.'

Once recovered, Charles Edward set about taking different dispositions to suit the new situations: the troops were called back from Aberdeenshire and stationed on the left bank of the Spey, where huts were built for their accommodation, and he placed Lord John in command of the area. In contrast to what had happened at

Stirling, the retreat was achieved in an orderly fashion without the loss of a man. It was soon to be followed by a number of sorties, the one to Keith, in which Elcho took part, being a spectacular success. The town was raided and its Campbell garrison all taken prisoner and taken to Forres where they were 'very ill used as they had plundered several gentlemen's houses in Banff and Aberdeenshire who were in the Prince's army'. They were later sent to France 'but this scheme of sending hostages was begun too late' and it was difficult to find ships to convey them. The problem of prisoners was becoming acute, for as Johnstone explains, 'having taken a great many English prisoners . . . it became difficult to know how to dispose of them. As our ambulatory army was continually in motion, they continually escaped so at last very few remained with us; and what was still worse they joined their different regiments so we had always to encounter the same men whom we had vanquished and whose lives we had spared. There were two ways of avoiding this inconvenience either to send them to France or to take no prisoners and put all the enemy to the sword, which might be deemed fighting on equal terms, as every Scotsman who was captured was sure to perish on the scaffold. Indeed it was the only kind of warfare that we ought to have adopted to infuse more terror into the enemy and to prevent us from having to combat the same individuals over and over again . . . Mr Peter Smith (brother to Smith of Methven) . . . suggested to the Prince a means of extracting ourselves from this dilemma, which was to cut off the thumbs of their right hands to render them incapable of holding their muskets.' Fortunately the Prince turned down this barbarous suggestion which, however, was saddled on Elcho, and was to stick to him throughout his life despite his repeated denials.

The next move was to prevent a junction between Loudon and Cumberland. So the Duke of Perth set off at the head of a large force to try and capture both Loudon and his army. He landed at Dornoch in a thick fog and fell upon what was believed to be the prey but which turned out to be only a portion of the enemy force. They were taken prisoner, although not before a warning had reached Loudon and President Forbes, who retired to Skye with eight hundred men. All the Jacobites were able to capture by way of loot were two ships loaded with provisions, whilst the war chest, which was what they were after, had been embarked in time on a naval vessel. However, the 'public monies' were still in the custody of the Earl of Sutherland, and McDonnel of Barrisdale was despatched to Dunrobin to get hold of them.

If this came to Elcho's ears he must have been deeply concerned, for Barrisdale truly deserved the appellation of 'bandit'. This fair-haired giant — he was said to be able to lift a cow unaided — was notorious both as a cattle rustler and the associated protection racket he operated known as 'blackmail'. He was, what is more, a sadist who had even invented an instrument of torture. On his arrival he discovered to his fury that his prey had flown, the Earl having escaped by sea carrying the precious monies with him. The ensuing confrontation with the Countess — Elcho's aunt — was nothing if not violent. 'One of their officers held a dirk at Milady's breast to get account where your Lordship was', wrote one of her husband's faithful retainers; he got no satisfactory answer and 'another officer pushed it by Milady's breast, the edge touching the skin . . . and although her ladyship prepared all good entertainment for them, they made a stable of your drawing room and stole one of the silver snuffers.' They seized all the horses, entered all the rooms and took away all arms and ammunition. Lady Sutherland complained to the Prince, asking for his protection. 'It is known over most of the kingdom my attachment to Your Royal Highness' family,' and had not all her horses been taken, she 'would have waited on you.' She had obeyed Barrisdale's instructions and had sent round orders that those clansmen who were in arms should go home 'in order that a proper draft be made of them for Your Royal Highness' service.' However, she doubted she would be obeyed, 'but if matters were further at my disposal the fencible men in Sutherland would be at Your Royal Highness' service as I am quite afrighted.'

After having taken part in the expedition against Lord Loudon,

Lord George went off to Atholl in response to an appeal from the now occupied people of this area. Thanks to his intimate knowledge of the country, Lord George was able to surprise the enemy, making many prisoners in the process. He then laid siege to his old home, Blair Castle, now defended by a tough old Scotsman, Sir Andrew Agnew, who was not one to allow himself to be intimidated. Not having the necessary cannon to breach the walls, Lord George endeavoured to reduce the garrison by starvation, and he might well have succeeded had not the Prince of Hesse come to the rescue. During the ensuing skirmishes the Jacobites captured a Hessian officer who turned out to be a Swede with whom Lord George conversed in Latin. He was soon on his way back to his commander bearing the request for a cartel. This Hesse would have been perfectly willing to grant seeing in Lord George a courteous and honourable opponent. But it was vetoed by Cumberland who would have no truck with 'traitors'. The Hessians showed little inclination to fight an enemy believed to give no quarter, so Lord Crawford, who had been so kind to Elcho in Flanders, now appeared on the scene. He was not the most energetic of commanders, but Lord George now found himself so greatly outnumbered that he was obliged to lift the siege and return to Inverness, where his enemies were putting about that he had spared Blair Castle because it belonged to his brother, and that he had had a treasonable correspondence with the Prince of Hesse!

Charles Edward was more persuaded than ever that his general was a traitor. These suspicions were widely held, notably by d'Eguilles and were fanned by the Irish who hated the Scots as much as they were hated by them. 'What displeased the people of fashion was that [the Prince] did not seem to have the least sense of what they had done for him, but on the contrary would often say that they had done nothing but their duty as his father's subjects were to do; then, as he had his head full of notions of commanding his army as if they had been mercenaries, and had their fortunes dependant upon his will and pleasure, he never consulted with any of them or let them know in the least any of his schemes, but managed all his affairs in a hidden way with his favourites Sir Thomas Sheridan, Mr O'Sullivan, Murray and Hay.' Hay of Restalrig had replaced a now ill Murray of Broughton, as the Prince's confidential secretary.

The party was already deeply divided when the Prince learned that 'the French had laid aside all thoughts of sending any men over either to England or Scotland, and that Duke of York was in Paris' and no longer with the projected landing force at Dunkirk — up to then Charles Edward had always spoken of his brother's landing in England as being imminent. Now his talk was about a Swedish expedition of three hundred officers whom the French were about to send out. Needless to say these never materialised. In the hope of bolstering up a sagging morale at Inverness he gave balls and even danced at them, which he had never done at Holyrood, and when approached he would aver that the 'Duke of Cumberland's soldiers would be so conscious of the highness [sic] of fighting against their true and lawful Prince that when ever he appeared they would certainly run away. [Although] he believed this firmly, he had difficulty in persuading other people of these notions who were in any ways acquainted with the English soldiers.'

Elcho felt free at this stage to visit Inverness, no doubt attracted by the presence of such charmers as Lady Ogilvy, Mrs Murray of Broughton and 'Colonel Anne', for he dearly loved female company. What he found must have filled him with gloom. 'The preference the prince gave to the Irish over the Scots, which he did on all occasions' was causing bitter resentment. 'His reasons for that were that they were of his own religion and always paid more court to him in their discourses. As they had nothing at stake and were only there to gain his favour and protection, whatever he proposed they were for, whereas many of his schemes were very ill formed, and as the Scots had their lives depending [on them] they sometimes took the liberty of representing against them which the Prince took highly amiss.' At the best of times Scots did not get on well with the Irish and 'knowing that we disliked them they had inspired in the Prince a hatred for Lord George Murray, Lord John

Drummond and his old banker, Mr Aeneas MacDonald who had always been loyal to him.' He might had added his own name to the list.

Another subject of complaint was food, for although there was no real shortage of oatmeal or salted beef, which to the disgust of the French had become the staple diet; their distribution had become deplorable since Hay of Restalrig had taken over from the efficient Murray of Broughton. What was even more damaging was the almost total lack of funds, there being no 'public monies' to purloin, or Whig landowners to blackmail and castles to plunder. Cullen, whose owner Lord Findlater had 'refused to pay a contribution to the Prince', had been occupied earlier on, but Cumberland had promptly retaliated by withdrawing his protection from the ladies, with the result that the Dowager Duchess of Perth found herself confined to Edinburgh Castle (whilst the three above-mentioned charmers were to be arrested whilst making preparations for the ball which was to celebrate the Jacobite victory of Culloden).

'There was great discontent in the army . . . both among the officers and the soldiers. As money was very scarce with the [Prince], he paid his troops mostly in meal which they did not like and [they] very often mutinied, refused to obey orders and sometimes threw down their arms and went home; it would have been impossible for him ever to have marched in the face [sic] of an army over the Spey without money, for people who would have willingly fought [at] Inverness would never had marched out of the country without pay. This led to the Irish representing the Scots as being a 'mutinous people fighting for themselves rather than for him,' and they were careful to remind him of 'their bad behaviour towards King Charles first', with the result that 'at the battle of Culloden he thought all the Scots were a parcel of traitors . . . but the care they took of him whilst he was in hiding made him change his mind . . . private gentlemen who had no command were very much to be pitied . . . and some were of very good estate who never either spoke to the Prince or ate with him; and as he knew nothing of the families of this country he used to look upon them in the light of common dragoons.'

The situation was hopeless, a fact of which both Lord George and Elcho were well aware. Writing to his wife just after Falkirk Lord George Murray with a presentiment of doom said he regretted not having been killed 'as I imagined to myself that by that means to save my family from forfetry.' Ever since Derby it had been abundantly clear that as a political force Jacobitism was dying, that a restoration was nothing but wishful thinking, and that the only sensible thing to do was to negotiate a surrender, which at this time could have been obtained on reasonable terms: the Jacobites were still undefeated whilst Cumberland was longing to get back to Flanders, where in the absence of the British troops, Saxe was flying from victory to victory. But 'as in his conversation [the Prince] used always to swear he would never lay down his arms as long as two men would stick to him, nobody ever thought of asking terms from the Government, but on the contrary stand by the cause whither good or bad as long as it would last.' As Charles Edward persisted in his belief that the Highlanders were invincible, and that Cumberland's soldiers would not take arms against him, nothing could be done about it. *Le Vin etoit tiré, il falloit le boire* wrote a dispirited Elcho. Morale was already low when it was learnt that a French sloop carrying a handful of soldiers and a good supply of funds, had been chased up to the north coast of Sutherland by a frigate of the Royal Navy, H.M.S. *Sheerness*, where it had been captured by the Whiggish Mackays, who duly delivered up the prisoners to the authorities, but retained the funds. 'The loss of this money was inexpressible', wrote Maxwell of Kirkconnel; 'the Prince's affairs never had so bad an aspect [for] notwithstanding all the care was taken to conceal it, it disheartened the army. The soldiers began to murmur afresh, and some of them deserted . . . The Prince was never so much at a loss what resolution to take.'

Lord Cromartie now marched into the northern Highlands at the head of his Mackenzies. His orders were that his son, Lord Macleod, should go to Sutherland, recapture the gold, put the delinquent Mackays to 'fire and sword', persuade the hesitant Sinclairs to join the Prince and lay his hands on whatever 'public monies' there were to be had, whilst he himself would go with O'Sullivan to Dunrobin to see if Lady Sutherland had either recruited her husband's people for the use of the Prince — which was most unlikely — or had had them disarmed. Should this not be the case, they too, must be 'put to fire and the sword'. It was a most unpalatable mission for he was friends with the Sutherlands, and more especially with Lady Sutherland with whom he was connected, for as we have seen, his grandfather, the first Earl, had been married to her great-grandmother, Margaret, Countess of Wemyss, and the families had been friends ever since. He and O'Sullivan were received with great amiability by Lady Sutherland, who stressed her attachment to the Cause, but bitterly complained about the treatment she had received at the hands of Barrisdale. O'Sullivan assured her that the Prince had been greatly shocked and had taken steps to prevent it ever recurring again. He then disclosed his instructions: her husband's people must lay down their arms or pay the penalty. She assured him that she had done all in her power to see that this was done, but that they stood in fear of the Caithness people — presumably the Sinclairs — who were hereditary foes and that they would only disarm after these had marched through. Cromartie now offered to remain at Dunrobin until the disarming could take place, and O'Sullivan departed wondering if she was as attached to the Cause as she pretended to be.

When he returned it was only to discover that 'Lord Cromartie was no more advanced than when he had left him.' Embarrassed, 'the Earl began to speak high and assured Lady Sutherland that the next day he would burn three or four houses of the officers that were in the mountains with her men. The lady wrote immediately to the officers to return, and begged Lord Cromartie to abstain for two days which he did, and found himself a prisoner at Dunrobin, the delay having enabled Captain Mackay of the Sutherland militia to trap the Jacobite men'. Whilst his mistress was entertaining

Cromartie and his officers with copious libations, Mackay had first bolted the Castle gates, after which he fell on the now leaderless clansmen and routed them with a heavy loss of life. In the meantime Lady Sutherland, who had no wish to see her old friend arrested under her roof, hid him under her bed, from where he was unceremoniously pulled out by the all too energetic Mackay. The prisoners were bundled on to a sloop and arrived at Leith 'pouring out bitter reflections, curses and imprecations on the Countess of Sutherland.' Cromartie and his son were brought to London where he was condemned to the scaffold and Macleod to a long period of detention. However both were reprieved. Indeed the latter was to finish as Colonel of his own regiment of Highlanders in the British army. One would like to think that this happy ending owed something to Lady Sutherland, to her charm and to the prestige she had acquired by means of her brave action. This episode took place on the very eve of Culloden, and Elcho cannot have been aware of it at the time. What we do know is that he was very hurt when the Sutherlands refused to see him a few years later when on a trip to the Continent. He was never able to come to terms with the unfortunate fact that his Whig relations, and more especially those who had been so kind to him, resented the way he had joined the rebellion thus becoming a traitor in the eyes of the law.

In the meantime the Prince summoned all his troops to Inverness on news that Cumberland was advancing from Aberdeen. To Lochiel in distant Lochaber he wrote 'Those that love me will follow me'. 'It is not to be imagined with what joy the first news of this march was received in the Prince's army', wrote Maxwell of Kirkconnel, 'the prospect was now entirely changed, the affair must be decided in a few days.' Cumberland reached the banks of the Spey on April 12, 1746 where he encountered a detachment of Life Guards sent to gather information. Their Commander, Hunter of Burnside, had his horse shot beneath him, and only escaped capture by scrambling on to that of one of his troopers. There was never any question of defending the passage, the river being low and fordable in many places. Perth, who was now in command, ordered a retreat to Culloden, which took place in good order with no losses on the way. Cumberland pitched his camp at Nairn whilst the twenty-eight ships carrying his provisions anchored close inshore, as was their wont. His advance was too speedy for Barrisdale and the MacGregors to join, or more surprisingly for the Macphersons from nearby Badenoch.

Elcho reached Culloden House on the evening of the 14th to find Charles Edward in residence. 'I supped there that night with the Prince, who had no doubts as to the issue of the conflict, he had a most exalted idea of his cause, and believed it would be difficult to get the English soldiers to attack him; indeed his mere presence would be sufficient to frighten them away. Those who spoke of a retreat and waiting for the 3,000 soldiers who had not as yet turned up were not listened to [in all probability Elcho is referring to himself] and when asked for a rendez-vous in case of defeat, he answered only those who were afraid could doubt a victory. In short his boastfulness that night was unworthy of a Prince.'

It was thought that the battle would take place on the following day; so the men took up their battle stations on a flat stretch of moor chosen by O'Sullivan against Lord George's advice, who pointed out that it was ideal for troops trained to manoeuvre on the fields of Flanders but fatal for Highlanders who needed to charge down a hill and preferably with a bog to hamper the enemy cavalry. There the men remained stationed for five hours before Elcho was sent to reconnoitre. He remained three hours in sight of the enemy before returning with the news that the Duke was celebrating his twenty-fifth birthday with his men. So the clansmen were dismissed and told to find what food they could, Hay having omitted to get the necessary bread baked. The Prince now called a council-of-war, the first since Derby, the one at Crieff having been imposed upon him. Lord George suggested a night march to surprise a camp sleeping off the repeated toasts to 'our Billie' — Cumberland was popular with his men. Surprisingly the suggestion was universally approved of, even by the Prince, and the departure was fixed for seven that night.

The plan was to attack the camp from three sides, cut the tent ropes and stab the soldiers smothered in the canvas before the alarm could be raised. Unfortunately Lord George had overlooked the fact that the heavily equipped troops of the *Royal Ecossais* and the Irish regiments had no training in what we would call commando tactics, or any experience of marching over treacherous terrain in the dark. The army set off in three columns headed respectively by Lord George, the Prince and Lord John. But the pace proved too fast, and Lord George was soon receiving desperate demands for a halt. This he refused, but he did slacken the pace with the result that they arrived in sight of the camp as the first drums were being beaten. All hopes of a surprise were over, and after consulting with Lochiel, Lord George ordered a retreat without first waiting for instructions from the Prince. These were to go on, and Charles Edward immediately jumped to the conclusion that he had been betrayed. It was then that he ordered the two Irishmen to shoot Lord George should he show any sign of treacherous behaviour. By the time the senior officers reached Culloden House they were so exhausted that all they could do was to slump down wherever they found room to stretch their weary limbs. One wonders if Elcho remembered the time he had been the Lord President's guest, and how the kindly old man had warned him whilst crossing the Firth, not to get involved in the Rebellion?

Two hours later trumpets sounded, drums were beaten, pipes wailed; the enemy had come into sight marching in perfect order as if on the parade ground. The senior officers hurriedly mounted their horses and went off to rally their hungry and sleepy men; some were so exhausted that they were to sleep right through the din of battle. The Life Guards were posted with what was left of the Jacobite cavalry to the right of the line with a view of preventing it from being outflanked by Cumberland's dragoons. This they succeeded in doing, thus saving the Prince from falling into the hands of the enemy. It was said that Cumberland never forgave Elcho for having prevented him from capturing his cousin, and that

that was the reason why the latter never received the pardon after which he was always to crave.

As is well known, the battle started by a fierce cannonade which claimed a great many Highland lives, soon followed by the usual mad onrush by the men of Atholl headed by Lord George, and followed by the Camerons, the Mackintosh regiment and the rest of the right wing. They pierced the first line but were halted by the second, the enemy using their slanted bayonets to good purpose. The scene now became one of utter confusion. The Clan Donald regiments on the left made as if to charge but wavered and took to their heels with most of the left wing. It soon became clear that the battle was irretrievably lost.

'The Prince, who at the beginning of the action was behind the Irish Piquets guarded by sixteen of Fitzjames' horse, turn'd about his horse and went off as soon as the left wing gave way, and never offered to rally any of the broken corps.' According to some account he was led off the field by O'Sullivan. But his nerve had given way as at Derby. He was soon followed by some five hundred men, for the most part officers in search of instructions. Elcho had ridden off the battlefield in company with Lord Balmerino, of whom he does not seem to have seen a great deal during the Rising, Balmerino being one of these devoted souls who believed the Prince could do no wrong. But Elcho was horrified to hear the old man say that it was his intention to give himself up 'should the Prince's troops not reassemble. I did all in my power to dissuade him saying that he would lose his head. He answered that of this he was fully aware, but that he was too old to survive such a disaster either by hiding or by seeking refuge abroad, and he knew he would meet death with calmness and thus enhance his reputation. He surrendered the following day and was beheaded with the Earl of Kilmarnock. No one died on the scaffold with more coolness and courage.'

A deeply moved Elcho rode off in search of the Prince, whom he found some four miles away 'in a deplorable state. Having always been flattered with false hopes that the Duke of Cumberland's army would take flight as had those of Cope and Hawley, he came to believe that all that had happened was by treachery, and he became afraid of all of the Scots whom he believed capable of delivering him up to obtain peace and the £30,000 placed on his head. He consulted no one, indeed spoke to no one except the Irish who were still with him. He asked them if all their officers had obtained a superior rank which might prove useful on their return to France. He appeared to be only concerned with their lot and not at all about the fate of the Scots. Seeing that the number of Scottish officers was increasing, he ordered them off to a village a mile away where he would send his orders'. These proved to be to disband and fend for themselves.

'I remained on and asked him if he had any orders for me. He told me I could go whereever I liked; as for himself he was about to leave for France. I said I was surprised by a resolution so little worthy of a prince of his birth; that it was unworthy of him to have got all these people to sacrifice themselves for him and then abandon them because he may have lost a thousand men in battle; that he ought to remain and place himself at the head of 9,000 who remained and live and die with them . . . I also pointed out that finding themselves without a leader, his followers would disperse and thus find themselves in the vengeful hands of the Duke of Cumberland. All these arguments made no impression upon him, and that his intention was to seek safety in France. Upon which I left resolved never to have anything more to do with him.' Elcho's parting words were 'There you go you damned Italian coward!' These are not to be found either in the *Narrative* or the *Journal*, but under the pen of Sir Walter Scott, who had them from the lips of Elcho's nephew Sir James Steuart Denham of whom he saw a great deal in his later years. They have the ring of truth and betray months of frustration when Elcho had been obliged to look on helplessly whilst this stupid young man allowed himself to be manipulated by his Irish friends, who ran little risk themselves and were out to get all they could out of the situation, and at the same time doing all in their power to harm their traditional opponents, the Scots.

Having got his followers into this mess Charles Edward was now far too frightened to take to the hills and wage the commando war which might have led Cumberland to offer decent terms of surrender. Instead of which he was fleeing to France abandoning his followers to their fate! Thinking back to the days of his youth, no wonder Elcho called him a 'damned Italian coward' [See Appendix].

Elcho now decided to seek out his old friend Aeneas MacDonald, the Paris banker, who had come over with the Prince, and had been working for him every since. He was at the home of the Kinlochmoidart family among the mountains of western Inverness-shire with his lieutenant colonel, Maxwell of Kirkconnel, and two of his six servants, the others having surrendered with his possessions after the battle. It had been hard going. 'On reaching Loch Arkaig we heard that the Prince had passed by there with Mr O'Sullivan. The roads were now so bad that we dismounted and proceeded on foot. [At] Kinloch Moydart we were received by Mr MacDonald, who was just back from the island of Barra, where he had gone to recover money left there by a Spanish ship', and which he was about to deliver to the Prince. This he proceeded to do, and returned from Borodale with the news that 'the Prince had despatched a man to Stornoway to hire a ship to take him to France, and had been advised to write to the chiefs fixing a rendez-vous when he would put himself at their head.' This was a ruse 'intended to distract the attention of the Duke of Cumberland and thus facilitate his escape . . . I received one of these letters'. It was seemingly written by O'Sullivan who begged Elcho 'in the Prince's name to gather up those of the Guards and others who were in the neighbourhood and go and join Lochiel, and that he would go and join them. Lord Elcho did not answer the letter but said, as was reported, that he was sorry enough for the folly and that he would never join the Standard.'

It must have been on the strength of this letter that Lochiel, encouraged by the arrival at the end of April of two large privateers from France with a large quantity of *louis d'or*, turned down

Cumberland's offer of terms on condition his clan lay down their arms, with disastrous results. Charles Edward now left for the Island of Lewis in company with O'Sullivan and another Irishman, Captain O'Neil, only to discover on his arrival that the vessel which had been chartered to take them to France had sailed away. Suspecting who his mysterious passenger would be, the captain refused to take the risk of being captured by one of the naval vessels soon to be patrolling the area. This was the start of Charles Edward's time 'in the heather' when his backwoodsman upbringing and his physical courage were to stand him in good stead and earn him universal admiration.

It was the end of April when 'Mr Macdonald having received word that the Duke of Cumberland, the Duke of Argyll and General Campbell were preparing to send troops to the Highlands', Elcho, Maxwell and Aeneas MacDonald took to the hills where they built themselves a bothie in sight of the sea. 'One day when I was walking I saw two large ships enter the Loch Nan Uamh, cast anchor and send boats ashore with a number of people. As my telescope enabled me to see that these mingled readily with the Highlanders led me to believe that they were French.' They sent a messenger who returned with the news that the ships were the *La Bellone* and *Le Mars* thirty-six gun privateering frigates and that they had been sent by the court of Versailles with arms and 36,000 gold louis for the Prince.' Elcho and Maxwell left immediately for Borrodale, but Aeneas MacDonald chose to remain, only to be arrested, tried, condemned to death, reprieved and finally pardoned.

The news of the French ships had spread fast and on arriving at Borrodale they found that they had been preceded by the Duke of Perth, Lord John Drummond, Murray of Broughton, Hay of Restalrig, Sir Thomas Sheridan, the Lanarkshire laird Lockhart of Carnwath, and a great number of Highland officers who were all complaining at 'having been abandoned by the Prince.' There was a great deal of recrimination. 'Mr Hay had the baseness and the effrontery to use I should remain and help keep the Highlanders together. I asked him why he intended to go to France? He

answered that the Prince's affairs demanded his presence — I
answered that my personal safety demanded mine.' Elcho was in
an aggressive mood. 'I once asked Secretary Murray why he always
took sides with the Prince against the whole army, and this when
he was fully aware that the advice he was giving had no rational
basis. He answered that the Prince was very stupid and could not
endure any opposition. In order to rule him one must always give
in to him, he added that he very often changed his mind . . . In a
word Mr Murray spoke of the Prince with the utmost contempt.'

On the day following his arrival Elcho was invited to dine on
board *Le Mars* whose captain, M Rouillé as commodore in overall
command was in dire trouble. He was aware 'of the Prince's
departure even though it was to be kept secret,' whilst the
Highlanders were clamouring for the six barrels which contained
the gold coins. These were in the charge of an Irishman called
Brown, who was refusing to deliver them without a written
permission from the Prince. But the Prince was out of reach, and
the Highlanders, who felt the money should be theirs, were
threatening to board the ship. The situation was all the more
dangerous that they had partaken liberally of the brandy which
also formed part of the cargo. In the absence of the Duke of Perth,
now too ill to take any action, Lord John Drummond was the senior
officer present. But he was in French pay and loath to go against
King Louis' orders. Elcho was under no such obligation, having
openly broken with the Prince. So after discussing the situation
with Lord John, who agreed with him that the money should
remain in Scotland, he had Brown arrested and frightened into
giving his consent. The 'Treasure of Loch Arkaig', of which Elcho
tells us that neither he nor Lord John ever touched a sou, was to
line many a pocket and cause a great deal of trouble.

'Having received notice from the French commander to hold
ourselves ready to embark, and that boats would be sent to fetch
us, we went to the seashore before daybreak on May 3rd. At dawn
we saw three English ships enter the Bay.' The ensuing battle,
which was to last three hours, was watched with the keenest

interest from the shore. 'It might have been a show put on expressly for our benefit, and at times the ships were so close that we could hear the words of command.' One who died was Major Hales of the *Royal Ecossais* 'when the ship of the English commodore began to fire', Elcho recorded, 'the captain of the French ship called on him to throw himself on his face. Major Hales answered that he was not in the habit of doing that, and was killed'. Outgunned but not outmanoeuvred, the English left in search of reinforcements, and the French spent the afternoon feverishly repairing the sails, fearing that the enemy would return in greater strength. Lord John, Elcho, Maxwell and Lockhart of Carnwarth embarked that evening on board the *La Bellone*, where a dying Perth had been hoisted in a blanket. He did not survive the journey and was buried at sea on *Le Mars* thus avoiding disputes about the Prince's behaviour, which was beginning to come under censure. Murray of Broughton remained on shore to look after the gold, as he said, adding to Elcho's and Maxwell's suspicions about his honesty.

As he entered the sea up to his waist before scrambling on board *La Bellone*, it cannot have occurred to Elcho that he would never again set foot on Scottish soil.

CHAPTER NINE

The Refugee

It was the June of 1746 when the two privateers dropped anchor at the mouth of the Loire. The crossing must have been a nightmare and the stench almost unbearable, for Elcho cannot have been alone to still be wearing the clothes in which he had fought at Culloden. No wonder that an epidemic had carried off a number of lives. 'We lost the Duke of Perth who died of a fever and was buried at sea; he was a very brave and gallant man and entirely devoted to the House of Stuart.' It was therefore a ruffianly looking crowd which scrambled out of the sloops which had brought them to Nantes, where its arrival caused a scare, it being mistaken for a pirate raid. 'However when it was learned that we were officers of Prince Charles Edward's army people could not have been kinder and more attentive.' They were escorted to the house of Antoine Walsh, the wealthy Irish ship owner and slave trader who had provided the vessel on which the Prince had come to Scotland. 'Mr Walsh did a great deal for us, providing us with fresh linen, whilst M. Roullie (sic), who had treated us somewhat roughly, would accept no payment for our passage and we parted good friends.'

Two days later a bathed, deloused and decently clad Elcho left for Paris in company of Lord John Drummond, now the Duke of Perth. After the western Highlands, with their 'horrible mountains', their heather-thatched bothies, their perennial shortage of food to which was now added the feared presence of the redcoats, Touraine, with its vine-covered slopes, fertile fields, fruit-laden orchards, its fine *chateaux*, delightful manor houses, prosperous villages and expanding towns was little short of paradise. Angers must have reminded Elcho of the happy days he had spent there

acquiring those martial skills he had so recently put into practice.
In Paris he automatically gravitated to the Hotel Imperial, unofficial
headquarters of the Jacobite diaspora where he had stayed with
Francis three momentous years before.   On his arrival he was
greeted with the welcome news that Lord Ogilvy had escaped to
Norway, where he had been arrested on orders of the pro-English
King of Denmark. However, he had soon been released, and was
now on his way to Paris.

In the meantime the Duke of Perth — as he now was — had
gone to Versailles to report. His was the first reliable information
about Culloden, which had been variously reported as a victory
and a defeat. The Court was not particularly moved, all eyes being
then fixed on the Mediterranean, where the French were suffering
reverses at the hands of the Imperial army backed by the Royal
Navy. He was soon followed by old Sheridan, who went to plead
for more support for the Prince. His plea went unheard, and indeed
their reception was lacking in warmth. Tencin complained angrily
about the mistakes which had been made: Why had the Prince
sent only Sir James Steuart? To which Sheridan answered that King
Louis has sent out d'Eguilles, adding, perfidiously, that they had
been in the hands of the Scots, thus shrugging off all responsibility
for the disaster.

Elcho's first visit was to his brother-in-law, from whom he must
have learned all that had happened since they had last met in
Edinburgh, when he had connived at Sir James' bogus arrest.
Steuart's instructions had been to act in close collaboration with
the Earl Marischal, whom the Prince had put in charge of his affairs
before leaving for Scotland. However he only arrived to discover
that the old man had left after having fallen from grace with the
French. On learning that the Royal Standard had been unfurled at
Glenfinnan, Marischal had gone to Paris in the hope of obtaining
that support which, according to Murray of Broughton, was already
on the way. But the French had no intention of supporting a venture
planned and executed without reference to them. The situation
had utterly changed since 1745 when Fontenoy had wiped out

Dettingen; Saxe was now master of Flanders; Paris was no longer in danger and there was no urgent need to get the British troops brought home, whilst it would be unwise to alienate the German allies who had no wish to see Cousin George toppled from his throne.   So Marischal had returned empty handed from the interview he had with the Marquis d'Argenson, the new Foreign Secretary. This had pleased not only Sempill and Balhaldie, but also O'Brien who was jealous of his status as the Chevalier's official representative at the Court of Versailles. Discouraged, Marischal had left France, and was soon replaced by the Duke of York, come to further his brother's interests.

Everything had changed after the Prince's triumphal entry into Edinburgh, followed by his victory at Prestonpans which caught the imagination of the French. He became a hero overnight; he was not the 'Bonnie Prince Charlie' of legend and song who has ever since haunted romantic imaginations. King Louis now declared his support for the Rebellion; Argenson signed a Treaty of Alliance with O'Brien, and plans were laid for an invasion of England with a force commanded by the Duc de Richelieu, who hoped it would earn him the greatly coveted *baton de maréchal*.   Enthusiasm for the Cause was at its peak, and the diaspora in a fever of expectation when Sir James Steuart arrived in Paris. His first task had been to help Voltaire draw up the proclamation Richelieu was to distribute on landing.

While the Highland Army began its southward march into England the expedition got bogged down with delays and disputes. Walsh, who had been put in charge of the naval preparations, was at daggers drawn with Lord Macarthy, an arrogant, hard-drinking, foul-mouthed Irish ex-naval officer who claimed to represent the English Jacobites. At a higher level Richelieu and the Duke of York did not get on: the Frenchman feared the Duke's Italianate piety — he 'would genuflect like a verger' — would harm the Cause in Protestant eyes, while the Duke was horribly shocked by Richelieu's dissolute way of life. Nor did the invasion command universal approval.   Saxe, for one, was opposed to it, fearing that it might drain men and guns away from Flanders. The plan was that Charles Edward would celebrate Christmas in a recaptured London, but it was already December 23rd when Richelieu set out for Boulogne in company of York and a bevy of smart young noblemen who formed the latter's household. They were followed more discreetly by Sir James Steuart.

However, neither Richelieu, nor anyone else had taken into consideration the fickle nature of the winter weather and the effectiveness of the Royal Navy, with the result that the armada got bottled up in the Channel ports. Finally, the news that the Jacobite army was in retreat from Derby led to Richelieu returning to Paris, leaving poor York on his knees at Boulogne praying for a miracle. Efforts were made to support the Rebellion in Scotland; but as we have seen, they had come to naught, and the Ministry soon lost interest. In his despair Sir James turned to Spain, which angered the French. But it was in vain, and he was now living quietly in a small house in the suburbs of Paris in company of Lady Fanny and their small son. She had been arrested when Cumberland withdrew his protection from the Jacobite ladies; but she was soon released and had been able to rejoin her husband.

The couple must have been relieved to find Elcho safe and sound, but somewhat embarrassed by his open-mouthed condemnations of the Prince. The sea voyage had done nothing to calm his anger; he could not forgive Charles Edward for having deserted the Scots, leaving the Jacobite clans defenceless to face the redcoats allied to their hereditary foes, the Campbells. Before leaving Nantes he had had a flaming row with old Sheridan with the result that York had refused to receive him. He was still young and in some ways incredibly naive, and he had never as yet had to bridle his tongue. 'I would often say what I thought of the Prince ... and as I expressed myself freely on the way he had preferred the Irish to the Scots when in Scotland, I antagonised all the Irish in French service', a dangerous thing to do for they wielded a great deal of influence. 'Later these became the enemies of all the Scots without distinction, partly out of jealousy and partly out of national antipathy.'

Up to now Elcho does not seem to have bothered about his own future, so obsessed was he with what had happened in Scotland. Remembering the Master of Sinclair, Balmerino, Lord George and all the other Jacobites of his acquaintance who had received pardons after the '15, he never doubted that he would soon be home. His intention was to get married, as he had promised Francis he would do, and endeavour to bring some order into his father's muddled affairs. He never seems to have realised what an outstanding figure he had been, and how his behaviour had been resented by all those who had endeavoured so hard to prevent him from getting himself into trouble.   So it came as a great shock when he read in the press that he had been attainted. His first reaction had been to write to the Duke of Argyll, asking him for his protection and reminding him that his late brother had been a friend of his grandfather, the Colonel and the guardian of his brother, Francis. 'I am ready to surrender myself immediately and give all assurances whatever that for the future I shall make His Majesty a most peaceable subject.' His handwriting betrays how distraught he was. This letter was followed by others addressed to the Duke of Queensberry, Lord Fletcher of Milton, Lord Lincoln and no doubt other pillars of the Hanoverian establishment.   Writing to the Duke of Newcastle, Milton pointed out 'had his Lordship been sooner sensible of his obligations as to have followed my advice he had not been in the situation he finds himself at present.'   Not only did his letters remain unanswered, but he had the unpleasant surprise to see one of them published in the *Gazette d'Utrecht*.

He certainly had a very bad reputation: 'Lord Elcho has written to Lord Lincoln to solicit his pardon', Horace Walpole told his friend, Horace Mann, 'but as he has distinguished himself amongst all the rebel commanders by brutality and insults and cruelty to our prisoners I think he is likely to remain where he is.' Elcho had fallen a victim to his ungovernable temper, for he had been outraged at the way officers captured at Prestonpans had broken their parole on orders from Cumberland, in whose eyes Jacobites were outlaws and traitors with whom one should have no truck. He also suffered from the vindictiveness of the Irish who had saddled him with the suggestion to cut off the prisoners' thumbs, an accusation he was always hotly to deny, but which was to dog his footsteps to the end of his days. [The true culprit was the brother of a Perthshire laird]. Had it been true he would most surely have forfeited the friendship of such honourable men as the Earl Marischal, Lord George Murray, Lord Ogilvy and the new Duke of Perth, or indeed the respect of his fellow combatants, with whom he was always to remain on very good terms.

Having lost all hope of an immediate pardon — he never lost hope of returning one day to Scotland — he left for Boulogne, from where he intended to get in touch with Francis by means of Smith, the Jacobite merchant and agent who had been the first to welcome him to France, and who maintained close links with his native land. It was arranged that Francis would continue to pay an allowance in exchange for the donation of the Colonel's legacy and his share in the Wemyss estate. This, added to the interest of the Colonel's legacy which his father was still holding on to, left him comfortably off and free from having to rely on the Prince for his upkeep, as was soon to be the case of his unfortunate fellow combatants.

The arrival on the scene of one of the principal participants in the Rebellion must have caused a considerable flurry in a town which had so many links with the Jacobites. 'I went to see the Commandant . . . in whose company I was often to be seen. The conversation often turned on the Prince, and being young, I often said what I thought of him. I have every reason to believe that he reported all I said to Versailles, and I soon realised that I was regarded at the French Court as being detached from His Cause.' He had effectively been placed under surveillance, and was reported as living quietly in the house of a village *curé* and frequenting, for the most part, merchants. He was probably working out ways of getting his money, it being illegal to send any to Jacobites.

Elcho was still in Boulogne when Lords Kilmarnock and Balmerino were executed. As we have seen, Cromartie was reprieved largely thanks to his wife, who had softened the heart of the Princess of Wales by bringing her children, and conveniently fainting after having seen the King.   Kilmarnock had not figured largely in his life. He came from a Covenanting family and had, as a boy, taken part in a search for Mar during the aftermath of the '15.   But he had joined the Prince after Prestonpans against the entreaties of his wife but in fear of being disinherited by the Jacobite Lady Errol, for he was desperately poor. He was certainly sincere when he recanted, and he bitterly regretted having to sacrifice his life for a cause in which he had never really believed. On his appearance, a tall youthful-looking figure dressed in black from head to foot, leaning on the arm of a friend and accompanied by a Presbyterian minister, for he had reverted to the faith of his youth, the huge crowd was seized with pity.

By way of contrast, Balmerino, 'the most naturally brave old man' Walpole had ever seen, appeared jauntily dressed in his 'rebellious regimentals' still bantering with his jailers, as he had done during his captivity. His last act before leaving the Tower, was to drink a large bumper of wine to the health of King James, whom he proclaimed to be the legitimate monarch as he laid his head on the block. The crowd was now filled with admiration. Elcho cannot have been either surprised or even shocked, knowing full well that the penalty for rebellion was the block.   He may even have been relieved not to figure amongst the forty commoners who had been hanged, drawn and quartered on the previous day. But the sad news must have brought back to his mind the last conversation he had had with his gallant old kinsman, as they had ridden away from the field of Culloden. Balmerino might still have been alive if only the Prince had taken to the hills, as Elcho had urged him to do, instead of running away.

It may well have been in connection with these sad events that Elcho fell out with Sir James Harrington, who had come to France in company with 'Mr Goring an old captain in the service of the Queen of Hungary . . . in the hope of getting support for the Prince'. Harrington taxed Elcho with treachery and only just escaped having a rapier thrust through his fat body. It was dangerous to insult so expert a swordsman. Elcho became fond of challenging his detractors, and none were courageous enough to take up the challenge. Harrington and Goring were soon to enter the Prince's service.

Elcho now returned to Paris preceding the Prince by only a few days. The five months Charles Edward had spent 'in the heather' stood in contrast to an otherwise dismal career. Then he really was the 'Bonnie Prince Charlie' of legend and song. He was now freed from the responsibilities incumbent on a commander-in-chief, as well as from the intrigues of Sheridan. On his arrival in France people were struck how fit he looked despite all he had had to endure. He landed at Roscoff in Brittany in company with a Lochiel wracked with guilt, for had he only responded to Cumberland's advances his people would not have had to suffer at the hands of his troops. After a few days' rest the Prince left for Paris. A defeated hero, when young and attractive is always a romantic figure, and 'all the way to Paris exceptionally large crowds lined the route of this man who had become so celebrated.' As we have seen he had always thrived on flattery, and what could be more flattering than a hero's welcome? He soon came to see himself in that light, and looked forward to the day he would drive through cheering crowds to a right royal reception at Versailles. What then was his disappointment when told that he must remain incognito until O'Brien could negotiate an invitation to Fontainebleau, where the Court was then in residence.

Before the invitation had been issued the welcome was muted and his peremptory demand for twenty thousand men to undertake a cross-channel invasion was promptly turned down. Although great pains had been taken to rescue him, and a great deal of money had been spent on the operation, Charles Edward's presence in France was proving an embarrassment. The country was desperately in need of peace: the coffers were empty and all the steps taken to fill them had failed. Tentative negotiations were then starting at Breda, and the King had been told that 'nothing must be done to shock the English, and the less that was done for the

Stuarts in France, the less they would feel their fall when they would have to be abandoned after peace was signed.' Louis was shy and never felt comfortable in the company of strangers; the Queen proved more forthcoming — she was closely related to the Prince through his mother. But it was the Pompadour who retained the power, and she had never favoured the Cause. Charles Edward never recovered from the blow thus dealt to his pride, and from then on he went out of his way to make a nuisance of himself. In this he was greatly helped by the popularity he enjoyed with the Paris mob whose darling he had become. He would go every night to the play or the Opera where he would always receive a standing ovation.

In the meantime refugees were flooding into France. Amongst the first to arrive was Lord Ogilvy, for whom Sir James Steuart managed to get a regiment with the help of the Duke of York, after having first obtained the consent of King James whose policy it was to encourage his 'subjects' to go into foreign service. There ended up by being three Scottish regiments, all attached to the Irish brigade, whose leaders were prejudiced against them. Ogilvy was fortunate in that having preceded the Prince, he was from the start under French protection, whilst the unfortunate refugees who came later were left to the tender mercies of Charles Edward, with the result that some were later reduced to near starvation. This need not have been so, for with this contingency in view he had been offered a very handsome pension which, however, he refused, not wishing to be in any way beholden to King Louis.

As peace began to loom large on the horizon the Prince's behaviour became more and more erratic. He had set his heart on thwarting every effort to expel him in accordance with the Treaty of Utrecht, by which the Stuarts were banished from French soil. His popularity made him a redoubtable opponent, and all his whims were met in the hope of making him more reasonable. He now demanded the arrest of all the British then residing in France with that of Lord Morton in view. The 14th Earl of Morton was a distinguished member of a very distinguished Scottish family. He was a scientist of some renown, a member of the Royal Society, and was later to become a foreign correspondent of the *Académie Francaise*. But he was a Whig, a staunch supporter of the Protestant Succession and as such was loathed by the Jacobites. He was living in Touraine for the sake of his wife's health, and as was then the custom, he had not been molested. Already in 1744 Murray of Broughton had suggested that Charles Edward should get him arrested. But at that time this was not in his power to do. But things had changed, and the Earl was now thrown into the Bastille in company of his ailing wife and small daughter whilst the other British residents were also rounded up. This arbitrary move was unanimously approved of by a completely besotted public opinion. Lady Morton and the child were soon released for fear of retaliation. This angered the Prince. 'He would never give his consent . . . but should there be any proposals of exchange, he would give his opinion on the subject . . . he had been very shocked at the way Lady Morton had been released without his permission.'

Elcho was shocked. Morton was a neighbour at Wemyss, and he had dined with him during his last stay in London. This arbitrary action brought home how vulnerable he was, there being no one to whom he could appeal for protection. 'I had no intention of going to see the Prince having openly declared I had left his party for ever. But I was persuaded by the Duke of Perth that it would look very odd in French eyes should I not do so. So I yielded and went one evening. Sir John Graeme, whom I found in the anteroom undertook to announce my arrival. He returned to say that the Prince had no wish to see me as I had written to England to ask for a pardon. I returned home and made no other attempt to see him . . . That night all the Scotsmen then in Paris came to see me to tell me how they disapproved of his conduct, for it could not be denied that one who had not only risked his life for him but had been condemned to lose his head, and had lost his fortune and his title did not deserve being refused an audience. Had I been dependent upon him for my fortune I would have been ruined, for nothing could be got out of the French but through him.' As was his wont, Elcho did not keep his feelings to himself and echoes of what he had said were to reach the Prince's ears. 'He complained to the Court and I received the visit of a gentleman sent to tell me that should I speak ill of the Prince I would be sent to the Bastille.' Having no wish to join Morton he decided to leave 'despite the fact that the Duke of Perth offered me a company in his regiment, as well as a captaincy for Mr Hunter. The Duke, Lord Ogilvy and many others shared my opinion of the Prince, but being in need of his protection, they were obliged to behave more prudently.'

Elcho now left Paris in company of Hunter of Burnside, who had been an officer of his in the Life Guards and they never drew rein until they reached Basel and safety. He was now able to relax and take notice of his surroundings. 'The Grisons are very mountainous but there are pretty valleys. The inhabitants are all equal, each man having a say in the running of the country as from the age of twenty-five ... The inns, which are usually run by officials are very expensive, I had to pay a louis d'or for a small trout, two fresh eggs and bread and wine ... ' They were heading for Venice where they were to meet Earl Marischal. He had also been under threat of the Bastille, having run foul of not only Sempill and Balhaldie, but also of O'Brien who felt that he alone had the right to negotiate with the Ministry. He had then gone to Courland to stay with his friend Baron Braekel in the hope of rejoining his brother, now a field marshal in Russian employ. His plan was to settle in Astrakhan, but the British ambassador persuaded the Czarina to withhold the necessary permission with the result that Marshal Keith soon went into Prussian service. The Earl Marischal now plumped for Venice, which had always been pro-Jacobite and where living was cheap. 'It was impossible to find any part of Europe where both the laws and the customs are contrived on purpose to avoid expense.' He had rented a small palazzo standing on a back canal where Elcho and Hunter were to find him. They now settled comfortably in an apartment with 'valet, cook and two gondoliers,' and they were able 'to entertain all who came to see us.'

Needless to say the arrival of such prominent rebels as Marischal and Elcho did not go unnoticed, and Sir John Gray, the British

Representative, 'called on the authorities to expel us, giving as a pretext the Empress of Russia's refusal to allow Earl Marischal to settle in her dominions. By way of a reply he was told that the Republic was an independent state open to anyone who did not plot against it, and in general we were well received. But Sir John continued to give us proofs of his animosity by preventing the English from frequenting us. He even had the impudence to threaten Cerestesi for having presented me in public. M. Cerestesi, who is a Florentine answered that he was indifferent to the English Court and would continue to render me all the services owed to an old friend.' This was all the more to the Italian's credit that he was poor and largely depended on the generosity of his English friends. More touching still was the Comte de Wemyss who wrote from the country where he now resided, that he was too old to come to Venice. 'but should I need it during my exile he was willing to share with me the little he possessed.' Elcho was able to reassure his generous old relative that 'despite my misfortune I had the wherewithal to live.'

Marischal introduced him to his Italian friends and to some minor German royalties who had come to Venice for the Carnival. Yet Elcho found Venice dull. 'There is little social life for foreigners, the homes of the nobility not being particularly agreeable. One seldom goes there except for balls, of which there are a great many, a cardinal's hat or a seat in the Senate being celebrated in this fashion by the recipient's family, some of which I attended.' He evidently missed the Pomfrets and their pretty daughter, Lord Lincoln, Sir Francis Dashwood and Horace Walpole with whom he had last been in Venice, and in whose eyes he was now a rebel if not a traitor. He still had hopes of a pardon: 'he affirms he did not see the Pretender's son when in Paris' noted a disbelieving Gray, 'and hopes to obtain His Majesty's pardon.'

Boredom drove him to the gambling tables; 'one day I staked the six hundred sequins I had received that day from my banker and lost them. On leaving with Mr Hunter I discovered that I had one left in my pocket and asked him to return to the tables and stake it. He was soon back with the six hundred sequins I had lost and we went home to our supper well pleased with our luck. However, the news of my imprudent behaviour soon reached the ears of Lord Marischal and on the following day he took charge of my purse only doling out what was required for my daily requirements 'til Lent closed the Ridoto'. Elcho soon found himself in another scrape which might well have had serious consequences.

'The imprudence of youth was to get me into trouble with Lord Marischal who in his kindness was to overlook the incident. Next to his house lived a noble called Canale who had a very pretty daughter. I saw her at her window, we exchanged salutations and in a few days we came to a good understanding by means and signs and words spoken at a distance. One day, Milord being in the country and his house in charge of his German housekeeper, I managed to lure Mademoiselle Canale into it, this being the only means I had of speaking with her at close quarters. Having got the housekeeper to dress like a lady, I gave her my arm and walked in front of the young lady's window, behaving towards her as if she were of gentle birth. A few days later I asked her to call describing herself as the wife of the foreigner who had come to live next door, Lord Marischal being as yet unknown in the neighbourhood. The ruse worked; the housekeeper was received with all the honours due to a lady of rank and Mademoiselle Canale returned the call on the following day. Whereupon I introduced myself and whilst entertaining her seized the opportunity of declaring my love. A rendez-vous was arranged for the near future. However, warned by another servant of what was going on, Lord Marischal came home, looked into the business, turned out the housekeeper and warned the girl's parents to be on their guard. I was fortunate in that I never had an opportunity to seeing her again, it being very dangerous to have an intrigue with the daughter of a Venetian noble. His Lordship never referred to the subject, whilst I soon felt ashamed of this youthful indiscretion which had led me to deceive him.'

Elcho's time was soon given up to a quite different matter. 'One evening, as I was sitting in the pit of the opera house I was addressed by name by a masked figure who was sitting behind me. Surprised, I looked up to see that it was Lord George Murray who had arrived by coach from Germany. We dined and supped together every day during his stay in Venice,' where he was able to renew his acquaintance with Lord Marischal.' After the men who had gathered at Ruthven in Badenoch had dispersed on the Prince's orders, Lord George had 'lurked in the great pine forests in Glenlyon until conditions had allowed him to reach the continent, where he intended to 'live a family life in company of his wife.' He was now on his way to Rome to disculpate himself from the charges of treachery brought by the Prince against him. But he was evidently not looking forward to his audience with the Chevalier, and Carnival being in full swing, he lingered on until Lent brought the merrymaking to a close. He then departed bearing a letter in which Elcho assured James of 'his duty', and begged to be forgiven 'for having taken certain steps for the recovery of my property without permission, as the matter pressed.' He was back in time for the Feast of the Ascension, which always attracted many foreigners to Venice.

Lord George had been well received at the Palazzo Muti. James had had the charges investigated by both Sir James Steuart and the Head of the Scots College in Paris, neither of whom had been able to find any written proof of treachery. Nor could O'Sullivan produce any convincing argument to that effect, and all that could be raked up was a 'want of respect', which Lord George readily admitted, and for which he was willing to ask the Prince's pardon. This Charles Edward was in no mood to grant. On hearing that he had been seen in Venice in company of Elcho, he had immediately jumped to the conclusion that they were hatching some sinister plot against him. 'Have him detained' he wrote to his father. King James gently pointed out that this was neither grateful nor wise, and referring to Elcho, he wrote 'I am very conscious of the zeal he has shown for our service . . . Persons like him can do both good and hurt . . . It would manifestly be of prejudice could they be able to say that their former services could be disregarded', and he ended up with a plea that the Prince should 'receive Lord George's submission with goodness.' The Feast of the Ascension once over the two friends went to Padua where that of San Antonio was about to take place. Lord George then left for Paris, where he hoped (vainly) to get back into Charles Edward's good graces. Being debarred from accompanying him by the threat of the Bastille, Elcho decided to remain in Padua. He had happy recollections of his last visit in 1741. He made the acquaintance of the local aristocracy, who unlike the proud and aloof Venetians, took him to their hearts.

The Paduans were poor, and as such despised by their arrogant Venetian rulers...'Their estates consist only in fields meadows and vineyards with no heritable jurisdictions. They are very heavily taxed by the Republic and as the only money they receive is when they are serving in the armed forces, they have to live very economically. They fare badly at home as their Italian vanity obliges them to keep a great number of servants, who, if the truth be told, cost them but little, as well as a carriage and horses and the gala garments, they display at the feast of San Antonio. The nobility never entertains to a meal at home but arranges picnics at a country inn. They would often dine with me at my inn, but I was never invited back. However, in every other way they showed me every kind of attention.'

Little had changed since his last stay. This agreeable if somewhat monotonous way of life was suddenly disturbed by the unheralded arrival of Signorina Vigano, a charming little actress who had done much to enliven his stay in Venice. It was a repetition of what had happened in Paris, but this time he did not have to send her away. He did not pretend to return her passion, nor was he faithful; but he had a taste for female company, and even for domesticity which, under other conditions, would have led him to the altar with Miss Graham or some other girl of that ilk. But in his present circumstances he could only marry an heiress, and what heiress would bestow her hand upon an outlaw with an unwarranted reputation for cruelty? He was attractive to women, and kind enough when his temper was not roused, and for a time the relationship seems to have satisfied both parties. Nor did it raise any eyebrows, it being common practise at the time.

He soon received an invitation from Lord George to join him at Cleves, where he was now living. However, before leaving Elcho went to say goodbye to the Earl who was spending the summer at Treviso with his *menagerie*, as the old man called his odd assortment of retainers. He found him ill with fever. This may well have been a blessing in disguise as it provided Marischal with an excuse for refusing Charles Edward's request to take charge of his affairs, which were now in an awful mess. Marischal had never had a high opinion of the Prince, whom he had known since childhood, and all that he had heard from Elcho and Lord George had done nothing to improve it.

CHAPTER TEN

From Refugee to
Man About Town

Elcho left Treviso in September 1747 taking Hunter, the Aberdeenshire laird who had been his Lieutenant-Colonel in the Life Guards, and the Vigano with him, and they travelled at a leisurely pace stopping on the way to see the sights: Augsburg 'which was very beautiful'; Heidelberg 'a fine city' where they were taken to see 'the Great Barrel, the largest in the world'; Mannheim, where they watched the Elector Palatine and his wife at their devotions, and where Hunter left them to join the French army; Frankfort-on-Main, where they visited the Hall where the Emperors are crowned and where the inns were magnificent, 'more like houses belonging to the nobility than inns'; Dettingen, where he 'went over the battlefield' (he never missed exploring a battlefield); Mainz where he hired a boat to go down the Rhine noting the castles and the names of their owners as they went along; Cologne 'a very large city where the Papal Nuncio resides', to finally reach Cleaves where he was welcomed by Lord George Murray.

Lord George had chosen Cleaves as a place of refuge, it being in Prussian territory and therefore safe from both British and French interference, Frederick being then courted by both. After parting from Elcho at Padua, he had gone to Paris in the hope of making his peace with Charles Edward, but a peremptory message from the Prince warned him that he must leave at once if he did not wish to end up in the Bastille. So he went off to see the Duke of Perth, (who was besieging Bergen-op-Zoom) where he was received with full military honours.

Cleaves turned out to be a 'pretty town in a very beautiful tract of country half a league from the Rhine'. Here Elcho settled down happily enough, having been provided by Marshal Keith 'with letters of introduction to high ranking officials; all these gentlemen invited me to dinner and treated me very well.' Elcho was still enjoying the protection of the Earl Marischal, now settled at Potsdam.

Unfortunately his equanimity was soon to be disturbed by the news that in Scotland Colonel Charteris' legacy had been confiscated. Wishing to find out how things stood, he sent his faithful servant, Tiddman, to Edinburgh from where he returned with the information that Francis was suing the Government under pretext that the legacy had been in his possession even before the rising. The Earl of Wemyss had returned to County Durham, no doubt chased by the hostility of his Whig subjects.

Maybe it was as well that Elcho had not received his pardon for he would have had a bad time had he returned to Wemyss. Tiddman had been arrested on boarding the ship which was to bring him back to the Continent, and had been cross-examined by no less a personage than the Secretary of State, Lord Chesterfield. He was soon released, but it was clear that his master was looked upon with deep suspicion.

'At the beginning of 1748 Lord George left for Königsberg from where he wrote to me, as he did from Poland. As far as I could guess he intended to buy an estate, live there under a false name and circulate the rumour that he had died so that his son could inherit the title and fortune should Duke James predecease him.' Lord George now disappears from the pages of the *Journal*. They were never to meet again.

Elcho soon became bored with the purposeless life he was now leading. His intention was to claim, as soon as he could, the commission King Louis had promised to all those who had served as officers in the Prince's army. But for the time being he was still under threat from the Bastille. However, that would be removed when peace had been proclaimed, for Charles Edward would have to quit France, as stipulated in the Treaty of Utrecht. He should not have too long to wait as negotiations were then taking place at Aix-la-Chapelle. In the meantime he would go to Liege where Scottish officers were recruiting for their regiments. Liege was 'a large town which stands on the Meuse. Its inhabitants have a bad reputation, and the streets are not safe at night'.

The War of the Austrian Succession came to its weary end in October 1748, leaving everyone dissatisfied with the exception of the Prussians — Frederick having kept Silesia — and the Dutch, there having been no repetition of the terrible invasion of 1682 when only the opening of the sluices had saved Holland from a French invasion. Louis' subjects coined the adage *bête comme la paix*, whilst Horace Walpole reported that 'it does not give the least joy'. The continent was overrun by robber bands made up of deserters from all the armies.

Peace having been signed, Elcho left for Boulogne which he intended to make his headquarters. He stopped a fortnight at Lille, staying with Lord Macarthy, an old acquaintance from his Cocoa Tree days, and where he frequented yet more Scottish officers in French pay. All the towns he rode through 'were full of French troops, and in Brussels chargers were being sold for 6frs.' He found Boulogne full of Scottish refugees, all of whom called upon him. Amongst them were his friends the Ogilvys, who had rented a house where he was to spend a great deal of his time. Lady Ogilvy had been arrested after Culloden, but had made her escape from Edinburgh Castle by exchanging clothes with her maid, and had travelled to London in guise of an invalid. One cannot help suspecting that the authorities were turning a blind eye, being only too happy to get rid of these tiresome Jacobite women.

The principal, indeed the only subject of conversation must have been the Prince's recent expulsion from France. As we have seen the low-key reception he had received at Court upon his arrival from Scotland had dealt a blow to his pride from which it was never to recover, and he had set himself out to be as tiresome as possible. Nothing would appease him, not even the arrest of the whole

Morton family including the child.

Two highly publicised affairs — one with his poor besotted little cousin, the Duchesse de Montbazon (their mothers had been sisters), whom he deliberately compromised in what can only be called a caddish fashion, the other with the much tougher and more experienced Madame de Talmont who had kept him in the public eye.   Disgusted by such behaviour, his straight-laced brother left secretly for Rome, where their father had arranged for him to receive a cardinal's hat. This Charles Edward was never to forgive, and although he did not break openly with the Chevalier, the latter lost whatever influence he had ever had over him. In the eyes of many Jacobites the Duke of York's action was an even greater tragedy than Culloden, and the diaspora became more divided than ever, this time between Charles' supporters and those of his father.

Peace was naturally anathema to the Jacobites, any hope of a restoration depending on France being at war with England. During the peace conference the Prince had endeavoured to raise as many obstacles as he could be means of theatrical gestures. But in vain. 'Under the Treaty of Aix-la-Chapelle the English had demanded the expulsion of the Prince. This had put the King of France in an embarrassing situation as he had given the Prince in writing a promise of asylum. The Prince insisted on it being honoured as he wished to remain in France. The Marquis de Puysieux was sent to tell him that he must leave, his departure being one of the Treaty's stipulations, and the country was in no position to start a new war. Should he leave with good grace he would be received by the Canton of Friburg in Switzerland, where a mansion would be rented and got up for him by the French, and he would be universally addressed as 'Your Royal Highness'; he would receive a pension of six hundred thousand livres or more . . . and any wish he might have in favour of his fellow exiles would be carried out.   By way of an answer the Prince took the Marquis by the arm and shoved him out.   On hearing his Minister's report, the King said 'since the Prince acts as a madman he must be treated as such' and gave orders for him to be arrested without, however, any harm being done to him. The Prince was in the habit of carrying pistols in his pocket and had bragged that he would defend himself, so on his leaving the Opera ten or twelve sergeants-at-arms sprung out, bound him from head to foot with a silken cord like a roll of tobacco and put him into a postchaise. The first night was spent in the Chateau of Vincennes, whilst his household spent a few days in the Bastille. It is said that by resisting the King he had hoped to win the approval of the English nation, and that he had acted on the advice of Sir James Harrington and Mr Goring.'

Elcho was not long settled in Boulogne before he was summoned by his mother to Basel. She wanted him to escort her to Lyon, where she would be met by the Steuarts, now settled close to Angouleme. He was not too happy at the prospect of meeting Sir James, with whom he had fallen out in Paris on the subject of the Prince, to whom the latter had been very attached. (Sir James had not witnessed the Prince's craven conduct in the immediate aftermath of Culloden). However, he could not decently refuse her request. But on reaching Dijon his heart failed him, so he sent her on with the faithful Tiddman and returned to Boulogne stopping in Paris on the way. Here he could not refrain from going to the Opera, a pleasure of which he had for long been deprived, and where he ran into Lord Albemarle, who had recently been appointed British ambassador. It must have been an embarrassing moment for both as Albemarle had been Cumberland's second-in command. But it went to show Elcho that he could visit Paris with impunity.

Back in Boulogne he rented a house where Vigano gave birth to a daughter who was soon to die. By the end of the year he grew restless. Life was monotonous as all he had by way of company were his fellow refugees. The French 'people of quality' who lived in the *Haute Ville*, did not mingle with the *Basse Ville*, the merchant quarter where foreigners were allowed to live. Some of these were very dubious characters indeed. Nor was life at home without its problems. He had grown tired of Vigano and was having an affair with an English woman who had also borne him a daughter. Their recriminations were soon more than he could stand, and he packed them off to England after having taken the child in charge. He had hoped they would find new protectors, and the English woman did pass out of his life; but not the still enamoured Italian. However in their absence he was free to return to Paris.

He now took up his residence in a bagnio run by a Sieur Bielle and situated in the Rue Richelieu, which was long to be his Paris headquarters. It was comfortable, and above all it was cheap. 'Here one could stay with one's servants for half a crown a day. A hackney coach cost three hundred livres a month and a hired servant thirty sous a day'. The fact that it was a house of ill-fame did not worry the grandson of Colonel Charteris, who was notorious for having frequented this sort of establishment. He dined every day at the Hotel Notre Dame in company of his old friend, Sir Hector Maclean, young Glengarry who had served with him on Lord Marischal's staff in 1744, and no doubt other Jacobite cronies. He was naturally unaware that Glengarry was 'Pickle the Spy.' A great deal of the talk must have been about the 'Arkaig Treasure', of which 1,200 *livres* had been recently brought to Paris.

The Ogilvys were now in Paris, and it was at their house that he made the acquaintance of Lord Selkirk, who despite his firm support for the Crown, had remained friends with his old schoolfellow, Lord Ogilvy. His behaviour was in sharp contrast to that of Lord Charles Douglas, Drumlanrig's brother, with whom Elcho had been at Winchester. 'One evening at the Comedie Francaise I entered a box where my cousin . . . was sitting. He left immediately.' Elcho was hurt; it was the first rebuff he had suffered and he had evidently forgotten that he had been present when Drumlanrig had been plundered by the Jacobite army. 'On the following day I met him again gambling at Lord Albemarle's table. Lord Selkirk, who supported the Crown and had raised troops during the rising, asked the Ambassador if it was against the law to frequent Lord Ogilvy and myself. The Ambassador answered that he, for one, did not think so, but he was sure it would displease the Court, to which Lord Selkirk answered that he had nothing to ask from the Court, and that he would continue to see his old friend'.

Reassured, Elcho now set out to enlarge his circle of acquaintances in which he was greatly helped by the Colberts, one of whom, the Abbé, was to become a life-long friend.

Colbert and his brother, an officer in the *Royal Ecossais*, had started life as Scottish Protestants, but they were now Catholic Frenchmen having been adopted by the family of Colbert to whom they were related. However, they had not forgotten the land of their birth, and the Abbé took Elcho under his wing, and presented him to his French friends. Clearly these did not belong to the same glamorous set which once frequented Lady Sandwich's salon. But in those days Elcho was a young milord well received in London society and with a peerage in sight. Now he was a stateless refugee who had fallen between two stools, being a dangerous rebel in the eyes of the British authorities, and a traitor in those of the Prince and his, mostly Irish, followers. He was, however, something of a hero in those of his brethren-in-arms, judging by the way he was received when he visited their messes.

The expulsion of the Prince had necessitated new arrangements for the distribution of the forty thousand livres allocated to those who had fought in the '45, and of which, needless to say, Elcho had not had a penny. A new list was being drawn up and he was advised to send in his name. But when it was published his name did not figure on it. He was understandably indignant: no one had sacrificed more than he for the Cause. His new friends arranged for him to have an audience at Versailles with the Cardinal de Tencin. 'I pointed out to him that my name had not appeared on the list of awards granted to the Scots and that, moreover, the Prince owed me the twelve hundred louis d'or I had lent him in Scotland. The Cardinal answered that he had not been surprised to hear that I was no friend of the Prince; as for himself he knew him well and had a poor opinion of him. He sent his secretary to the Marquis de Pausieuix [sic] to ask if there was a vacancy on the list. The secretary brought back word that there were twelve hundred livres to spare. His Eminence offered them to me saying that he was sorry that the sum was not larger, and I gratefully accepted the offer'.

What with clearing up his position in regard to the Ambassador, making new friends and the 'gracious manner' with which he had been received at Versailles, Elcho departed well satisfied with this his first long sojourn in Paris since the Rebellion. His mother must have brought about a reconciliation with his brother-in-law, for he now left for Guiscal, a place the Steuarts had rented close to Angouleme, and where his mother was now living. It must have been hard for Sir James to face up to the unpalatable fact that Jacobitism, of which he had been so ardent a supporter, was now, politically speaking, dead. But he was too intelligent to cling on to a quarrelling Diaspora and he had discreetly slipped away, first to Sedan, then to Angouleme where life was cheap and the climate pleasant. Here he found many intelligent and well-read people, who were able to appreciate those brilliant conversational gifts which had led so many Scots to adopt the Cause.

Elcho found his mother happily settled and 'paying Sir James £400 a year for her board, and she moreover kept a carriage for the use of the household.' It was a pleasant place in which to reside, for Sir James 'kept open house and was visited by all the local gentry and nobility, Angouleme is one of the French provinces where life is cheap and food very good.' Elcho must have thought himself back at Rheims. He noted that although the gentry were 'poor, badly dressed and their houses ill-furnished, they lived very well . . .The peasants are, on the contrary in a miserable condition. Their clothes consist of linen smocks, breeches and wooden clogs. They sleep on straw and their bread is as black as a chimney. A great deal of brandy is made, the best coming from Cognac.' He thoroughly enjoyed his stay which was often to be repeated. It was followed by a trip to Spa where he took the cure, no doubt necessitated by a surfeit of delicious food. 'I stayed at an inn where there were many English people who dined at the *table d'hote*. Having learnt who I was, they abandoned it so as to mark their attachment to the Government.' This brought home how notorious he was in England. However this reprobation was not universal and there were still brave souls willing to eat their meals in his company.

His life was now made up of sojourns in the Rue Richelieu, trips to Angouleme, an occasional cure at a spa, and above all, frequent visits to the Scottish regiments, Boulogne, where he had parked poor Vigano, being still his headquarters. It was a purposeless existence and would have soon become intolerably dull had it not been for the vivid interest he always took in the world about him. He would never miss a sight if he could possibly help it. He went to Versailles to see the King being dressed or eating his dinner, both of these events taking place in public. He witnessed the solemn conferring of the Order of the Saint Esprit and Louis reviewing his Body Guard on the plain of the Sablons, and he was also present at the opening of the *Parlement de Paris*. All these provided him with pleasant ways of whiling away the time, whilst the manoeuvering of troops remained an inexhaustible subject of interest.

It was on his return to Boulogne after one of these trips that three friends came to tell him of the arrival 'of a young lady, Miss Mynshull by name, who it was said would have £70,000 one day. What is more, she was very pretty and they urged me to remain in Boulogne and ask for her hand in marriage. She turned out to be very pretty indeed, and I arranged for a little trip in company of her mother and some friends, after which I asked for her hand, having been assured that in England she was reputed to be very rich.' However, the damsel demurred: she was half engaged to a Mr Turner and she asked Elcho to go away and give her time to make up her mind. He departed for Paris in company of the still enamoured Vigano, who had just borne him a daughter, but from whom he must now part. Her passionate Italian nature made the process so painful that he was never again to have a steady relationship with a mistress. He now had two small motherless children on his hands.

With matrimony in view, he asked the Chevalier to procure him a French commission, which would invest him with the legal status which he did not as yet possess. He was literally an 'outlaw', and as such unfitted to become the head of a family. 'I received a detached captaincy and was attached without a salary to the cavalry regiment of St James. That is all that he could procure for me, so low was his credit at this time.' Was it by inadvertence or by malice that he found himself attached to the one regiment where his presence would be resented? For as we have seen, it had served in the '45 and was imbued with all the anti-Scots feeling then rife amongst the Irish.

Elcho's sojourn in Paris coincided with the arrival of the Earl Marischal as Prussian Envoy to the Court of Versailles, and he returned to Boulogne bearing letters of introduction to the *Haute Ville* which made life far more agreeable. Miss Mynshull was now looking forward even more to becoming one day the Countess of Wemyss, that she had fallen in love with him. But on investigation her fortune proved to be only sixty thousand *livres*, not seventy thousand pounds, and she was reputed to be secretly married to Mr Turner. Marriage with her would end in disaster. The best thing he could do was to break off. But remembering what that had entailed with the enamoured Vigano he set about the business with enough tact for them to remain friends.

He had painted so pleasant a picture of life in Angoulême that the Mynshulls decided to settle there, and he offered to escort them to their new home. They stopped on the way at Chantilly, where the Ogilvys were now living, and from there went on to Paris, where he took them to the play and the Opera. He also invested, at her mother's request, Miss Mynshull's fortune, for he had inherited some of the Colonel's flair for finance. He then took them to Touraine 'where the finest scenery in France is to be found' — it was before Jean-Jacques Rousseau had made snowy peaks and romantic caves fashionable. At Amboise they parted, the Mynshulls going to Angoulême where they were to settle, whilst Elcho hurried back to Paris where the Earl Marischal was waiting for him.

The Earl Marischal's appointment as Prussian Representative to the Court of Versailles had created a furore in London, where the King took it as a personal insult. Diplomatic relations were almost severed. Frederick was quite willing to cock a snook at his uncle George, whom he disliked, and with whom he was at odds about Prussian vessels captured by English privateers during the late war. But this was not the reason why he had despatched the wily old Jacobite to Paris in exchange for another Jacobite, Lord Tyrconnel, whom Louis had sent to Berlin. He was bent on retaining Silesia which Maria Theresa was planning to reconquer, and he saw in France a possible ally. Marischal's task was to negotiate a formal alliance, which he failed to do although through no fault of his own.

Marischal's first duty now lay with Prussia, and he exchanged the green riband of the Thistle for the black one of the Prussian Eagle, a gesture greatly resented in certain Jacobite circles where it was seen as an insult to King James. Charles Edward, on the contrary, saw in the appointment a Heaven-sent opportunity for implementing a plot then being hatched to put him on the throne, and Goring was soon in Paris clamouring for a secret interview. Marischal was probably already aware of what he had come to reveal; Elcho most certainly was. Had he not gone to Chantilly to make the acquaintance of its author, the Hon Alexander Murray, brother of Lord Elibank, who was staying there with his niece, Lady Ogilvy? Murray was a well-known figure in Jacobite circles, having gone to prison for contempt of the House of Commons, before which he had refused to kneel and ask pardon for the violence he had incited during a by-election.

> He had seen the Prince in Flanders where he was living with Miss Walkinshaw, who had come over from Scotland in 1751 to join him. Murray had spent the summer with the regiments, the *Royal Ecossais* and *Ogilvy* and had conceived an ill-formed plot to establish the Prince in England. MacDonald of Lochgarry and Dr Cameron were to go to the Highlands to get the Highlanders to take arms. In the meantime he would go to London with some officers of the Ogilvy regiment, where he said he could find enough friends to form a company of a hundred strong, who would present themselves at St James' Palace with swords and pistols and lay hands on the Royal family; upon which the Prince, who would be concealed in London, would show himself to the people. Murray asserted that many persons of consequence were in the plot . . . including Earl

Marischal. As he had heard that I was no supporter of the Prince, he displayed much distrust when we met. He was unaware that I was informed of his plans.

The arrival upon the scene of his old patron was to change Elcho's way of life. He now became the Envoy's constant companion, accompanying him to Versailles and frequenting the *corps diplomatique* amongst whom he was to make many friends. He was discreet and took a detached and somewhat cynical view of the situation, thus providing a welcome relief from all the plots and intrigues in which Marischal now found himself involved — he was getting too old for this kind of activity. However, Elcho was not introduced to Marischal's *philosophes* friends amongst whom he would have cut a poor figure, abstruse speculations not being at all in his line.

It is to this time that Elcho's narrative of the '45 can be dated. This his '*Short Account of the Affairs of Scotland in the years 1744, 1745 and 1746*' reads as if directed towards someone with a close interest in the conduct of a military campaign. I strongly suspect that this was Marischal himself. Internal evidence corroborates this. Indeed, at this time of shifting alliances, it may have been Marischal's then master, Frederick of Prussia who had asked for an analysis of the campaign of 1745-6.

In the meantime Lady Wemyss had invited her children to spend the Carnival season with her in a house she had rented in Angoulême, and his sisters, the Ladies Helen and Walpole (Polly) arrived in Paris from where he was to escort them down to their mother.   He lodged them in the respectable hotel where he had taken up his quarters in view of their arrival, and he showed them the sights.   Their presence in the capital created something of a stir; 'all the Scots called upon them whilst the Earl Marischal paid them much attention.' But, having more exciting things to attend to, he sent them off in charge of Tiddman.

Mr Murray was still organising his plot;   Lieutenant Colonel MacDonald and Mr Cameron had left for Scotland; the Prince went to London . . . as did the officers of the Ogilvy regiment, and last of all Murray himself. Some days before his departure he invited me to sup with him in an inn with the Earls of Kellie and Airlie, and as he still mistrusted me he said, announcing his departure from Paris, that he was going to Venice; and the better to deceive me, asked me for letters of introduction to Venetian nobles. Being well-acquainted with his plans, I replied with a hearty laugh that when he did set out for that city I would give him the letters. That evening I went to see his niece, Lady Ogilvy, and told her what had passed between us. She had no love for him and on his return she told him how I made fun of his plot. On arriving in London his courage failed him and he returned to Paris; the officers rejoined their regiment and the plot he had conceived in his folly ended by the capture of Mr Cameron and his execution the following year. Lord Marischal closed his doors upon him on his return. The Prince went back to the Low Countries from where he would come back to Paris to see Murray, whom he looked upon as his Minister.'

By his jeering Elcho had made an enemy for life.

He found Angoulême full of merrymakers come from afar to join in the fun. The usually closed mansions of the feudal nobility — the Jarnacs, De la Rochefoucaulds and others of that ilk — were open, their owners having abandoned for the Carnival Versailles or their great *chateaux*, whilst the more modest houses of *La Cloche*, as those whose titles derived from municipal appointments were slightingly called, were crammed with friends and relations up from the country. Elcho had a low opinion of the last, know as *hobereaux*, that is country squires. 'They are, or have been , in the services, and are very ignorant as they never read, they not having had a proper education. They enter the army at the age of sixteen and leave it with a pension of four or five hundred livres and the cross of St Louis. They then go back to their estates and spend Carnival in town.'

'Life was very pleasant. Morning visits were the prelude to great dinner parties held in town and followed by gambling; in the evening there were supper parties and balls, whilst a good deal of singing took place during meals. The food was delicious;

Angoulême is one of the towns where one eats best . . .Two officers paid court to my sisters'. One courtship came to nothing, but the other ended in the marriage of Lady Polly with 'M. de la Barthe who belonged to the *bonne noblesse du Givaudan*. His brother owned a small estate close to Angoulême.' At first Elcho was not too happy at having a *hobereau* for brother-in-law; he felt his sister could do better for herself. But Labarthe was to prove helpful, caring, and touchingly attached to his wife's family.

The merrymaking once over, they all returned to Guiscal. Unfortunately, Lady Wemyss had spent without counting and was now up to her ears in debt. This affected the Steuart's very restricted budget, and so when Elcho returned to Paris, Sir James went with him in the hope of getting some of the famous forty thousand livres allotted to the Scots. They put up at Bielle's establishment, and Sir James, who had not been attainted, left cards at the embassy. His call was returned as the ambassador wished to find out who this Steuart might well be. His Excellency must have been somewhat taken aback to find himself in a bagnio, and even more so when confronted by Goodtrees, whose house had been commandeered for him when he was in Edinburgh. 'However he pulled himself together and talked for a long time with Sir James, who asked him to procure him a permission to return home — he was told to draw up a memoir and bring it to the Embassy, which he did but with no result'. Lord Albemarle then brought up the subject of Elcho, who was hiding in the room next door, accusing him of having been violent in the '45. 'Sir James took my defence saying that the charges laid against me were false, and pleaded in my favour.'

The brothers-in-law went to Versailles in search of the money; but by now the Jacobites had become such a nuisance that they were none too well received; nevertheless, Steuart was granted a small pension. They spent a great deal of their time with the Comte de Jarnac, one of Steuart's Angoulême friends, who told Elcho that 'the Duc de Saint James had not been at all happy at his joining the regiment, some of his officers having served in the '45.' Whereupon Elcho called on the Duke to explain that this was none of his making; he had wanted to join the *Royal Ecossais*. They 'parted good friends' but Elcho was not transferred as he had hoped would be the case.

Sir James returned home. He left Elcho with a greatly enlarged circle of acquaintances, to whom were added all the gossiping Scots, whom he had long avoided, not knowing quite how he would be received. He was to have a brush with Alexander Murray who 'gave out that he would pay me out for having laughed at his plot; but although we met everywhere he never said anything. As his lack of courage prevented him from speaking himself, he put about a tale by which an Irish officer was alleged to have told me off at the play.' Elcho searched the man out, discovered that it was just a pack of lies and got a written apology.

Sir James was soon followed by the Wemyss girls who arrived in Paris with the devoted Labarthe in tow. They were again made much of by the Scots, and after having visited the city they left for Boulogne accompanied by their brother, who had managed to foist his 'natural daughters' upon them. After having embarked them for Scotland, he left for Lille where many regiments were assembled under the command of the Prince de Soubise. He was curious to find out more about the 'strict discipline then being introduced into the army.' He was 'introduced to the Prince and often dined at his house.' Life proved very pleasant: 'the colonels kept open house; there was also a good theatre and one could spend one's time very agreeably.' But it was the drill which really interested him and he spent a great deal of time watching the manoeuvres with the practised eye of an experienced soldier. He now returned to Guiscal where he spent that winter in company of his mother.

His brother James turned up in the spring; they had not met since 1741. Having served in the West Indies, the youngest Wemyss was now on half pay, and rather than return to an empty Castle and a hostile tenantry, who still resented the Jacobitism of his father and brother, he had set out on a mini-Grand Tour in order to complete his neglected education. Avoiding Rome, where his name would have had Jacobite connotations, he had started by Turin, from where he had gone to Florence to finish up in the university town of Montpellier. He was now on his way to London, and hopefully to a new commission, and he intended staying in Paris on the way.

The brothers, who had not hit it off, travelled separately to the French capital where James put up at a reputable hotel, whilst Elcho returned to his bagnio. However they did not air their differences in public and whilst Elcho presented James to his French friends — but, needless to say, not to the Jacobite Earl Marischal, for James was a convinced Whig — James presented Elcho to a fellow guest, the Comte de Lubersac, with whom he had made friends. Lubersac had his *entrée* in the world of the rich *fermiers generaux* such as M. Herbert 'who kept open house every day. There were eighteen places at his dinner table and all his acquaintances could go there whenever they wished. When the places were filled the porter would tell the latecomers that he was not at home . . These open tables are an admirable way of knowing what was going on in Paris and Versailles.'

As was the custom, James called at the embassy, but his call was not returned. So, donning his naval uniform, he attended a service at the embassy chapel where he pointed out to the chaplain that although he was Elcho's brother 'he was on English service'. The call was returned but he was never invited to dinner, which confirmed his fears that Elcho would prove an impediment in his career, which effectively was to be the case. For the time being, however, he was soon appointed lieutenant on board HMS *Orford*. Elcho was equally apprehensive as to the future. 'I told my brother-in-law that should my father die leaving him his property he would prove a bad brother as far as I was concerned. He had been in the Royal Navy since his youth and had been badly brought up'. Elcho was being unfair. James was to prove supportive and even generous and this at a time when he was struggling to put to rights the inheritance his father had dilapidated, whilst his manners were polished enough to make him acceptable in any society.

His brother once gone, Elcho returned to Marischal whom he found greatly perturbed by what he had just heard about the Prince.

After the collapse of the Elibank plot Charles had taken to 'skulking', as his followers had done in Scotland before the rising, and moved, duly disguised and under a false name from one place to another, accompanied by Clementina Walkinshaw and their little girl. They would occasionally make surreptitious visits to Paris. 'This came to Lord Marishal's ears in a very odd way. A certain gentleman arrived shortly after and sat at a table close to his. They started to quarrel: the gentleman called the lady a slut; she replied 'Your Royal Highness, though you are a Prince you are no gentleman', and after a great deal of abuse they took to blows.' Marischal had no difficulty in guessing who the couple were. A few days later Goring turned up at his house 'where he confirmed the story, told a great many more and finished by begging his Lordship to get him some other form of livelihood.' Marischal took him to Berlin where the King gave him a commission. The poor man was to die the following year. Elcho felt himself to be justified: 'In 1746 this Mr Goring had tried to pick a serious quarrel with me, saying that I never sang the Prince's praises. At that time I knew the Prince well. He too came to know him well, and what he was to tell was far worse than what I ever did.'

In 1754 the Earl Marischal had asked for his own recall. He had failed to obtain a French alliance, having been outwitted by Kaunitz, Maria Theresa's wily minister, who had succeeded in bringing to an end the centuries old Hapsburg-Bourbon rivalry largely with the help of Madame de Pompadour. (He was one of the eminent personages whose acquaintance Elcho had made when in company of his diplomatist friends).The Franco-Austrian alliance was unpopular and remained so. It was to be one of the causes of the French Revolution.

Frederick was soon to find himself fighting on the same side as his Uncle George in a war which was already in the offing. 'Men o' war were being fitted out in the dockyards of both England and France, there being trouble in their respective factories on the river Ohio', Elcho was to write the following year, but Frederick did not lay the blame at Marischal's door. He had grown very fond of the old man and had appointed him Governor of Neuchâtel, which he wrongly believed to be nothing but a pleasant sinecure. Before leaving Paris Marischal had placed Elcho under Prussian protection, and had recommended him to the 'Comte d'Argenson, the Minister for War and to Mareschal de Thomand (he was an Irishman) for a colonel's commission. But according to the usual behaviour of the Irish towards the Scots, he never did me a good turn, although he was polite when we met.' Elcho had many good reasons to be grateful to his old protector, thanks to whom he had risen from obscure refugee to elegant man-about-town.

No sooner had Marischal left Paris than Elcho was on his way to Guiscal. From there he went on to Bordeaux where he was to meet the newly-married Labarthes and little Marguerite (Elcho's daughter), whom they had practically adopted. As on his previous visit all those years ago, he stayed with the Scottish wine merchants Ainslie and Sandilands. He cannot but have admired the fine town then springing up on the banks of the Garonne. It was during this stay that he suffered a painful rebuff when his cousin, the young Earl of Sutherland, refused to see him. This must have brought home how much his involvement was still resented by his relations. It must have hurt, given how kind the young man's father had been to him. He also received a letter from Marischal telling him that Frederick would not have a French officer as chamberlain, which was understandable given the pending war.

Greatly to Elcho's distress, Lady Polly refused to live in Angouleme with her mother-in-law, and insisted on settling at Toulouse, where she was soon to die in childbirth. Labarthe now boarded little Marguerite in Montauban, no doubt with a Huguenot family, of which there were many in that area.

On his return to Guiscal Elcho found the house full of *Parlementaires* exiled by the King for refusing to register certain laws, and enjoying Sir James's company. Delightful as this was, it placed an extra burden on the Steuart's finances, already strained by the temporarily penurious Lady Wemyss. It was time to leave the area, whilst the boy's education provided a useful excuse. They settled in a modest hotel, whilst Elcho returned to his usual quarters at the Sieur Bielle's. However, this being no place for a respectable woman, and as he liked to spend a great deal of his time with his sister — they were very close to each other — he rented rooms for them. All three were soon much in demand by both Elcho's old Paris friends and by the Steuart's Angoulême ones, and they were soon constantly dining and supping with the *Parlementaires* now back in Paris, and who wished to return their hospitality.

CHAPTER ELEVEN

Milord Wemyss

In the spring of 1755 Elcho was summoned to Neuchâtel. The Governorship was not proving to be the sinecure Frederick had anticipated, and Marischal felt lonely and dispirited. Although he was having a good time in Paris, Elcho did not hesitate to obey the summons and went immediately in search of a permission to leave the country. This was granted all the more readily that he was personally acquainted with the Minister of War, the Comte d'Argenson. 'He received me very well, told me to sit down and laughingly reminded me of how he had wanted to shut me up for having spoken ill of the Prince. "At that time we would not allow anyone to speak ill of him but now we know him to be an obstinate fool, and you can say whatever you like about him". He then asked how old I was and finished by saying it was high time I should make my way in the world.'

There was nothing Elcho would have liked better to do. He had been sedulously attending the Minster's audiences 'where there were occasionally a thousand military men present', in the hope of getting a commission. But the competition had proved too fierce and nothing had come of it. This time Argenson was all the more gracious that what was being requested was a year's foreign leave and the permission to go to Neuchâtel. 'He entrusted me with compliments for Lord Marischal and gave me a passport valid for a year ... I left my sister and brother-in-law in Paris and departed on 4 May 1755.'

Elcho found his old patron installed in the fine medieval castle of Colombier which dominates the town of Neuchâtel. This stands on the shores of the lake of that name with the snow-clad Alps far away on the horizon, a truly magnificent sight. But Marischal was thoroughly disgruntled, for the Neuchâtelois had turned out to be independent-minded folk, deeply attached to their, to his way of thinking, outdated 'liberties' and shockingly indifferent to instructions coming from faraway Berlin.

Such was the place Marischal was called upon to govern. Unfortunately he was ill-fitted to do so. His experience lay on the battlefield and in the corridors of power, not with the intricacies of administration. His master, Frederick, was a *philosophe*, an enlightened despot, whose aim it was to drag his subjects willy-nilly out of their 'Gothic' darkness into the Enlightenment. Marischal fully shared these views, and like all *philosophes* he was obsessively anti-clerical. Anything to do with established religion was a matter of ridicule. He had therefore been shocked to hear that public penance, that is, Stools of Repentance, were still in use in the Principality.

As if these church matters were not enough to plague him, Marischal, who hated the cold, had just lived through an exceptionally hard winter. So on his arrival Elcho found him toying with the notion of resigning and retiring to Venice. In the meantime the arrival of this new milord in a place where the British were largely unknown, had excited a good deal of curiosity. 'Everyone of any importance in the town called upon me and I was able to meet them again at Lord Marischal's house' Interested as ever in his surroundings, he was delighted to accompany 'his Lordship to the Estates of Balengin and was present at the great banquet given in his honour.' He had entered a new world the like of which he had not as yet met. It was made up of free land-owning and self-governing citizens, in majority peasants, and where the aristocracy enjoyed but little power and very limited prestige.

He seemed to be set for a long stay. Yet after a month he was again on the road posting full speed to Lyon, a place where he had no friends and where he was to spend a seemingly aimless three weeks. This points to his having been sent on some secret mission, but all he notes is that he again ran into his Sutherland cousins by whom he was again snubbed.

Having accomplished what he had set out to do, he again took to the road this time at a more leisurely pace. He followed the same route as he had taken on the Grand Tour. In Turin 'the Earl of Bristol was then English ambassador. Having formerly known him in Rome, I wrote to him, begging him to intercede in my favour with the King of England, pointing out that I had not seen the Prince since Culloden; that I had not taken any part in his affairs since that day and was resolved never to do so again. He did not answer my letter, but he paid me the compliment of letting me know that circumstances prevented him from coming to see me or inviting me to come and see him, but that he wished me good health and a pleasant journey to Venice for where I was bound. One evening . . . I saw him in his box at the Opera; he came down to the pit and stood beside me. But as he did not speak to me, I did not speak to him and after a few minutes he returned to his box,' a kindly gesture which put some balm on poor Elcho's lacerated feelings.

From Turin his route took him to Milan, where he made a short halt, and where he met his old friend, Cerectesi before heading for Padua. 'After Bergamo I dined at a village and as I entered the inn the innkeeper, seeing that I had guns and pistols, said I did well to take these precautions for a gentleman and his servants who had dined with him on the previous day had been robbed and murdered in a wood through which I must travel by five bandits who posed as sportsmen shooting in the woods. I called my two servants and asked them if they were willing to be armed and accompany me, to which they agreed. It was hot and I had fallen asleep in the carriage when I was roused by one of the servants who told me that he had seen five sportsmen in the woods quite close to us. We all sprang out, and although the bandits had their guns slung over their shoulders, I told my men to aim at them and did the same, having every intention to shoot should they show any sign of handling their weapons. Seeing this they passed on and we continued our journey.'

In Padua Elcho found himself amongst old friends and he also made new ones in the persons of Count Algarotti and Nobile Priuli for whom he had letters of introduction. They in turn introduced him to the equally Venetian Madame Morisini, a well-known hostess who entertained the smart cosmopolitan set in her palazzo. French was their language and they looked to Paris, but they were at home in every European capital. Algarotti is described by Nancy Mitford as a 'combination of the manners, tact and intelligence of an ancient race, a childlike *joie de vivre* and an easy sexuality'. He had long been one of Frederick's boon companions. Elcho now shared his time between them and his old Paduan friends, upon whom these smart Venetians were inclined to look down, but who had been so kind to him during his last stay, and whose provincial way of life he seems to have enjoyed as much as that of the glamorous Venetians.

But he still preferred being with his fellow countrymen. Soon on hearing that there was a Scotsman lurking in the neighbourhood he sought him out with a view of celebrating St Andrew's day in his company. He turned out to be a Mr Forbes of Alford (in Aberdeenshire) who, having gone bankrupt in Rotterdam, was lying low. Although somewhat embarrassed at having been discovered, he accepted the invitation and they must have drunk copious libations to the homeland to which neither could return.

In December Elcho followed his Venetian friends to town where he had many acquaintances. Unfortunately his generous old Wemyss relative, who had befriended him when he was a friendless refugee, now lay dying in the country and he was unable to see him. He was the last of this branch of the Wemyss family. Elcho may have looked back with some satisfaction on those bad old days, measuring up how greatly his position had improved since then. 'Everyone, or nearly everyone was now friendly, even the British Resident who often had the goodness to ask news of me from Dr Rigolini whom I had known in 1747, adding that he was sorry that his position precluded him from seeing me.' Only Mr Hope, brother of Lord Hopetoun, whom he met at Madame Morisini did not call, an unpleasant reminder of the Jacobite occupation, and the levying of supplies which it had been his task to organise.

Amongst his letters of introduction was one for Madame Zenobio, reputed to be the most beautiful woman in Venice. Elcho called several times but was always told that she was not at home. 'Thus rebuffed I asked to see her husband and was admitted. I told him I had a letter for his wife; he snatched it from my hand and read it. I pointed out that it was addressed to his wife. He said he would give it her. He returned my visit the following day, but as to the lady, although I often pressed at her door, I was never to lay eyes on her. When in love with their wives Italians are very jealous. Nobile Priuli had a very pretty one and although I dined with him every week the lady was never there. One day, when we were talking after dinner, he asked me if there was anything of the Italian about him, for he prided himself on resembling the French. I answered that he had still a little of that nation's jealousy. "You are right my friend" said he, "but it arises from the intimate knowledge I have of the women of this country; they cannot resist advances, and as I love my wife it is my duty to preserve her from them."

'General Graeme arrived in Venice when I was there'. He had been a Major General in Dutch service and had just been appointed head of the Venetian army on the Earl Marischal's recommendation. 'After his arrival we spent most of our time together, and Madame Morisini, who had the best establishment in Venice, showed us much attention. Count Algarotti had procured for her a good French cook and she often had people to meals.' Graeme introduced Elcho to the Austrian ambassador who suggested he should enter Austrian service, 'saying that it would be a better way of securing my pardon. . . . To this I consented on condition I got a colonel's commission. But whether he got no answer, or that the Court refused my application it being about to go to war with England, I shall never know.'

Marischal's failure to procure a Franco-Prussian Treaty had led Frederick to bury the hatchet with his Uncle George and in January 1756 a Treaty was signed. This in turn induced King Louis to listen to Madame de Pompadour who had long been working for a Franco-Austrian alliance: the famous *Renversement des Alliances*. The French and the English had long been fighting each other in India, America and at sea and Elcho had heard from Sir James Steuart, now in Liege, that there had been a fight between 'the *Orford*, on which my brother was a lieutenant, and a French man o'war . . .The French ship had been captured.' The war was about to move to the Continent and it was time for him to return to Neuchâtel.

On this occasion he took the direct route by way of the Tyrol, where he fell ill.

> I called in the local doctor who arrived very much the worse for drink, I had some lemonade by my bedside. He asked me what it was. I answered 'lemonade'. 'Drink more wine', he said, 'It will do you more good'. He then proposed to bleed me; I did not want him to do so, but having been reassured by the innkeeper that he did so better when in that state than when he was sober, I gave my consent. He therefore bled me as one bleeds horses in my country, with hammer and lancet. He pulled me through.

And Elcho was able to continue his journey. On his arrival at Neuchâtel he was greeted with the news that his father had died. 'I was greatly affected for I had not seen him since 1745. . . I discarded my title of Lord Elcho and assumed that of Earl of Wemyss', and it is as Milord Wemyss that he is still remembered at Neuchâtel. In Bôle near Neuchâtel there is a 'Chemin Comte de Wemyss'. What 'Milord Wemyss' really felt about his father is hard to judge. The fifth earl had been an indifferent parent, and there is no word of criticism in the *Journal* for his having so disastrously encouraged his Jacobitism.

Elcho found Marischal settled at Colombier which acted as the Governor's summer residence. It was a delightful place standing in wooded country and surrounded by a fine garden which Marischal was doing much to improve, for he was a keen gardener. Elcho fell in love with the country: its forest and its vineyards which covered the hillside; its red-roofed villages with their solid stone-built houses inhabited by well-fed and well-dressed Swiss peasants whose prosperous appearance was in strong contrast to the miserable country folk he had seen in Angoulême. 'The country is very beautiful and it so pleased me that his Lordship suggested that I should buy a place of my own to become his neighbour,' to which Elcho assented, and Marischal said he would look out for one.

It was during this stay, that Charles Edward proposed to come to Neuchâtel, a suggestion the Governor turned down. He could not forgive the way poor faithful Goring had been treated. The Prince was now living at Basel with Miss Walkinshaw and their small daughter under the name of Dr and Mrs Thompson, and he had the reputation of being cruel to his wife. Rumours of his presence in the area had reached the ears of the British Representative in Berne, and were confirmed by a Neuchâtel contact according to whom Marischal had definitely broken with the Young Pretender. 'He had the lowest opinion of his character, a view also expressed by Lord Elcho who held Lord Marischal in such high esteem.'

After a pleasant sojourn, Elcho returned to Paris. He now took up his residence in his flat, recently vacated by the Steuarts, and which he set about furnishing, never dreaming that he would not benefit by his father's will. By now France and Britain were at war and the French had captured Minorca, which was to lead to the execution of Admiral Byng. This did not worry Elcho, who looked upon war with the professional eye of a soldier of fortune, and being attainted, he was free to fight the British if called upon to do so. However, he would have preferred to fight in Germany. Anyway, as he explained to his brother James, it was his intention to do his duty, but no more; he would not become a volunteer. What did worry him was the thought that he would be called upon to serve as a captain in an Irish regiment where he would encounter nothing but hostility. So he took to lobbying Versailles for a colonelcy in the *Royal Ecossais* without achieving any success.

The news that his father had not left him a single penny came as a shock. The whole estate was entailed on James, but with so many restrictions as to make it a poisoned gift. It would seem as if the Earl had wished to punish his sons one for his Whiggishness, the other for having fallen out with the Prince. In his distress Elcho

turned to the Old Pretender. 'I and my heirs lose the estate for ever',
he wrote to Edgar, the King's Secretary, 'I am no bragger but no
one that was in the Prince's affair lost so much for the cause as I
have done.' King James may have had a few twitches of conscience.
It was that unfortunate promise extracted out of a mere boy which
was responsible for Elcho's present plight, and he managed to get
him a colonelcy in the *Royal Ecossais*, but still without pay.

James Wemyss was also to be pitied. True, he was now head of
the family, a fact officially recognised by Lyon King at Arms, and
he enjoyed, on paper, an income of £2,000. But £500 must go to his
father's creditors and another £500 to his mother, who under
Scottish law inherited a third of her late husband's income. 'Quit
the service and establish yourself in the old castle and get married
immediately,' wrote Elcho with all his newly acquired authority as
head of the family, for it was as such that he saw himself. His advice
was followed; but quitting the Navy must have been a wrench,
James being greatly attached to his naval career. He married his
cousin, Lady Betty Sutherland, and set about restoring the family
fortunes.

'Milord Wemyss' future must be settled. He could not be left
with only his French pension of twelve hundred livres to live on; it
would disgrace the family. So James, Francis, and the Ayrshire laird
of Bargany who had married their sister, two cousins who bore
their name and Mr Anderson, an Edinburgh lawyer who had the
family's interest at heart, put their heads together and came to the
conclusion that the Countess must be persuaded to give up her
share of the Wemyss estate, she being amply provided for by her
father's will. So a document was drawn up and sent to Elcho for
him to present to his mother. He called to his aid his French brother-
in-law who promised to bring Lady Wemyss to Poitiers from where
they would all go to Paris.

Obtaining her consent proved a formidable task, for she was in
no mood to be generous. She had deeply resented being left at
Angoulême, and she laid the blame at Elcho's door accusing him of
having contracted the debts which had got her into trouble, a

ridiculous accusation for he was the most parsimonious of men,
and as careful with other people's money as he was with his own.
Elcho and Labarthe came to the conclusion that she had best reside
at St Denis in one of those convents which catered for wealthy
widows. During the whole journey the brothers-in-law pressed the
point home and finally obtained her consent. The precious
document was signed at Versailles, the event being followed by
what was reported as a very merry dinner. Elcho now took his
mother to St Denis and after having settled her comfortably in her
convent, returned well satisfied to his Paris flat.

Unfortunately insulting remarks about the Host during a
religious procession obliged the nuns to find her other
accommodation, and she was settled in rooms not far away but
where she was free from all supervision; as a result she became an
easy prey to the many sharks who roamed the French capital. Of
this her son was well aware. 'Knowing my mother's character,
and being aware that her faculties were failing, I feared she would
fall into the hands of cheats and rogues of which Paris abounds.
When I went to visit her at St Denis I warned her above all against
Dr Cantwell, a man called FitzGerald and Mr Alexander Murray.
When I realised that there was no other way of restraining her I
went to see the Comte de St Florentin to ask for a *lettre de cachet*
authorising her transfer to a convent in Chartres where she would
be very comfortable, as a large sum of money would be paid annually
to ensure that she was well treated . . . She was as much mistress of
her fortune as she had been in Paris.'

One of these rogues, 'Mr Leslie, a brother of Lord Rothes [and
incidentally a relation of the Wemyss] set about bringing her out
of her Chartres convent in the hope of getting her to marry him. He
was helped by Mr Crawford, a banker at Rotterdam to whom Leslie
owed a great deal of Money. They obtained from the States General
an order directing the ambassador in Paris to obtain her release
and a passport to leave France'. Elcho was with his regiment when
the 'ambassador did me the honour to inform me of what had
happened.' However, Leslie was followed by Alexander Murray

whose abject slave she was to become. After a spell at Spa, she
returned to England from where Murray was able to carry on a
blackmailing campaign, as the fact that they sent money to Elcho,
which was against the law, made his brothers vulnerable. The
passage in the *Journal* about these difficulties with his mother was
to have a curious consequence in the following century.

The year 1757 saw Damiens' attempt on Louis XV's life. France
was shaken to its very foundations, the monarchy having as yet
lost none of its aura. He was promptly arrested and condemned to
a barbarous death.   Needless to say Elcho was present at the
execution, of which he gives all the grisly details in his *Journal.* 'He
died . . . having screamed and sworn in torment for three hours. *La
Cour et la Ville* were present and it was noticed that none of the
ladies left their seats at the windows whilst many gentlemen
departed . . . Sometimes later I was attending one of the audiences
the Comte d'Argenson held at the Louvres, when a letter was read
out to the effect that Damiens had come from London and crossed
from Dover to Calais in a packet boat. As this was quite untrue I
fancy the rumour was being put about to rouse the credulous young
soldiers against the English soldiers whom they would soon be
fighting in Hanover.'

That same year saw the death of his friend Lady Ogilvy. Having
become a Catholic, her corpse was not submitted to the indignity
of being buried at night without prayers and in the presence of
only two mourners which was the fate of those who refused to
rally in time to Holy Mother Church.   She was on the contrary,
given a grand funeral attended by all the Scots then in Paris. This
was probably the last time that they all came together, for the
memory of the '45 was growing dim and Jacobitism was becoming
a thing of the past. Her husband's name disappears from the *Journal.*
He married again, became a general in the French army, defended
the Royal Family from the mob during the Revolution, was
pardoned and ended his life in Scotland as the Earl of Airlie.

The time had come for Elcho to join the *Royal Ecossais* now
stationed at Gravelines with the Ogilvy regiment. 'I was received

as its colonel by the whole regiment under arms on the parade ground…The officers and non-commissioned officers were all Scots as were some of the soldiers, the others coming from other countries. The uniform was blue with red waistcoat and facings, white breeches and white buttons. The Ogilvys wore the same uniform but with yellow buttons. I took my quarters in an inn where four places were set for officers of our regiment…The King's Lieutenant at Gravelines kept up a good establishment where he would often entertain us to meals and where whist was played every day. The summer was spent in manoeuvres and I also made little trips to Dunkirk', scene of his first encounter with the French army thirteen years before.

He returned to Paris a worried man, wondering what his mother would be up to now that she was in the hands of his arch-enemy, Alexander Murray. He was also short of money; campaigning was expensive, he was always without pay, and the war was making the despatch of funds more difficult. He felt so disgruntled that he wrote to Pitt who had just come to power at Westminster, but received no answer. He could no longer afford to live in Paris. So he gave up his flat, moved to a hotel, although not to Bielle's establishment which he may have thought unsuited to the Earl of Wemyss, and sent his furniture to Neuchâtel where Marischal had found him an estate. But he put off the move until after the summer campaign.

In the spring he rejoined his regiment now quartered at Dunkirk. The talk was of an invasion of England: 'the French Government having assembled boats all along the coast facing England, it was thought that the army assembled there was destined for a descent.' Elcho pooh-poohed the notion. 'The French never entertained such a plan; they were too sensible to risk an army without having the command of the sea.' However with the arrival of the energetic Choiseul as Prime Minister, Alexander Murray, who was acting as Charles Edward's representative, was pushing for a descent on Ireland. An interview was arranged with the Prince who arrived so drunk that a substitute had to found in the person of a Mr O'Dun who according to Elcho 'did bear some resemblance to the Prince.' It was no doubt with this expedition in view that the Irish General Roth came to Dunkirk to review the troops. The Governor of Dunkirk gave a great dinner in his honour to which 'Milord Wemyss' was pointedly not invited. 'Whenever I found myself in his company he affected not to speak to me. One day I told him that I thought it extraordinary that I received no pay after having served two campaigns at my own expense. He answered very dryly that the King was master of his gifts. Roth was Irish and hated the Scots.' Elcho got a fright, for he believed that his letter to Pitt had been intercepted; he was, however, reassured when he was invited to dinner by the Commander-in-Chief. Roth had probably been warned against him by Alexander Murray, now involved in a plan for a Jacobite descent upon Scotland's Ayrshire coast which was frustrated the following year by Hawke's great victory at Quiberon Bay.

That summer a series of English descents on the coast of Normandy put the troops on the alert. But Elcho must have wondered what would be his fate should he be captured. He was to ask Marechal de Belle-Isle for a 'paid colonelcy in the army in Germany', a request which remained unanswered as did most of those he ever made. Once the campaigning season was over he left the regiment intending to return to it in the spring. But the King 'published an ordinance by which all colonels attached to a regiment would have to serve as captains except for one day a year . . . Mr Stirling who had served under my orders during the '45, as had the other captains who had been my inferiors in Scotland, would become my superiors in France, I determined never to rejoin the *Royal Ecossais*.'

After a few days in Paris, he left for Neuchâtel. He was in a filthy temper for he knew it to be the end of his military career and he hated leaving Paris where he had so many friends. On arriving at Besançon he grew impatient with the postillion 'who would not go fast enough. So I got out of my carriage intending to give him a few strokes with my cane. When he saw me alight he set off at a fast gallop leaving me in the middle of the road. Fortunately one of my companions pursued him on horseback and overtook him, and although he made good his escape I got my carriage back. On the 3rd of October I arrived at my chateau of La Prise and on the following day I dined with Lord Marischal.'

The old man was probably in no better mood, for he too was having a difficult time. Shortly after Elcho's departure from Neuchâtel two years before, he had gone on leave to Potsdam resolved never to return to the Principality. He found Frederick facing a seemingly desperate situation, for Maria Theresa had managed to align against him a massive alliance made up of France, Russia, Sweden and Saxony; one hundred thousand men or more against his forty thousand. Her intention was nothing less than to wipe Prussia off the map, and reduce him to being the mere Margrave of Brandenburg. She had already divided his dominions between her allies. Frederick was at bay, and like all animals at bay he attacked. At first all had gone well; then his luck had turned and he suffered reverse upon reverse. He was on the verge of suicide when he first defeated the French at Rosbach then the Austrians at Leuten. He was now acclaimed as saviour of Protestant Germany

Such was the situation when Elcho turned up at Colombier where, however, the war was then uppermost in its inhabitants' minds; 'His Lordship (i.e. Marischal) often received letters from the King of Prussia written in his own hand, and giving an account of all the military operations. Although attacked on one side by the Russians, on the other by the Swedes and the Imperial armies he held out and defended himself like a lion. He invariably defeated the Swedes with a small force, compelling them to remain in Pomerania; and although he suffered a terrible defeat at the hands of the Russians in the battle of Frankfurt-on-Oder, he prevented them from wintering in Brandenburg and Pomerania. He was checked this year by Marshal Daun at the battle of Hochkirchen where Marshal Keith was killed. I was at the Castle of Neuchâtel when Lord Marischal received the news. Although his Lordship was greatly attached to his brother, he bore his loss like a 'philosophe', observing that he was not young and that he could not have had a better death.

Elcho had only been three months in the Principality when Frederick sent Earl Marischal to Madrid on a diplomatic mission. This left him alone to find his feet as best he could in his new role of landowner. He must have been disappointed — or possibly relieved given the parlous state of his finances — to discover that La Prise was far from being a 'chateau' in the given sense of the word — had it been thus named by some zealous official wishing to flatter the new proprietor? It was a well proportioned rectangular building, built in the style of the day, in a clearing of the forest which extended as far as Colombier. In front a lawn bordered with trees ended up with a view on the lake; a walled garden faced the front door and adjacent to the house were the farm buildings, as is often the case in Switzerland. With its woodlands, fields and pasturage, La Prise was a pleasant, compact little estate. But it was extremely isolated. No other building was in sight with the exception of Le Pointet, which stood across the fields in the neighbouring parish of Colombier. It belonged to old M. de Charrière who lived there with his two maiden daughters, whilst his son was a tutor in Holland. They were well-born Bernese who had sought refuge from religious persecution and were still looked upon as strangers, their only visitor being the local minister.

Marischal had warned the *Chefs de famille* who made up the parish council that a Milord would soon be living amongst them, and demanded that he should be elected *coutumier*, with all the privileges, such as grazing rights which went with it. But Swiss peasants are not easily bullied, and Milord Wemyss had to wait for three months before a delegation arrived from the village with the news that he had been duly elected. Elcho seems to have developed an excellent relationship with his neighbours. All in good time he was voted a pew decorated with his arms in the village *temple*, and at the end of his life he was regarded with 'veneration' by the villagers. One of the first things he did was to send for little

Marguerite, whom he officially recognised as being his daughter, thus going some way to mitigate her bastardy. She must have grown up on the farm, as was so often the case with children of the gentry, be they born in or out of wedlock. All goes to show that she was a lively and wilful child, not unlike her vivacious Italian mother.

That first winter spent alone at La Prise must have had a nightmarish quality for a man who had spent his whole life in the company of his peers, and who for the last few years had revelled in the delights of Paris society. With the spring the roads improved, it was easier to get about and he began to explore his new surroundings. Finally in July he went off to stay with Baron Braekel whose acquaintance he had made during his first stay at Neuchâtel, when they were fellow guests at the Castle.

Braekel, a Baltic Baron, was the man to whom Marischal had turned when hounded out of France in 1745, and had hoped to get an appointment in Russia. The roles were now reversed and it was he who had sought refuge in Switzerland from the Czarina's wrath. He had married a daughter of Sir James Kinloch, whom Boswell describes as having remained after thirty years' residence in Switzerland 'an old Scotsman, just an East Lothian laird.' According to the same witness, Braekel would have been about forty-five at this time: 'a good manly figure, reserved, polite, quite a man of the world', whilst his wife was 'a tall handsome, charming woman . . . The Baron was formerly in the French service in the regiment of the great Marechal de Saxe, with whom he was very intimate. I found he had been a wild rogue. It is curious to see a man, after a life of libertine conduct turned a grave father of a family.' However, it is the Scottishness of the Braekel background which provided the soil on which this friendship was to grow: 'I could scarcely think myself out of Scotland' James Boswell, wrote a few years later. The Braekels must have felt sorry for Elcho who was then going through a bad patch, for not only was he forced to live a lonely life but he had fallen out with his family on the subject of money. Marriage to an heiress was the answer to his problems and

Madame Gaussin, the Scottish wife of a Geneva banker was asked to find him a suitable bride.

> In September [1759] I went to see Baron Braekel . . . and from there we went together to see a M Gaussin who had married a Scotswoman called Forbes. It was now arranged that M. and Madame de Braekel, Madame Gaussin and I would go to Vevey in November where I would ask for the hand in marriage of a widow Madame de May . . . whose father had an income of 60,000 livres a year. Madame Gaussin, who knew the family, undertook to make the presentations. We all met at our rendez-vous at Vevey and we all stayed at the same inn. Her father called on us and invited us to dinner . . I found his daughter a very pretty woman of twenty-eight and she confided to Madame Gaussin that she liked me. We remained three days being invited every day to dine by her father. On the fourth, when we were about to leave, I despatched my servant with a letter asking for her hand in marriage. Her answer was neither yes nor no, and she asked for time for reflection.

Elcho was not alone in the field, she was also being courted by a 'Chevalier Wynn'. 'I wrote to her and she answered but without coming to a decision, but said in one of her letters that she found it difficult to make up her mind to marry a rebel.' Being called a rebel put Elcho in a state of fury: 'I sent my servant with her letters and demanded mine back; and at the same time wrote . . . that rebel though I was I had done her too great an honour by even thinking of her, thus putting an end to the business. Shortly after she married the Chevalier Wynn who took her to England'. An angry Elcho returned to La Prise, there to spend another solitary winter.

The year 1760 was to prove much happier. By now he had made his way in local society and had been elected a member of the *Club des Jardins*, rendez-vous of the local gentry. The Steuarts had settled in Tübingen for the education of their son, and where they were now rejoined by Elcho. He found them already well ensconced in the life of the University, having made friends with the principal professors and on the friendliest terms with the local nobility. 'Sir James took me round the neighbourhood introducing me [to various aristocratic families] as well as to Prince Hohenzolern Hechingen where we stayed several days on two occasions. The Prince is a very amiable nobleman whilst the Princess .. is very charming. He took us hunting .. and his land is stocked with stags, does, roebuck, wild boar, pheasants, partridges, quail, rabbits and hares' a real hunter's paradise. 'One eats extremely well in his house where concerts and dances are held every afternoon. I have never spent a more pleasant time.'

With the Steuarts he went to Karlsruhe, residence of the Margrave of Baden Durlach 'to whom we were presented. The Margrave is a well-educated Prince, who has travelled widely and speaks French, English and Italian. He governs his subjects well and his finances are in good order... He is well acquainted with English affairs and likes to speak about them. He spends a great deal of his time in his library'. They were then presented to the other members of the family and Elcho describes at some length this little German Court modelled, as they all were, on Versailles. They then parted, the Steuarts returning to Tübingen whiles Elcho wended his way back to La Prise, sightseeing as usual on the way.

> On my return from Germany I received a delegation of four Councillors sent by the municipality of Neuchâtel to offer me the freedom of the city, which, I gratefully accepted. The King of Prussia gave his consent and I was entertained at a great banquet given in my honour by the magistrates, when Burgomaster Montmollin presented me with a parchment conferring upon me and my posterity the freedom of the town. It was dated 22 December 1760. I was now enabled to enjoy all the privileges inherent to Switzerland'.

No wonder that he felt grateful: after fourteen years in the wilderness he was now a Swiss citizen which then, as now, was an enviable thing to be. 'In return I invited all the magistrates to a banquet at my house.'

CHAPTER TWELVE

Bourgeois of Neuchâtel

From having been no more than a stateless foreigner, Elcho was now a member of a well-established community which belonged to the greatly respected *Conféderation Helvétique*. No longer did he haunt the corridors of the *Ministère de la Guerre* in Paris in the hope of being received in audience. He was free to go wherever he pleased. But the community into which he had been admitted was far from being peaceful, being beset with religious disputes.

Although he was far from being devout, he did not share Marischal's obsessive hatred of religion, whilst what he had seen at Wemyss, where the hostility of the Kirk had been one of the factors which had driven his father to live in England, had inspired him with a healthy respect for the influence exercised by the clergy. It may well have been he who alerted the Governor to the serious situation which had arisen during his absence over the friction that had arisen between him and the Church.

At first Marischal turned a deaf ear. He was now in England, where he had been well-received, and where he was having a good time. But the situation had now reached the stage when it could no longer be ignored, and he returned to the Principality where he arrived in February 1762. 'I called on his Lordship' wrote Elcho, and while discussing local affairs pointed out that he had only to allow the appointed minister to take possession of his temporalities to put an end to the troubles, and the people would be content. He thought this very reasonable and said he would follow my advice.' But Marischal changed his mind, believing that his opponents were pro-French. This was all the easier to believe in that the Neuchâtelois did favour the French cause, without, however, taking any active part in the business. 'I warned him that . . . the Council of State, which had been waiting for his return to thank him for having calmed things down, would act despite his orders. He replied they would not dare do this. He was irritated with me and asked me why I was meddling. I answered that my interests were at stake: I was fond of him and it was to be near him that I had settled in Neuchâtel where my happiness, my pleasure and my interests made me hope he would end his days. But knowing him as I did, I knew full well that should the Council of State receive the minister without his consent, he would take it to heart and leave the country. This is exactly what happened.'

Deaf to Elcho's entreaties, Marischal not only backed his candidate who had been rejected by the Church but prevailed on Frederick to do so too. The affair went up to Berne for arbitration, when the King was blamed for having endeavoured to tamper with his subjects' liberties, with the result that Marischal was discredited and became very unpopular. 'In 1763 his Lordship went back to Scotland to sell his estate and from there returned to Berlin where the King gave him a house close to Sans Soucis.   He never set foot again in Neuchâtel where he had been greatly loved and esteemed, being an honourable and disinterested gentleman'. Sadly this unfortunate affair was to bring to an end an eighteen year old relationship — one might almost say discipleship — for one of Marischal's well-known traits was that he never made up a quarrel. However, Elcho, who had greatly benefited from the old man's protection, did not forget what he owed him, and not one unkind word figures in the *Journal*. He was well aware that, by taking the line he did, he was risking to lose Marischal's friendship, but he wanted to prevent his old patron from throwing away the respect he had once enjoyed.

Elcho then learnt that his other friend, Sir James Steuart was in trouble. The house where Sir James Steuart was staying at Spa had been surrounded by a company of hussars who had taken him off despite his being ill with the gout, and that he was now a prisoner in the fortress at Charlemont. This sent Elcho posting off to Paris where he returned to the Sieur Bielle's establishment. 'In Paris I was told that a letter addressed in cypher to him [Steuart] and containing a plan for an attack of St Domingo which he was requested to lay before the British authorities had been intercepted. It also contained the address of a Bordeaux merchant to whom the reply could be sent. The merchant was arrested and the Duc de Choiseul sent the Intendant of Valenciennes to try and extract the name of the writer. Sir James was well aware of his identity — the culprit owned property on the island from which he was getting no revenues and wished it to be captured by the English and thought that the hope of obtaining his pardon in exchange for so valuable a piece of information would be enough of an inducement for James to carry out the request. However Sir James pretended to have no knowledge of the business, as he feared to put the life of the writer in jeopardy'.

'I went to see the comtesse de Rohan Chabot [one of Steuart's influential Angoulême friends] and several other ladies to beg them to intervene in Sir James's favour. I also wrote several times to the Duc de Choiseul whose invariable answer was that if he revealed the writer's name Sir James would go free.' Fortunately for Steuart, the negotiations for peace, which had been dragging on for the last two years, were coming to a head, and the Treaty of Paris once signed he was released. He joined Lady Fanny in London where he was not molested, 'for it would have been too hard to clap him into an English prison having just been released from a French one.' The Steuarts retired to Coltness in Lanarkshire where he was soon to make a name for himself as a political economist. After a time he received his pardon largely thanks to Lady Mary Wortley Montagu, who pleaded his cause with her daughter, Lady Bute, wife of George III's Prime Minister.

By now Prussia was out of the war. Frederick, who did not believe in miracles, was saved by one, for he was pretty well at the end of his tether when the Czarina died. She was succeeded by Czar Peter III who was one of his fervent admirers, and who ordered his army to change sides. This obliged Maria Theresa to negotiate a peace. by which Silesia remained in Prussian hands. Louis did not get off so cheaply as he was obliged to cede his American and Indian possessions to England.

The war being now over, the disbanding of regiments began. Amongst these figured both the *Royal Ecossais* and the *Ogilvy*. 'Their Colonels pointed out that the King had promised that this would never happen, but the Duc de Choiseul said that as the men were no longer Scots the convention was no longer binding... The cavalry regiment of Fitzjames [which had served in Scotland during the '45] and the Irish infantry regiment of Lally shared the same fate.' This threw a great many mercenaries on the market and Elcho's friend General Graeme, who was then in Paris, suggested he should raise a regiment which he, Graeme, would propose to either Venice or Holland, countries with whom he had close links. Elcho was enthusiastic and set about recruiting officers and men, whilst Graeme endeavoured to find employers. Although the negotiations with the Venetians went very far, they did not go far enough and the enterprise had to be abandoned. This marks the end of Elcho's military career.

The peace being signed, the British returned in shoals to Paris. Amongst them figured Scots bent on discovering if Archibald Stuart, son of the late Lady Ann Douglas, was or was not the rightful heir to the estates of her brother, the Duke of Douglas, who had recently died. She had married Colonel (later Sir John) Stuart of Grantully (in Strathtay) but had kept the marriage secret fearing that her eccentric brother might — they said — cut off her allowance. The couple had lived on the continent, and Archibald and his twin brother, who died in infancy, were born in Paris in 1748. But the Hamiltons, who would have inherited the estates, claimed that Archibald was not Lady Jane's child, she being, in their view, past childbearing age. However, Archibald found in his aunt, the Duchess of Douglas, an energetic woman who would loudly proclaim her views in broad Scots, a fervent supporter determined to vindicate her dead sister-in-law. Now Elcho had been a friend of Sir John Stuart's whose home, Balcaskie, was in Fife, and he was therefore sought out by both sides as a possible witness. But as he had not been in Paris at the time of the twins' birth, he cannot have been of much help. The case became the *cause célèbre* of the 18th century, the Douglas cause, and it divided the Scots about to meet each other in company. Elcho lent his support to the Duchess. Finally, the Court of Session took sides, by one vote, with the Hamiltons, whose windows were broken by the Edinburgh mob which was supporting the Duchess. However, the verdict was reversed the following year, an event duly celebrated in the Scottish capital by bonfires.

For the next four years Elcho divided his time between La Prise and the Rue Richelieu, with trips to Yverdon to see the Braekels, and to Karlsruhe to stay with the Margrave of Baden-Durlach whose acquaintance he had first made in company of the Steuarts. They had since become great friends to the point of Elcho being decorated with the Durlach order. It was not a very prestigious decoration, but it meant that he was no longer alone amongst his peers not to sport a ribbon, he having been refused *Pour le Mérite*, the decoration instituted by King Louis for his Protestant officers.

In November 1764 he was back to Rue Richelieu where he was greeted by his nephew who had been sent over to discover how things stood. The Wemyss family was now in need of his help; their sister, Lady Anne, had left her husband, Hamilton of Bargany, and now living at Lille, seemingly alone and therefore an easy prey to any adventurer, as her mother had been. Elcho was best able to cope, but was he willing to do so? He had fallen out with his brothers, whom he accused of not having carried out the financial agreement they had reached in 1759. However, he proved amenable, and he soon met Francis Charteris. 'We met on the stairs of the house in which he was living without recognising each other; We had not met for nineteen years! I spoke about the £250 annuity which had not been paid for four years. He also promised to pay Sir James the £500 he owed him for having boarded my sisters at Goodtrees, and he wrote to Lord Marischal in Berlin to ask him to return the £400 he had lent him, which his Lordship proceeded to do'. Charteris then went to Bordeaux to fetch his wife, whom he brought to Paris so as to meet Elcho, whom she had not seen since her wedding day. The brothers were evidently happy to see each other again.

Shortly after Francis' departure Elcho received a letter from his sister suggesting they should set up house together at La Prise. This, however, did not suit him as he was courting a wealthy young woman. So after having fetched his sister at Lille and settled her financial affairs at Dunkerque, he lodged her in a respectable hotel in Paris, whilst remaining himself in the Rue Richelieu. But she soon felt out of her depth in the French capital. So he packed her off to Neuchâtel, where she was even more lonely and bored. She returned to Scotland where she was to die a few years later.

The marriage, originally suggested to Elcho by a brother officer, did not come off as the girl's father refused to give the dowry his daughter had suggested. Both she and Elcho were disappointed, for they had taken to each other. She was quickly married off to a titled officer, from whom she parted two years later. 'She settled in a convent where I often had the honour of being received', and where, one suspects, he was granted those favours which her miserly father had prevented him from receiving within the bonds of matrimony.

From 1755 Neuchâtel had been troubled by the presence of Jean Jacques Rousseau in the Principality. In 1752 his book, *Emile*, had been banned by the Parlement of Paris, and he would have been arrested had he not been warned in time by one of his influential protectors. Rousseau, who was an awful coward, was frightened out of his wits and took refuge in Motiers, a large village situated in the Neuchatel uplands, where his sister-in-law had a house. Here Jean Jacques settled after having sought the Governor's permission which was granted all the more readily that Marischal had a soft spot for the *Philosophes*. He took to Jean Jacques, who was in the habit of paying him regular visits, and whom he described to the Scottish philosopher Hume then a senior official at the British Embassy in Paris as being 'gay in company, polite and what the

French call *aimable*, and gains daily ground in the opinion of even the clergy here.'

In 1755 there had appeared Jean Jacques' *Lettres de la Montagne* which were a virulent attack on the clergy and ruling classes of Geneva. Hell was now let loose. Up to now Elcho had paid but little attention to the storm now raging in the Principality. He had little patience with the *Philosophes*, and was at this time wholly taken up by the Douglas cause, infinitely more interesting in his Scottish eyes than these wrangles. But the violence of this attack on Jean Jacques aroused his curiosity, and he wrote to Du Peyrou as 'Milord Wemyss', a fellow Neuchâtelois of foreign extraction. Elcho was now raised to the rank of champion of the much slandered clergy, and his church-going fellow *coutumiers* awarded him, by a unanimous vote, a pew in the church at Bôle bearing his arms. What could a village do more to show its gratitude?

In the meantime the situation at Motiers was becoming daily more explosive, aggravated as it was by Rousseau's mistress-housekeeper, a surly and suspicious woman who was universally detested. Marischal became seriously alarmed and wrote to Hume asking him if he could not arrange with Rousseau to take refuge in England. Whereupon Madame de Luze, one of his many female admirers, despatched her son in her carriage to take him to safety. Potsdam was their destination, but in Strasbourg Jean Jacques received an invitation from Hume to join him in Paris, from where they would proceed together to London. So the carriage now headed for the French capital where it deposited the Philosopher at the Temple, a grim fortress whose Governor was the royal Prince de Conti, a protector of the *Philosophes*, and young Luze at the Rue Richelieu where he was welcomed by Elcho, who was friends with his mother. Here he stayed until the party left for England.

This business, of which he was not particularly proud — it gets no mention in the *Journal* — had earned Elcho three visits from Hume, who was then in charge of the British Embassy. It is not clear what led the philosopher to seek out so notorious a Jacobite, thus risking a severe reprimand from the powers that be. Was it concern for Rousseau? Or did he wish to meet a man of whom he must have heard a great deal from General Sinclair, whose secretary he had once been?

Elcho must have come to regret Hume's departure, for had he still been in charge of the embassy he might have rescued his mother from the clutches of Alexander Murray, to whom the latter was related and of whom he had the lowest of opinions. It was Elcho's nephew, young Steuart, who discovered that his grandmother was living under constraint in Alexander Murray's Paris house. 'We went to see the *Lieutenant de police* and informed him that the countess was old and feeble-minded and that Murray was detaining her in order to get hold of her money; and we asked for an order for her release and entry into a convent at Charenton.' This the official was all the more willing to grant that Murray had already been brought before the Courts under serious charges, and owed his release to the protection of the Prince of Conti's very influential mistress, Madame de Boufflers, to whom he was related. The official 'who had received other complaints against him for other malversions sent a police inspector to Murray's house where he found the Countess and took her to the convent.'

Murray now went to the embassy where he made a complaint to Lord George Lennox, who had recently replaced Hume as *chargé d'affaires*. It should have been turned down given that Murray was then acting as agent for the Young Pretender; but Lennox was newly arrived and not too sure of his welcome; so he yielded to pressure and wrote to Choiseul asking for her release under pretext that 'being a peeress of Great Britain she could not be detained in France.' This the Minister consented to do on condition, however, that she should leave French territory. 'On the day fixed for her discharge' says Elcho, 'I went to the convent, found Murray in the street and challenged him to fight. He refused, upon which I showered abuse upon him which made him return to Paris, and that day the Countess remained in the convent. Whereupon Lord George asked me by means of my nephew not to put more obstacles in the way of her release'. She came out a few days later and left at once for England where she was soon followed by Murray.

Her two other sons brought the case before the Courts; it was to go up as far as the House of Lords, where it was lost. Murray having made much of the fact that money had been sent to Elcho, who being protected had no right to receive it. Not long after both Murray and poor Janet died, seemingly on the same day. Her sons gave her a decent burial. Echoes of Murray's shocking behaviour were to reach Jacobite ears.

The Old Pretender died on the 1st January 1766. The same year young Boswell, fresh from Corsica, picked up some gossip about the Prince from the elderly Scots *emigrés* at Avignon. The Prince, said old Lady Inverness, had been heard to say that he was still fixed in his longing and ambition to be King, and that for him all else was 'brown bread'. With the death of the Old Pretender disappeared Elcho's last link with the Jacobite cause, for he had never ceased feeling grateful for the good time he had enjoyed in Rome, and the way James had overlooked his repeated requests to King George for pardon. In his own words he remained to the end 'penetrated with the utmost gratitude for the goodness Your Majesty has all time shown me.' He had up to now refrained from demanding the return of the £1200 he had lent Charles Edward on the eve of their entry into Edinburgh, not wishing to add to the burden already borne by his unfortunate father, King James. But he was in need of the money, for Marguerite, who seems to have inherited her mother's wilfulness, had fallen in love with Lebel, a Protestant who combined the roles of factor and secretary. Elcho had objected to the marriage finding that the disparity in their ages was too great. But she had taken the matter into her own hands and had eloped, which had led the local *pasteur* to marry them. The problem was where would they live? La Prise was not large enough to contain two households; he must therefore buy a house in the village or build one on the estate. But this would cost money. So after having officially summoned Charles Edward to repay his debt, he left for Rome. He took the now familiar road by way of Lyon and the Mont Cenis, by Turin and Milan, where he fell in with his old friend Signor Cerestes, before reaching the Eternal City, where he intended spending the winter. Little had changed during the last twenty-five years except that the Palazzo Muti was now little more than an empty shell in which a drinksodden Charles Edward sulked, the Pope refusing to recognise him as a king. There were the same spectacular Church ceremonies; the same intrigues surrounding the papal throne; the same influx of foreign visitors come to enjoy the winter sun. As of yore the British kept themselves to themselves. None called upon Elcho with the surprising exception of Lord Glenorchy, heir of the third Earl of Breadalbane and a firm supporter of the Hanoverian throne. Elcho must have been all the more pleased that Lady Glenorchy was a sister of the late Lady Sutherland who had been so careful to avoid him a few years before. It really looked as if the hatchet was at last being buried! 'Lady Glenorchy was very amiable and I often attended musical parties at her house'.

He called on the French ambassador by whom he was 'ever well received' and he started frequenting that cosmopolitan society which was in the habit of wintering in the Eternal City. He again took to sightseeing, which he had somewhat neglected of late, and spent much of his time 'seeing palaces, churches, pictures, statues, antiquities and villas.' It was the Grand Tour all over again.

However he did not neglect the purpose of his visit. He started by addressing himself directly to the Prince, but in vain. He then applied for help to the French ambassador, who being friends with Charles Edward, refused to interfere. He was more fortunate with the Secretary of the French Embassy, who took him to see the Baillie de Treteuil who represented the Knights of Malta, and the Abbé de Viri who looked after the interests of the French Church. 'These three gentlemen entertained in a large way' and Elcho often dined at their houses, where he made many useful acquaintances. But he was still without access to the Palazzo Muti where the Prince had put himself up in company of Hay of Restalrig, Urquhart and Lumisden. Urquhart, whom he had known during the Rebellion, came to see him and told him that Charles Edward was 'drunk every day and that he ill-treated his gentlemen, going so far as to beat Mr Hay'.

Having failed to get any response from either the Prince or the Cardinal of York, Elcho now asked the Secretary of State, Cardinal Torrigiani, if he could discover if the Prince acknowledged the debt. That answer was that he did, but that it would only be repaid when he 'came to the throne. I told the Cardinal that I considered that to be very far away and that I wanted to be paid at once.' Elcho was now asked if he 'wished to start proceedings against his legitimate sovereign. I replied that I did not recognise him as such, and that I would sue him if I were not prevented from doing so'. He would not be prevented from doing so, came the answer, but he must understand that the Prince 'enjoyed the protection of the Church being a zealous Catholic', to which Elcho retorted that he had renounced that religion. 'I know it', replied the Cardinal, 'but he is a good Catholic now'. York, to whom Elcho had written several times, asked the French Ambassador to restrain Elcho from harassing him. This, however, the diplomat refused to do.

Persistent as ever, Elcho obtained an audience with the Pope and after having been duly drilled as to how he should behave, he was received with all the honours 'due to a Scottish peer.' He presented His Holiness with a memorandum in which he asked that the Prince should not receive his pension until the debt had been paid. 'The Pope read the memorandum from one end to another and then said with tears in his eyes, that he had already hurt the Prince by refusing him the title of King, and that he could not take upon himself to interfere in his affairs any more.' This marks the end of Elcho's campaign.

The war, which he had won, had ruined Frederick, who was now looking for means to replenish his empty coffers. This had led him to farm out the taxes of Neuchâtel. His initiative roused the whole population against him. The affair was submitted to Berne where the *Avocat Général*, M. Godot, won the case. Hardly had the poor man reached home than he was besieged by the mob. A carriage was sent to his rescue, but it was unable to reach him, whilst the soldiers despatched to restore order fraternised with the rioters. Finally these broke into his house, where he was killed bravely defending himself. The neighbouring cantons had to be called in to restore law and order; some of the culprits were arrested, but made good their escape before being brought to trial. Frederick learnt his lesson and henceforth the Neuchâtelois were left in peace to govern themselves according to their own laws.

Elcho's first reaction had been to return to La Prise. Then he thought better of it; he was still a newcomer and as such had no wish to get involved in local disputes. So he spent that summer pleasantly enough in Paris and only went home the following spring.   Although immensely enjoyable, Elcho's Italian trip had not fulfilled its purpose, and he had returned poorer than when he had left.   Marriage to an heiress seemed to be the only answer. So he sought the help of his friends the Braekels. They, in turn, consulted Madame de Braekel's brother-in-law who was the minister of the Scots church in Utrecht, and who came up with Isabelle van Tuyll, or Belle van Zeulen as she is known to posterity. Boswell had been in love with her, and his biographer describes her as being 'something of a bluestocking, something of a flirt, was gay, charming and completely virtuous.' She was also given to deep fits of depression. When still very young she had met an entrancing Swiss officer in Dutch service called Constantin d'Hermanches. It was apparently love at first sight.   But he was married, and they carried on a ubiquitous and purely platonic love affair by means of a clandestine correspondence. It was he who introduced her to the fashionable French *Philosophes* of whom he was a follower.

Belle was now approaching her thirtieth year when girls turned into old maids. So she decided that the time had come for her to get married, and she announced to her long-suffering father that she was in love with Charrière, Elcho's neighbour, who had been her brother's tutor. He had long been in love with her, but was too modest to aspire to her hand.   Her father objected: she could do better for herself. 'I have received another proposal in marriage which I have submitted to Father', she wrote to there brother. 'This man will come in May . . . Did I mention his name? . . . It is Milord Wemyss. He was once a rebel in Scotland . . . I shall marry him as if I were taking the veil. I intend to remain virtuous, but I shall remain indifferent.'

Whilst asking Elcho not to divulge what was being planned, she could not refrain from confiding in Charrière. He was horrified. Milord Wemyss was of a kind she could never love, he being 'debauched, violent and despotic.' Her cousin, Lady Athlone, to whom she was greatly attached, was equally distressed and begged her, with tears in her eyes, not to marry that 'savage'; and she brought up the tale of his having wished to cut off the prisoners' thumbs. Somewhat shaken, Belle turned to Hermanches for advice. 'Milord Wemyss is looked upon in Switzerland as a somewhat extraordinary personage and very licentious and he is believed to have behaved badly towards his sister. She may well have been in the wrong, but she has certainly turned public opinion against him. He is forty, good-looking, and a colonel in the French army'. And he advised her to marry a German suitor who was then on hand. 'All you tell me confirms what I had heard', came the answer. But as she was sure she would make her husband unhappy, Belle felt Wemyss was more deserving of this fate than his German rival, who being young, could still make a happy marriage.

Elcho was in Paris where he intended to remain. He had entered into the negotiations in good faith, but he had been warned of what he was letting himself in for, and he was now looking for a way of wriggling out. For the time being the wedding of the French heir to the throne provided him with a good excuse for remaining in the French capital. 'In the beginning of May 1770 Princess Marie Antoinette of Austria arrived in Paris to wed the Dauphin. I went to see her arrival. The road from St Denis to La Muette, where she was going to sleep, was crowded with carriages: the whole of Paris was there. She sat in a carriage with the King and the Dauphin'. The King brought his new mistress, Madame Du Barry to sup with the Princess who was married to the Dauphin on the 16th.

Elcho was shocked to see the way Louis had introduced this fifteen-year-old girl to a woman who was nothing better than a trollop.

The Du Barry had started life as a prostitute. She was then kept by a man called Dubarry who married her off to his brother. He in turn planned to make her the King's mistress. So he bribed the King's valet, Lebel, to introduce her into the royal bedchamber after having first instructed her how to deal with an ageing monarch worn out by debauchery. So well did she manage that on the following day the King confided to the Duc de Noailles that in the hands of his new mistress he felt like a man of twenty-five, to which the Duke answered, 'It is clear that Your Majesty has never frequented brothels'.

On the 16th a splendid fete was held at Court in honour of the royal wedding, and among other sights there was a magnificent display of fireworks in the grounds of the Chateau [of Versailles]. The whole garden was lit with lamps; and so great were the crowds that when the first carriage stopped at the gates of Versailles to allow its passengers to alight, the vehicles behind it stretched as far back as Paris, four leagues away. I saw all this with my own eyes, I being on horseback. The fireworks let off on the place Louis Quinze [now Place de la Concorde] were not so successful, for unfortunately one of the exits was blocked and several people were knocked down; others fell on top of them as the crowd surged forward, and a hundred and thirty people were crushed to death and more than six hundred wounded.

There were also several great entertainments.

The Austrian ambassador gave a splendid one; but the most magnificent of all was the one given by the Spanish ambassador. It was held in the Vauxhall of the Boulevards to whose halls had been added a very large *salon.* It started by a great dinner attended by three hundred ladies and gentlemen of the highest rank. At midnight more than a thousand masked guests, who held invitations, were admitted and dancing took place in several rooms. In others faro, biribi and trente-et-quarante were played for very high stakes. Everyone could call for the food and drink of their choice, and were served at once, four battalions of Swiss guards acting as waiters. All the entrees, roasts, sweet dishes, deserts, wines, liqueurs, tea, coffee, refreshments, ices, etc. that can be imagined were at the call of the guests. The service went without a hitch and the entertainment continued until eight next morning. I saw women staking eight hundred *louis d'or* at trente-et-quarante and men six thousand on a single throw.

The festivities once over, Elcho declared he must remain to find out if his name figured amongst those who had been awarded the *Ordre de Mérite*; 'indeed a childish ambition for an attainted Lord who has done nothing for France', scoffed Belle. She finally lost patience and decided to marry Charrière. So she fed her still reluctant father with every piece of ill-natured gossip she could discover about Milord Wemyss, and having obtained his consent, Charrière was summoned to Holland and the couple were married in January 1772. A relieved Elcho returned to Neuchâtel where he spent that summer. The Braekels remained as attached as ever to Elcho.

CHAPTER THIRTEEN

Husband and Widower

It was September of 1771 when Belle and her husband settled in at
le Pointet with old Monsieur de Charrière and his two spinster
daughters. She and Elcho were now neighbours and Neuchâtel was
too small a place for them not to have bumped into each other —
Elcho already had a nodding acquaintance with her husband. But
neither her voluminous correspondence nor his *Journal* bear any
reference to an encounter. They evidently wished to forget the
whole unfortunate episode. Belle's marriage, which had created an
uproar in Holland where it became synonymous of *mésalliance*, seems
to have passed unnoticed in Neuchâtel, so obscure were the
Charrières. Her husband did not even belong to the *Cercle des Jardins*,
an omission which, however, was remedied when the couple started
frequenting the *salons*. This phase did not last long, and she was
later to publish an ill-natured description of Neuchâtel society
which made her very unpopular.

The time had come for Elcho to make himself scarce. But Paris
was out of the question, the financial hurricane which had recently
torn through France having left him much the poorer. So he decided
to try pastures new. He first plumped for Briançon, a large garrison
town, seat of a *Parlement* and 'winter residence of the wealthier
members of the Franche Comté nobility.' It also boasted of a good
theatre. But apparently his reputation as a good card-player and
witty man-of-the-world had not penetrated thus far, and he was
soon back on the road heading for Montbeliard, home of his
nephew's old tutor, now Councillor Goguel. The arrival of an
emblazoned coach-and-four carrying a milord and three servants

must have created a stir in this small provincial town which stood well off the beaten track, and boasted of no feature likely to attract the foreign visitor. He was quickly met by Goguel, who took him off to see the President of the Council of Regency, Baron Uxküll, who invited him to dinner.

On the following day he went to the Castle to pay his respects. The Prince and Princess of Württemberg-Montbeliard were away at Ludwigsburg in attendance on the Prince's elder brother, the reigning Duke, and Elcho was received by the eldest child, Princess Dorothea. 'On the same day I had the honour to play cards with Princess Dorothea at Baron Uxküll's. Although she was only twelve years old she was very advanced of her years both in stature and intelligence.' This proved to be the start of a friendship which was to last until the end of his life.

He now left of Karlsruhe, stopping on the way at Basel 'where one of the burgesses gave a fine party in my honour followed by a great supper party'. He noted with some amusement that 'under their municipal laws the burgesses are forbidden to display their wealth outside their houses; they are not even allowed to have a lackey behind their carriages. Their houses are splendidly furnished and their tables are sumptuously spread.' Strasbourg he knew of old and did not like despite it having a 'good French theatre and often a German one.'

'On 18 January [1772] I crossed the wooden bridge which spans the Rhine', and soon reached Karlsruhe, home of his friend the Margrave of Baden Durlach. He found the Court in a state of turmoil, the recent death of the Margrave of Baden-Baden having doubled both Durlach's dominions and his income. From having been what Belle unkindly described as a 'very small prince', he was now one of the most influential of the German rulers. Elcho had as a fellow guest the Hereditary Prince of Hesse-Darmstadt who took a great liking to him. He was probably familiar with his name as his father had been in command of the Hessian troops in Scotland during the '45.

Elcho could not resist a spectacular display of troops and this he was sure to find at Ludwigsburg where the Duke of Württemberg was about to celebrate his birthday. Karl-Eugène was renowned for his luxurious way of life. He had come young into his heritage, and as he enjoyed absolute power, as did all the German princes, he had been able to indulge to the full his taste for beautiful buildings and spectacular entertainments. As a young man he had spent some time in Paris, for the most part in company of chorus-girls, and had acquired a liking for both opera and ballet. His aim was nothing less than to rival Versailles, conveniently forgetting that he did not enjoy Louis XV's revenues. He had enlarged his palace at Ludwigsburg, giving it stables able to house no less than eight hundred horses. But his *chef d'oeuvre* was *La Solitude*, a real architectural gem which stood amidst beautiful gardens. No expense had been spared: the blue tiles on the roof were edged with gold, as were the varnished posts in the gardens and outhouses. 'His Opera rivalled that of Paris and the dancers were the best that money could procure.'

On his arrival Elcho found that all the accommodation was taken by envoys from various princes come to present their masters' good wishes to the Duke, and he was obliged to go elsewhere. The celebrations once over he returned with a letter of recommendation from the French envoy which led to his being presented to the Duke, who invited him to supper. On the following morning he called on all the principal officials, and his calls being returned he knew himself to be *persona grata*. 'Every morning at ten the Duke, attended by his whole court, more than five hundred persons, would go to the courtyard of the Castle to see his troops parade before him,' a sight which could not but have rejoiced Elcho's heart. He was more especially impressed by the Guards, 'the finest looking and the best disciplined men I had ever seen', resplendent in uniforms covered with gold and silver lace. 'The cavalry regiment was mounted on white horses, whilst the guns were all in excellent order'. The army furnished the Duke with his principal source of income, he being in the habit of hiring it out. This had been the case during the recent war, when greatly to the dismay of the other German rulers, it had fought with the French against the Prussians, and many men had deserted rather than fight against other Germans.

'The review over, and there being no shoot that day the guests would go and change into silk garments embroidered in gold brought by servants from the Duke's own quarters. Before returning to Court the gentlemen were ushered into a drawing room where the ladies were sitting, and were given a number by the Master of Ceremonies. Although these were seemingly drawn by lot, rank was respected. This method had been chosen in order to avoid quarrels in a country obsessed by precedence'. Elcho's presence seems to have posed a problem of etiquette for 'as everyone is in military or civil employment it is difficult to determine the place of a foreign gentleman who is in neither.'

> On his arrival the Duke is ceremoniously advised that dinner is served; he takes the hand of his sister-in-law, the Princess of Württemberg-Montbeliard; his brother takes that of the highest ranking lady present, and as the others advance the Master of Ceremonies calls out a number and the gentleman in whose possession it is takes the hand of his partner and they sit next to each other at table. There were a hundred places, all magnificently set out. The dishes were brought in by Swiss guards, preceded by trumpeters marching in order as if on parade, and handed in with military precision. A row of pages, all titled, stood behind the guests, and behind them a Hussar or a Chasseur, whilst a third row of lackeys received the food and handed it on to the pages who laid it before the guest. More soldiers marched through during dinner to relieve the sentinels stationed in the various rooms, and there was a continual playing of trumpets, cymbals, hautbois and clarinets. .

> After dinner the amusements consist of walking in the Plazza San Marco, a large square with shops on each side where one can purchase jewellery and stuffs. Here the Duke has rooms where he gives dinner and supper parties, and there are cafés where faro is played. It was after a visit to Venice that he had this square built. He has an Italian Opera which is as fine as anything I have seen in Italy, an Opera Bouffe, a German theatre and the best concerts I have every heard. The access to all these amusements is free. In the evening there is a ridotto where

masked dances are held and there are gambling tables.

There were also shooting parties on the same lavish scale.

> Of all the Princes the Duke is the one who displays the most taste and ingenuity in regard to entertainments. He likes taking his guests by surprise. During dinner the ceiling of the banqueting hall was thrown back to disclose an orchestra whose musicians were dressed as gods and goddesses, and which performed excellent music. During supper one whole side of the hall opened to reveal an illuminated lake into which gamekeepers were driving a number of big game by means of their horns which they proceeded to shoot in front of the spectators. At the Opera the back of the stage opens and one sees a whole tract of country lit up and where the Duke's troops, both cavalry and infantry perform military exercises and fight a mock battle before the eyes of the audience seated in boxes.

Elcho wondered where the money could possibly come from. True the Duke had a very large income 'estimated at six million French livres but even this huge sum is not enough to pay for such wanton extravagance.' A few years before the States had dared remonstrate with the result that Karl Eugène had deserted his capital in favour of Ludwigsburg.

At the time of Elcho's stay the Kings of Prussia, Denmark and England had sent envoys in the hope of patching up the quarrel. However, salvation was already on the way in the shape of a pious young *hausfrau*, Baroness von Lautrum, with whom the Duke had fallen passionately in love. He had recently installed her in a house in town, where Elcho was invited to sup in his company and where the guests were treated to a splendid display of fireworks. Under her benign influence Karl Eugène was gradually to abandon his evil ways and become a model ruler with the welfare of his subjects at heart.

Elcho now started for home. On the suggestion of the Prince, with whom he had made friends, he stopped at Montbéliard on the way. He could not but have been struck by the contrast between the simplicity reigning in this Lilliputian principality and what he had left behind him. Montbéliard was a small Imperial enclave surrounded by French territory, it having somehow survived Louis

XIV's invasion of Alsace. Its last ruler had been eccentric to the point of insanity. Declaring himself a Mohammedan, he had acquired a large harem and a numerous progeny.

The new Prince of Montbeliard had been in Prussian service where he had risen to the rank of Major General. He had married one of Frederick the Great's numerous nieces. The marriage was an arranged one, as was then the custom, but the couple were fortunate enough to fall in love and to remain so. The Prince had acquired those skills in administration for which Prussia was rightly reputed, and Montbeliard had prospered under his rule which had made him extremely popular.

Possibly because they liked a simple way of life, or more probably because they could afford no other (although prosperous in a modest way Montbeliard was too small to provide its rulers with a large income), life at the Castle was more that of a large country house than of a royal palace. Etiquette was reduced to a minimum and amusements were of the simplest kind, there being neither theatre nor orchestra. This did not prevent the Court from having a very happy time, as is shown in the delightful *Mémoires* of Dorothea's girlhood friend, Baroness Oberkirch. Much time was then spent in creating a garden at Etuppes, some four miles from the town, inspired by both Lenotre and Capability Brown. It was adorned by a great many monuments, mostly commemorating family events. The Princess was also in the habit of reading the letters from her beloved ones, shedding many a tear in the process, for she was sentimental as Germans are apt to be. For the time being, however, the children would play whilst their elders would dig, weed and water.

That summer La Prise was to see many visitors. Dorothea's brothers stayed on their way back from Lausanne, where they were attending school. They were followed by the good-looking Prince of Hesse who created quite a furore, many balls and parties being given in his honour. Le Pointet too had its guests, amongst them Lord and Lady Athlone whom Elcho entertained to dinner. One wonders what that fat, jovial woman thought of the 'savage' she had so feared her cousin would marry?

With the autumn came the *vendanges* when the whole population would be out picking grapes, after which the country houses would be closed for the winter. It was time for Elcho to take his departure, and he returned to Montbeliard. 'The Prince invited us to come to the Castle, and as it was the Duke's birthday we found ourselves in goodly company. We were introduced into the presence of the Prince and Princess surrounded by eight Princes — their sons, and four Princesses — their daughters, and during our stay were invited nearly every day to dinner or supper.' They returned to Neuchâtel delighted with their reception. Some three weeks later the emblazoned coach-and-four was again heading for Montbeliard where Elcho intended to spend the winter. The place had become a magnet for the man who had never enjoyed family life, having been dragged away from home at the age of five. So taken was he that he 'bought a house with a garden and orchard after having first written to the Duke to obtain his consent, which was granted in a most gracious manner'. He also notified the Council of Regency that he had been taken under the Duke's protection. Later 'he had the honour of entertaining the Prince and Princess to a meal followed by a small ball'.

He did not, however, abandon his old friends, and he went to pay his respects to the Margrave and Margravine of Baden, then 'touring their dominions in company of the Hereditary Prince. They were staying with the Grand Bailiff . . The Margrave kept me to dinner, as he did the following day. The day after he went to Basel to take possession of his mansion, during which time I accompanied the Margravine while she visited the sights of the town'.

For the next few years Elcho's life was to follow much the same pattern: the summer being spent at La Prise, where he would entertain many guests: old companions of-arms from the '45; young Scotsmen keen to meet the man who had commanded the Prince's bodyguard at Culloden, as well as French, German and Neuchâtelois friends and acquaintances. He had become one of those middle-aged bachelors whose witty conversation and skill at cards make them welcome guests, more especially when they are discreet and do not make mischief, as was his case, gossip being noticeably absent from the *Journal*.

Some echo of his movements must have reached the ears of Lord Leven, whose son, Lord Balgonie was then on the grand tour. The young man turned up at Montbeliard to the great joy of Elcho who had always suffered at the thought that he was seen as a traitor by his Whig relatives who had been so kind to him. 'This unfortunate noble cousin desires me to offer you his best respects,' Balgonie wrote home from Montbeliard. 'He is most sensible of your intention in sending me to wait upon him. He is in good looks, health and spirits, recalls the happy days of Kinnaird with pleasure, as well as those of Cupar races with many circumstances too tedious to remember.' Balgonie spent a whole day at the Castle where he played chess with the Prince 'beating him no less than three times', whilst the Princess 'scolded me heartily for having kissed the Pope's slipper'. He was just back from Florence where he had come across the recently married Charles Edward — or Duke and Duchess of Albany as the couple called themselves. 'He was looked upon with contempt, and the English did not scruple to talk to him'. But the young man was full of praise for the Duchess. He departed after a short stay, Elcho accompanying him as far as Strasbourg.

The Montbeliard children were growing up and their parents were beginning to make plans for their future. Dorothea, now a beautiful girl, was destined for Elcho's young friend, the hereditary Prince of Hesse-Darmstadt. He was greatly taken by her; she, however, was less enthusiastic. She may well have thought herself worthy of a more brilliant match. But she finally gave her consent and they were duly affianced amidst great rejoicings. The marriage was planned to take place in June 1776.

Whereupon couriers began arriving from Potsdam; something important was clearly afoot and there were rumours that she was going to marry the recently widowed Grand Duke Paul, heir to the Russian throne! The death of his wife in childbirth — she was a sister of Dorothea's fiancée — had been a terrible blow, and his mother, the Empress Catherine, had decreed that she must be replaced as soon as possible so as to ensure the succession. Prince Henry of Prussia, who happened to be in Russia at the time, suggested that his great-niece Dorothea would make a suitable bride, to which suggestion both mother and son agreed. Negotiations started at once and were quickly brought to a successful conclusion, to the great satisfaction of great-uncle Frederick, who saw his alliance with Russia thus consolidated. Dorothea was quite delighted. Never had she contemplated in her wildest dreams marrying the future Czar of all the Russias! Her friends shared her joy. Only her mother thought Russia a barbarous land with a well-established reputation for murdering its sovereigns. Events were to prove her to be right. Paul, who ended insane, was murdered after a turbulent reign during which his consort behaved with admirable courage and dignity.

Elcho must have found Montbeliard in a state of intense excitement when he arrived there in June 1776. 'The Court was preparing for a great journey. It was being said that the Princess Dorothea was going to marry the Grand Duke of Russia. But the Prince and Princess gave out that they were only going to Berlin. At length, on the 27th, the whole Court, thirty-four persons in all, departed in six carriages. The Princess wept bitterly on saying goodbye to her old friends. The next day I asked for the hand of the Chanoinesse Comtesse von Uxküll from her father, mother and grandmother, Baroness von Walbrun, and the transaction was quickly concluded.'

What under Elcho's pen sounds like an unpremeditated move on his part was, in fact, the culmination of a three years courtship. This goes some way to explain his attachment to Montbeliard. It had been from the first his intention to get married; but given his past experiences in that field he had decided to conduct the whole business himself. His choice first fell on Mademoiselle Groll. But the project had foundered on the dowry, her father being unable — or unwilling — to meet his demands. One therefore cannot but be surprised by his next choice, for the Uxkülls were poor, indeed so poor that the Duke had allowed the deposed official to retain his salary. One wonders what Elcho can possibly have seen in this shy and retiring girl of seventeen, who lived so unobtrusively in the shadow of Princess Dorothea that she is not even mentioned in the Oberkirch *Mémoires* which give so detailed an account of the Court of Montbeliard. It was most certainly not romance which on the continent did not enter into consideration when planning a marriage.

At first he may well have been moved by a feeling of pity. He too had had a neglected childhood, and further developments go to show that the Uxkülls were uncaring parents. The Baron was a brutal Prussian Junker wholly taken up by his four sons to the detriment of his only daughter. He had evidently decided that she would never get married for lack of an adequate dowry, and he had got her enrolled in a *Chapitre de Chanoinesses*, one of those well endowed charitable institutions which provided spinsters with long pedigrees and no money with the title of 'comtesse' and the assurance that they would end their days in a dignified manner amidst their own kind.

But as time went on he grew more and more fond of her. She was so different from the prostitutes, actresses, promiscuous ladies of fashion and girls willing to barter their dowries for a title and a place in society whom he had frequented up until then. No one in any way like her had as yet come his way. She clearly stood in awe of this fat middle-aged suitor (good food had played havoc with his figure) whose name was linked with tales of valour and cruelty and who reputedly possessed an ungovernable temper. But marriage was better than spinsterhood, and she could look forward to care and consideration.

To get married Elcho needed money. This, however, was in short supply for he had been badly hit by the financial blizzard which had recently blown through France. There was the Colonel's confiscated legacy which might possibly be retrieved with the help of German friends in contact with the Court of St James. 'I mentioned the subject to one of the Margravine of Hesse Cassel's ladies-in-waiting . . and we agreed that the English Court should be sounded with a view of getting [the young Countess Uxküll] a pension paid out of my confiscated ten thousand pounds on the grounds that she was to marry me.' He also confided his troubles to the Margravine of Baden-Baden. 'She said she would make her Lady-in Waiting . . . and she wrote to the Queen of England's brother, Prince Charles of Mecklenburg'. But in vain. Elcho could not shake off the reputation with which he had been saddled by his enemies. He then appealed to the Duchess of Albany, begging her to get Charles to repay his debt, but with no success. Finally salvation came from Neuchâtel where the great merchant Pourtales, (he handled amongst other things the East India Company's business with Russia) put him on to lucrative investments. He was now in a position to get married.

The marriage once settled, he left for La Prise to arrange for the reception of his bride. He then went to Briançon where the honeymoon was to be spent, before meeting the bridal party at a small town close to Montbeliard. It consisted of the Uxkülls and their daughter, the bride's grandmother, Baroness Wallbrun accompanied by Baroness Konigsee, Secretary d'Uvernois and the Chevalier Ramsay, an army friend of Elcho's who was to act as best man. It was distinctly a low-key affair.

> Secretary d'Uvernois had prepared the marriage settlements by which the Chanoinesse was to have at my death the house, garden and orchard at Montbeliard with all its furniture and an annuity of a hundred louis d'or. Her parents were to give her a dowry of a hundred thousand imperial florins to be paid in the course of the year [which they clearly had no intention of doing]. Next day, 9 September 1776, we went to Beutal to be married by the local minister who was Secretary d'Uvernois' brother; and after the marriage the settlements were signed. This once over, Baroness Wallbrun and Baroness Konigsee, who had come for the marriage, returned to Montbeliard.

The Uxkülls went home on the following day 'and on the 11th we took our leave of the Chevalier Ramsay and went to Besançon.'

It was a curiously hole-in-the-corner affair as if the Uxkülls were unwilling to go to any expense whilst being too proud to allow their son-in-law to bear all the expense.

It is rather touching to see with what care Elcho went about arranging the honeymoon. His aim was to lift his bride gently out of the obscurity to which she had been so long confined without making her feel either awkward or shy. He asked two friends to show Madame la Comtesse de Wemyss round the town, which they certainly did with that mixture of deference and gallantry used by the French when dealing with a married woman. 'We went to the theatre where we saw the Marquis de Segur who commanded the province and the Marquise his wife'. This too was a new experience, there being no theatre at Montbeliard. They left three days later for La Prise where, however, they did not stay long.

On hearing that the new Bishop of Basel was to make his official entry into Bienne — the Bishops had been debarred from Basel since the Reformation — Elcho took his bride to one of those official functions in which he always delighted. This powerful prelate 'made his entrance escorted by a large number of Alsatian nobles and the whole of his Court. A thousand very well-dressed soldiers were under arms with a train of artillery, a company of mounted dragoons and a company of *Chasseurs à Pied* whilst a number of carriages followed the procession. The Bishop alighted at his residence and shortly after I went with my wife to pay our respects. He invited us to supper. After supper His Highness was to receive the congratulations of the magistrates and clergy.' But the Wemyss' were to miss this part of the proceedings, 'for the Prince Bishop had directed his Master of Ceremonies to place the guests, and as I found myself in a place other than the one to which I was entitled by birth and military rank I left the Prince's table and did not return to see him,' This did not prevent the couple from attending the ball held on the following day at the Hotel de Ville. They then returned to Neuchâtel where their welcome was such as to soothe Elcho's ruffled feelings. 'All the ladies and gentlemen called on us and many banquets and balls were given in our honour. In short we were treated with the utmost courtesy. Neuchâtel is certainly one of the most civilised of the small states.'

They returned to Montbeliard in November 'visiting a pretty collection of bibelots on the way'. The Prince and Princess were just back from Memel where they had parted from their daughter. 'The Prince had been given the Order of St Andrew; the Princess the Order of St Catherine with a large number of diamonds, and all the members of the household had received presents from the Grand Duke of Russia'. Elcho had not been forgotten. 'The Princess had induced the Duchess of Brunswick to write to her brother the King of England, asking for my pardon.' But Elcho was again doomed to disappointment: 'I have at last received an answer from the King of England,' wrote the Duchess. 'He is unwilling or unable to pardon Lord Elcho. I know not where he learnt the name, for I was ignorant of it; but I am sorry that my efforts have not succeeded as my dear friend is interested on his behalf'. Baroness Uxküll was no more successful. 'She arrived from Berlin where she had tried to induce the King of Prussia to ask the King of England for my pardon, but His Majesty refused to interfere. Thereupon she persuaded Prince Henry to write to the Empress of Russia asking for her help'. Never was there a man so persistent as Elcho, nor one so unsuccessful. His efforts to obtain a pardon and recover his debt were only to cease with his death. But neither George III nor his cousin, who now called himself Charles III (Prince Charles), would listen to his repeated pleas.

All this time the Lutheran Princess Dorothea of Württemberg was being turned into the Orthodox Grand Duchess Marie of Russia so that she could one day become the consort of the Czar of all the Russias. The process was taking an unconscionable long time and the Montbeliardais were impatiently waiting to hear that the wedding had taken place. So when 'Monsieur de Tomanoff, captain in HM the Empress of Russia's Foot Guards, decorated with the Order of St George' finally arrived with the welcome news that the marriage had been celebrated on 5th October 1776, the jubilation knew no bounds. He was to stay three months, and was joined by other Russians. Never had Montbeliard been graced with so many distinguished visitors. That winter was also memorable for Elcho who was awarded the *bourgeoisie* of Montbeliard. He could also have sported the Grand Cross of The Order of Württemberg had he so wished, for 'the Duke proposed through one of his agents that I should pay 120 *louis d'or* for the honour, but I made no reply and the matter remained in suspense.'

In May the couple returned to Neuchâtel at a leisurely pace for the roads were bad and Lady Wemyss was with child. La Prise was now constantly full of visitors, for the Neuchâtelois had taken her to their hearts; she was described as having 'much charm and graciousness'. In the words of Pasteur Bonhome, who certainly got to know her very well, she was 'young and very attractive' and 'evoked from all sides tributes of respect'. She was evidently very devout, but her piety was of that quiet, gentle, unaggressive kind so often to be found amongst Lutherans. 'Every day the Countess of Wemyss would spend some precious moments with her God, conversing with Him in prayer and reading His Word. By these means she learned to know her duty of which she never lost sight and discharged it with exactness'.

But it is the will she wrote a month before her death, of which she seems to have had a premonition, which gives us most clues as to the character of what must have been an exceptionally nice young woman. It is addressed to her husband and was confided to his daughter, Madame Lebel, who was to deliver it to him in the event of her demise. 'I beg of you, my dear Lord, as a last token of your love for me to execute these my last wishes'. Her dowry was to be divided between her four brothers, the younger ones getting a larger share 'their means of livelihood being less than that of the two elder ones'. She also bequeathed to them her few humble possessions: 'red garnets, an etui with porcelain fastenings, a porcelain bottle with a gold stopper'. 'You will keep a thousand livres and use them to purchase a ring with my monogram and containing a lock of my hair for my child when it grows up'. Should it die this too must go to the brothers. Her maid was to get two hundred *livres*; Elcho's grand-daughter, Marianne Lebel, her 'pink woollen dress and the taffeta one dyed in pink'; to the girl's mother 'my dress made in capuchin material and my blue pekin dress. The rest of my wardrobe, dresses, linen, objects are to be sold and the money divided between my brothers'.

Four hundred *livres* were to go the poor of Montbeliard 'I mean those who are ashamed of their poverty and hide it from the outside world [a revealing clause] and seventy livres to the church of Bôle and its poor. I request to be buried at night, without any pomp or ceremony, in my white dimity housecoat and one of my muslin caps trimmed with lace, and your portrait is to be placed in the coffin beside me. You will cut off some of my hair, my Lord and make a ring to remind you of one who truly loved and esteemed you, and whose attachment would have withstood any trial. I more especially commend to you my child. You will give it all your tenderness and care, lavishing upon this beloved one the love you had for its mother. May heaven make it resemble in all things its worthy father'. Of her parents not a word.

'While we believe ourselves to be at the summit of human bliss we are overtaken by calamity; and that which we looked upon as being a fountain of joy becomes all at once a fountain of bitter tears!' It is with these words that Pasteur Bonhome described, in his funeral oration, the fate which had befallen Elcho. Lady Wemyss had enjoyed 'perfect health' during her pregnancy; but the child was late and the doctor summoned from Montbeliard on the advice of her family had been in the house since November 3rd. 'The labour only started on Monday 19th at six o'clock in the evening' and Elcho goes on to give a minute by minute description of a particularly painful delivery which lasted no less than two days. 'It was a fine boy, 16lbs in weight, 22 inches long and with a head of a child of six months. It was buried the next day at Bôle'. Alas! the ordeal was not as yet over. The poor woman was overtaken by fever and diarrhoea. In vain did her distraught husband summon the best physician Neuchâtel could produce, she 'died at twenty minutes past five on the afternoon of 26th November 1777. She was twenty-

one years, three months and one week old, having been born at
Ludwigsburg in Württemberg on August 18th, 1756. I lost in her
the most virtuous and the most worthy young woman. She had no
faults and was the joy of my life. I am inconsolable'. This was no
less than the truth, this heartrending account being written ten
years after the event.

When his friend, Colonel Morel, came the next morning to offer
his condolences, he found Elcho in a state of utter collapse and
was obliged to take him home 'where he and his sister treated me
as if I were their brother'. Elcho was in no state to attend the funeral
and in the absence of any relative, Morel had to act as chief mourner.
So poor Lady Wemyss went to her grave unaccompanied by any
member of her uncaring family, her mother not having bothered to
be present at the birth of her first grandchild. There being no one
to open the will, she was buried with the pomp and ceremony she
had wished to avoid being 'carried to her grave by four Knights of
the Order of *Pour le Merite*. The Neuchâtelois had streamed out to
pay their last respects to the earthly remains of a young woman
who had won their love and respect in the very short time she had
been amongst them. The news of her demise spread far and wide;
and it was whilst changing horses many miles away, that it came
to the ears of young Chambrier, who extols her merits in a letter to
her father. After spending a few days with the kindly Morels, Elcho
went on to the Braekels, where he stayed a fortnight before ending
up with his fellow Scot, old Kinloch. He was now in a fit state to
face the world, and after a short stop at La Prise he left for
Montbeliard intending to carry out his wife's last wishes. 'I
presented a copy of the will to her father who, however, refused to
take it, saying that according to Montbeliard law he was his
daughter's sole heir'. Elcho held out with his usual pertinacity,
bringing up every argument he could possibly think of to get his
way. But his unfeeling father-in-law had the law on his side. The
business was to drag on until 1779 when the Court rendered its
verdict in favour of Baron Uxküll, who, however, was commanded
to pay 400 livres towards the funeral expenses. These Elcho donated

to the Montbeliard poor. It was the only one of her wishes he was able to carry out: her clothes, linen, and pathetic little trinkets being all despatched to her father. There was no money to return, the long overdue dowry having never been paid.

Elcho now set about honouring her memory. He had already ordered a tomb 'to hold us both it being my intention to be buried beside the most honourable lady I have ever known during the course of my whole life.' It is a fine 18th century monument, and still adorns, the corridor which leads into the very humble place of worship where he and his wife must have often sat in the emblazoned pew given by his fellow *communiers* in gratitude for the way he had stood up for the clergy then being hounded by Rousseau's fanatical supporters.

But this did not satisfy him; it was his wife he wanted to honour. So he decided to donate a bell and a clock. He went himself to the village where the bell-caster was and brought him back to Bôle, where they worked out together the best way of carrying out his wishes. These did not win universal approval: country folk are conservative and change is often resented. 'In the year 1779 I was named Comtesse. I owe my existence to Milord the Comte de Wemyss who donated me to the community as one of his liberalities. The clock which is placed beneath me is another of his gifts. Ever since he did us the honour of becoming one of our *communiers* he has never ceased furnishing us with proofs of his generosity'. On 19th August 1779 'Comtesse' rang out for the first time 'to the satisfaction of all the opponents', and three days later the parish council 'resolved to heighten the bell tower so as to make the bells more audible and find room for the clock'.

The emotional strain proved too much for even Elcho's iron constitution, and he fell seriously ill. His fellow *communiers* were greatly concerned and a delegation went to La Prise to find out the real state of affairs. It returned to the village much relieved to have found him 'convalescing'. He was to recover his health, but he never entirely recovered his spirits: the gay and lascivious man of the world was gone for ever.

CHAPTER FOURTEEN

The Laird of Cottendar

Lady Wemyss' legacy to her sorrowing husband was the home life he had never as yet enjoyed. He had planned to have children who would bear his name, and a son who would inherit his title at least abroad, although he never quite lost hope of getting a pardon. But these dreams were now buried in the churchyard at Bôle, for he had no intention of getting married again. So he turned his attention to his grandchildren: young David called after him, and Marianne to whom his wife had left the pink dress which was now being worn by some unknown woman of Montbeliard.

Elcho had shown himself to be a responsible parent, if not a particularly caring one. In that he did not differ from his kind, for children played little part in the lives of the 'carriage-folk' until Jean Jacques (who put his own into an orphanage) had made them fashionable. But Marguerite had been happy enough. She was proud of her illustrious father, for whom she had long kept house, whilst the gracious manner in which she had yielded the place as mistress of the house to her youthful step-mother had endeared her to her father. Her husband had long acted as secretary and factor to Elcho, who now took the necessary steps to make him acceptable as the future owner of La Prise. He first got him elected *communier* of Bôle, then bourgeois of Valengin, where bourgeoisies were easy to obtain. He also took him to Montbeliard, where he treated him as a friend rather than a retainer. He would leave enough money for Marianne to have an adequate dowry, whilst young David would enter the French army. As a first step in that direction he took him to Strasbourg, where he put him into an establishment similar to the one he had himself frequented at Angers.

The snag was that in France, as indeed in most European countries, only those of gentle birth could become officers. Now the boy's mother was born out of wedlock, whilst his father was of even humbler origin. Fortunately, status was linked to the possession of a *terre nobiliaire*; but, alas! La Prise did not belong to this privileged category. However, by diligently delving into the archives Elcho discovered that it had once formed part of the estate of Cottendar, which possessed this precious attribute, and he set about getting it reinstated. This meant knocking on many doors and answering many enquiries. Was his own birth worthy of the honour? On that count he passed with flying colours as he was certainly the highest ranking inhabitant of the Principality. Had he acquitted all his dues? Here too he could not be faulted.

'The King [of Prussia] did me the honour of erecting my possessions in the Principality into a barony under the title of Cottendar. I presented myself before the Council of State to request that the patent should be registered. The Council bade me be seated — an honour never paid to a citizen — and unanimously recorded the registration, after the President had taken each Councillor's opinion'. The conferring of the patent put a final seal on his status as a distinguished member of the Neuchâtel community. As such he was invited to the many ceremonies which marked the arrival of a new Governor. These started with a solemn installation, which took place in the presence of the clergy, magistracy and representatives of the local communities, when as the Prince's representative he swore to maintain the liberties and franchises of the Principality,' no light matter as Marischal had discovered to his cost. This was followed by a great banquet of ninety guests amongst whom figured 'Milord Wemyss'. Then came a tour of the different communities, to which Elcho was invited to four out of the five, the fifth being Catholic Boudry, which did not conform to local customs. The whole thing ended with a great reception at the *Société des Jardins*, where the President presented the Governor with the keys of both the building and the gardens, and which was followed by a ball.

All these marks of esteem and affection did not make Elcho change his habits, and he went on spending the winter at Montbeliard.   It was here that he received a letter from his old friend, Clementina Walkinshaw, who was in need of his help. This was not the first time that this had occurred. Already when he was in Paris in 1763 she had asked him to come and see her in the convent where she had sought refuge with her small daughter, Charlotte. 'I went and was told her whole story: how unhappy she had been with the Prince who had hit her up to fifty times a day with a stick; he was so jealous that when they slept together he would place chairs round the bed topped with a small table on which he placed bells which would necessarily ring should anyone approach the bed . . Not only did he refuse to contribute to their upkeep, but he refused to write the letter the Duc de Choiseul insisted on receiving before giving a pension. Had it not been for the Cardinal of York the poor ladies would not have known where to lay their heads. Miss Walkinshaw suggested I should find a husband for her daughter', a strange request given that the girl was only ten years old. But early marriages were then common practice and she was keen to see Charlotte provided with a protector at a time when her father was doing all in his power to lay his hands upon her.

'A little later I brought them a rich Englishman, who after having seen the young lady, was willing to leave her £10,000 at his death. But when everything had been settled they fell out when Miss Walkinshaw was too zealous in her defence of the Jesuits.   He said he would never have a friend of the Jesuits in his house, and they never saw him again'.

Charlotte was never to marry, but she had an affair with no less a personage than Prince Ferdinand de Rohan Guemenée, Cardinal Archbishop of Bordeaux, by whom she had several children. Now although she was of royal blood she was without a title, which precluded her from mixing freely with the friends of her distinguished lover. To remedy this unfortunate state of affairs she became a member of the *Chapitre Noble de Migrette* which stood close to Besançon. It is not clear who pulled the necessary strings, Elcho or the prelate; but is was the former who acted as surrogate father at her installation as *Chanoinesse honoraire*.   'On our return to Besançon she was called upon by the municipality and awarded military honours by the Commander. We were invited to dinner both by the Archbishop and the suffragan bishop, as well as by the Commandant, the Intendant, the Premier President and the Maréchal de Camp. Her mother was treated with great respect in all the houses where she was entertained'.

Courtship, marriage and the death of his wife had long filled Elcho's mind to the exclusion of all else, and it was 1778 before he realised that America was in a state of rebellion. On hearing that 'the English Ministry was endeavouring to arrange peace terms with the rebels I wrote to Lord North pointing out that since the Government was negotiating with the American rebels they should extend a little of their clemency to me, a rebel Scot, and allow me to return to my native land and see my relations after an exile of thirty-two years'. Although conveyed by safe channels, this missive remained without reply, as had been the case of its predecessors. Elcho was absolutely furious: 'The English are the most inconsistent people in this world when they have their enemies in their power. For thirty-two years I have asked in vain to return to my native land.   This had been consistently refused although it is known that I have not seen the Stuart Prince, nor held any intercourse with him since my exile, and that he is despised by all those who served under him. Today they see they cannot conquer the American rebels who have continually defeated them.   So they humble themselves before them and offer them all sorts of terms .. whilst they treat their Scottish rebels with the utmost haughtiness and cruelty. .What difference is there between the Americans who wish to form themselves into a republic and the Scots who renounced the sovereignty of George III to recognise a prince of the Scottish House of Stuart in place of the House of Hanover, which is foreign and German? They are as attached to freedom as are the English, and would not have endured arbitrary rule under a Stuart monarch . . A generous sovereign and people would have forgiven the Scots for having been attached to the family of their ancient kings, seeing that they were ready to abandon them on becoming convinced of their incapacity to rule them. Their animosity towards those who live in the same island is such that the appointment of the Bute ministry caused a storm; yet without Scotland what would they do? The Scots are their mainstay in all their wars!' There speaks the Winchester schoolboy who had learnt to 'fight with his fists' so as to defend the honour of his country.

From now on he was to follow with great interest not so much the war itself, as the part being played by the Scottish regiments, noting that 'Fraser, Agnew, Campbell, Abercrombie and Pitcairn had all laid down their lives, whilst not one Englishman of the same rank had done so'. This in turn focused his thoughts on the '45, and he decided to write an account which would be published by his Neuchâtel friend, the Baneret d'Osterwald, who ran a flourishing publishing business specialised in books forbidden in France, and for which there was a great market in that country and elsewhere. He tackled the task in a businesslike fashion, sending for a whole lot of books dealing with the question; and he returned to Paris probably in search of old companions who could refresh his memory.

By 1781 the work was in the hands of the Baneret who, however, felt that it was too full of names having little meaning for the foreign reader. 'I quite agree, Monsieur, that we must cut out the names of the simple gentlemen and only keep those of the higher nobility. We must also keep all those of the Highland chieftains, for it is they who played the principal role in this business'. Five months later, he cancelled the whole thing. 'There are several reasons for my decision which I will confide to you when next we meet'. Unfortunately we will never get to know what they were. He must have enjoyed writing these reminiscences for it was then that he started the *Journal* for the sole benefit of his family.

He was clearly happy to be back in Paris after an absence of nearly ten years. His first visit was to 'his old friend and fellow countryman the Abbé de Colbert, now bishop of Rodez'. The event of the day was the birth of the Dauphin. 'Three days later the King, accompanied by the Royal Princes and escorted by his Guard went to Notre Dame for a *Te Deum*. For three consecutive nights the city was illuminated, food and drink were distributed to the populace and musicians played in the streets.' A welcome occurrence was a visit from his French brother-in-law 'his regiment being at St Denis on its way to Valogne.' Even more welcome was the arrival in Paris of the heir to the Russian throne and his consort, who were travelling as the 'Duc et Duchesse du Nord'. They were given a tremendous reception, every sort and kind of entertainment being provided for them. However Dorothea had not forgotten her old partner at cards. Elcho was summoned to the Russian embassy where he was officially presented by the Russian Ambassador to the Grand Duchess, who in turn presented him to the Grand Duke. 'Their Imperial Highnesses treated me with the utmost kindness'. The official part of the audience being thus over, the Grand Duchess Marie reverted to being Princess Dorothea and took her old friend into her private sitting room.'I was asked why I remained in France during the war; I answered it was in spite of myself' without, however, revealing the reasons. 'On June 8 I was present at a *bal paré* the King gave in their honour.' On that occasion Elcho donned, probably for the last time, what he calls in his will his 'royal effects'; this may well have been the fine embroidered coat Francis had given him all those years ago, duly enlarged to fit his now portly person.

'On 20 January 1783 peace was declared in Paris. The Margravine [of Baden] arrived on 4 April and died at the Hotel d'Angleterre on the 8th at 1pm. She had been to the Opera on the 4th and to the Foire St Germain on the 5th. She was the most amiable and worthy Princess and had twice interceded with the King [of England] to get my pardon'. It is with these words that the *Journal* comes to an abrupt end. He must have felt sad and lonely, for his brother-in-law Sir James Steuart — Denham as he now called himself having inherited another baronetcy — had died in 1780. His death had been followed first by that of kindly old Sir James Kinloch, then by that of his son-in-law, Baron Braekel, who had been Elcho's great friend. However, he was soon to be cheered by the unexpected arrival of his nephew, now known as Sir James Denham the Younger, who had his other nephew, William Wemyss, in tow.

William had been educated at the High School in Edinburgh where had had been in the charge of the same tutor as Sir Walter Scott and other Scottish luminaries. From there he had gone to Oxford before joining the Coldstream Guards as a lieutenant. He was a keen soldier and burned to win promotion on the field of battle. After France declared war in support of the American rebels, it had been considered advisable again to raise the Sutherland fencibles, who had been disbanded at the end of the Seven Years' War. They had then been raised and commanded, as was the custom, by their Chieftain, Elcho's cousin, Lord Sutherland. But he had since died and the Chieftain was now his daughter who was the countess in her own right. She was only too willing to raise the clan and would have commanded it had this been possible. Unfortunately 'Colonel Anne' did not form part of the Hanoverian establishment, and she suggested that her soldier neighbour, Lord Mackay, should take on the job. This raised objections amongst the clansmen, the Mackays being traditional enemies. She now turned to her closest male relative, James Wemyss of Wemyss, who also represented the county in Parliament. But he demurred, he was a sailor, not a soldier, but he suggested that his son should take his place. So William found himself at the tender age of nineteen raising, training and commanding the Sutherland fencibles with the rank of Lieutenant Colonel. The war once over he left for the continent where he joined up with his cousin, Sir James the Younger who, having gone through Angers like his uncle, was now serving in the British cavalry where he was going to make his mark as a cavalry officer.

Elcho, who had always remained in touch with young James, was quite delighted to make the acquaintance of this as yet unknown member of the family, and the two young men remained

many months in their uncle's company, both in Paris and at
Cottendar, avidly listening to all he had to tell about his adventures
during the '45. In vain did James Wemyss summon his son back,
pointing out that it was time for him to get married and stand for
Parliament; the answer was that he had not as yet found a girl he
wished to marry, and that he was in no hurry to enter politics. When
he finally took his leave he presumably carried with him both the
Narrative and the *Journal*.

We know very little about Elcho's last years. He had, however,
come to an age when one does not easily change one's habits, and
one can safely surmise that he divided his time between Cottendar
and Paris with short stays at Montbeliard. He exchanged the hotel
where he was looked after by his devoted Swiss servant, Droz, who
had married his wife's old maid. Here he must have entertained old
comrades-at-arms and newer friends from Neuchâtel, such as his
banker M. de Rougement, and passers-through like Porutales, de
Luze, Chambrier and others. Here too he would receive respectful
calls from Neuchâtelois officers serving in the Swiss Guard — the
one which was soon to be ruthlessly massacred by the revolutionary
mob when defending the French Royal family.

He died in Paris 'on April 30 1787 in his house rue St Lazard as
the result of illness and in the Protestant faith,' leaving Cottendar
to his daughter and the Montbeliard house to the Drozes. Although
the savage laws by which the mortal remains of heretics were
dragged naked through the streets and literally thrown to the dogs
had long been in abeyance, Protestants were still interred at night
without ceremony, in an unnamed grave dug in unconsecrated
ground and in the presence of only three mourners; and Elcho was
accompanied to his last resting place by Droz and two officers from
the Swiss Guard. The cemetery was soon to be vandalised during
the Revolution. Thus it is that his bones do not lie, as had been his
wish, beside those of his wife. On hearing of his demise, Charlotte,
who was now looking after her drink-sodden father, wrote to her
mother: 'Milord Wims (sic) is dead. He was a nasty man who
endeavoured to hurt my father by making unfair claims upon him'.

How wise the Master of Sinclair had been to warn Elcho against getting involved with the ungrateful Stuarts; and how foolish he had been to pay no heed to the warning.

Poor Elcho! He died an exile in a foreign land with only strangers about him; the unfortunate victim of an ideology to which he had never really subscribed, and of a Prince whom in his heart of hearts he had always despised.

Postscript

At the time of Elcho's death Jacobitism was already moribund, and became extinct the following year with the demise of the Count of Albany, as Charles Edward now called himself. Soon men's eyes were fixed on Paris. But the French Revolution was to prove divisive for Jacobites. Some so hated the powers that be that they welcomed it — Robert Burns was to send a present of guns to the French Legislative Assembly; in others it only increased the aura which surrounded their concept of monarchy, leading them to transfer loyalties to the Hanoverian who ruled Great Britain.

The excitement then reigning in men's minds was to favour the development of the romantic movement, of which Sir Walter Scott was so brilliant a protagonist, and it was he who was to make Scotland fashionable. (One still comes across in France Scottish baronial halls complete with minstrels' galleries!) In 1813, Scott's *Waverley* took Britain by storm. From this novel and its successor, *Redgauntlet*, Jacobitism rose phoenix-like from its ashes and a romantic picture of 'Bonnie Prince Charlie' became imbedded in the public mind. The Jacobite phenomenon had also begun to penetrate the realm of serious history. This was taken further by the young Robert Chambers, busy collecting contemporary accounts, as well as by the elderly Sir Walter now writing straightforward history.

All this time Elcho's manuscripts had lain in Wemyss Castle. The family had decided to keep the *Journal* under lock and key, not wishing to disclose poor Lady Wemyss' unfortunate involvement with that adventurer, Alexander Murray. The General (as William had become) kept the *Narrative* in 'his own closet with his private papers'. However, it remained largely unread, the womenfolk, who had a taste for refined literature, having declared it to be 'hastily written'. But, he liked regaling his cronies with tales about his notorious uncle, and would occasionally show them the *Narrative* from which his cousin 'Jamie Coltness', as Sir James the Younger was known, copied some of the more relevant passages, which he eventually passed on to Sir Walter Scott, with whom he was friends. Indeed he must have told him a good deal more than what figures in the *Narrative* (which was to form the basis of the '45 as told in the *Tales of a Grandfather*). Although Scott did not have access to the *Journal*, he clearly knew something of its contents through 'Jamie Coltness'. General Wemyss died in 1822 and was succeeded by his eldest son, James Erskine Wemyss. James had joined the Navy at the age of twelve as a volunteer, and had served all through the Napoleonic Wars, retiring as a Captain when peace came. He was later raised to the rank of Rear-Admiral. As can well be imagined, his formal education had been of the scantiest, and he took no interest in the past. He was elected MP and sat as a Whig, as his father and grandfather had done before him.

In 1832 James received a letter from Sir Henry Steuart of Allanton (in Lanarkshire) informing him that Chambers wanted to publish the *Narrative* which Sir Henry had been shown by General Wemyss, with whom he had been to school. He had also heard a great deal about Elcho from his neighbour, Sir James Steuart of Coltness (son of Sir James of the '45), under whom he had served in the army. The request could not have come at a more inopportune moment, for James was then in the middle of an election campaign and under tremendous pressure from his Tory opponents, who were accusing him of having changed sides. A family which had produced a Jacobite like the 5th Earl of Wemyss, they argued, ought to belong to *their* party. But Elcho's youngest brother had always been a Whig, and Jacobitism in the family had been an aberration. However the pressure was real and he lost the seat. However this was only to recover it with a greatly increased majority at the election for the first reformed Parliament.

He therefore sent a curt reply to the effect that he did not wish the *Narrative* to appear in print, and that he would consult his cousin, the Earl of Wemyss, to whom he complained that he was being 'teased to death' not only by Jamie Coltness, but also by the 'Bookmaking Baronet' who was pressing for it to appear in Chambers' 'four bawbee trash'. In order to get rid of the whole business he sent the manuscript of the *Narrative* across the Firth 'in a box by coach' to his cousin. Lord Wemyss had 'never read the papers of Lord Elcho of the '45, but had heard from his grandfather and others that they contained very little that was not known [and] that they were written in bad style'. However on reading the *Narrative* when it reached him he found it 'of greater interest than he had expected' and that 'there was nothing in it but what was creditable to Lord Elcho'. He believed, however, that the latter would not have wished it to be published because of its 'hasty style and open manner'. And there the matter rested, for the remainder of the century.

As to the *Journal*, throughout the mid-Victorian decades it continued to lie under lock and key at Wemyss, almost, but not quite forgotten. So when in the 1870s A G Ewald was writing his *Life and Times of Prince Charles Stuart*, he asked to be allowed to study it. The request was addressed to Mrs Erskine Wemyss, the widowed daughter-in-law of Admiral Wemyss. She was taken by surprise having no notion of its existence. However she complied without first reading it. She was too busy bringing up her five children and running her late husband's estate, which comprised opening up new coal pits and caring for the men who worked in them, to tackle a manuscript about a man of whose very existence she may well never have heard.

Ewald was terribly shocked by what he read, for it was completely at odds with the picture of the gallant young hero of legend and song which was then — and still largely is — the accepted image of Charles Edward Stuart, although it is now much queried. He launched a violent attack on Elcho, begging the reader to 'attach no credence' to what the (still unpublished) *Journal* said and went on to describe Elcho 'as of a violent and jealous temper, and as unsparing and unscrupulous in his enmity'. Elcho did have an ungovernable temper and his was not a forgiving nature; but this does not necessarily invalidate what he says; it only means that his bias must be taken into consideration.

Not until 1907 was the *Narrative* published. This was by the Hon. Evan Charteris, the youngest son of the 10th Earl of Wemyss, under Elcho's own title *A Short Account of the Affairs of Scotland in the Years 1744, 1745 and 1746* with a long introduction which drew from the *Journal*. However this introduction did not do justice to the *Journal*. Charteris, perhaps, was not fully in sympathy with its author. And for want of the full-length portrait of Elcho which only the *Journal* in its totality can give, the *Narrative* itself, right down to the present day, has failed to have the decisive impact on Jacobite historiography which it merits.

Ewald was to find a latter-day disciple in that distinguished Jacobite scholar, Henrietta Tayler who was to publish the part of the *Journal* bearing on the '45 under the title *Portion of the Diary of David Wemyss, Lord Elcho* in the *Jacobite Miscellany* which the Roxburghe Club brought out for the bi-centenary of the '45. This first came into my hands at a time when I had only just taken up the study of Jacobitism, and I brushed it aside because of its rather unwieldy format, and returned to the typescript of the *Journal* in English whose mistranslations I was trying to redress. I did not read the introduction, nor did I pay any notice to the footnotes, not wishing to obscure the picture of Elcho which was then beginning to form in my mind.

Such was the situation when a chance remark of a fellow-historian, who asked me what I thought of Henrietta Tayler's footnotes, led me to take it up again. I was in for a shock for what I had before me was a subtle character assassination done by means of editing an authentic document! There follows an introduction in which she gets her facts wrong. True, Elcho is not easy to follow, his deadpan style and the absence of comment makes it a tedious task, but what comes out most clearly is her almost morbid dislike of her subject. She obviously could not stand him. This is understandable for in her eyes, as in those of the Prince, Elcho was little short of a traitor; but that surely does not justify departing from the truth.

To begin with the Wemyss family had not always been attached to the family of Stuart. On the contrary they had been originally attached to 'Dutch William', and it was only through a series of accidents that they found themselves Jacobite. She then rightly goes on to say that Elcho started the grand tour in charge of a Jacobite tutor in 1738 at the age of 17, but she goes on to describe him as a 'discomforted schoolboy' during his interview with the Old Pretender which took place nearly three years later when he was already a pretty sophisticated young man of the world. It would seem that he was marked out from the very start to be commander of the Body Guard for which his education at Angers had fitted him, for it was not, as Miss Tayler put it, one of 'the various French riding schools' but a preparatory school for cavalry officers, probably the best of its kind; as such it was attended some forty years later by the future Duke of Wellington. She was also wrong to complain that Elcho's 'a few days of soldiering [when at the Scottish camp in Flanders] was the only qualification . . . for acting as Colonel of the Prince's Lifeguards and the sole justification for criticising such military veterans as Lord George Murray, Colonel O'Sullivan and Brigadier Stapleton'. This is wrong. In the first place he had the greatest admiration for Lord George and never criticises him, and he had probably as much knowledge of tactics as O'Sullivan who had started life as a tutor and was given a commission by Maillebois in Corsica where he cannot have seen much fighting. But she is right, however, to refer to Elcho's obvious disapproval of the Prince, although this comes out mostly by implication.

But what Henrietta Tayler really resented is Sir Walter Scott's publication of Elcho's famous words 'There you go for a damned cowardly Italian!' though these words are exceptionally well documented, as Sir Walter transcribed them in his diary shortly after he had heard them from Elcho's favourite nephew, the only member of the family he had known since childhood. However she points out that they 'do not occur in the *Narrative* or the *Journal*' though they are consistent with the *Journal*. I am perfectly sure that Scott was right when he writes 'Lord Elcho called after him (I write the very words) . . ' If ever words have the ring of truth it is these, the stress being on the word 'Italian'. Elcho was clearly in a rage and the image which must have risen before him was that of the foolish, ignorant and conceited young prince whom he had got to know so well in the gardens of the Villa Borghese in Rome.

Although, like Sir Walter, I fully believe the story, I do not think the incident took place on the field of battle (as he explained in the lengthy note on the matter he wrote for the *Magnum Opus* edition of *Waverley*) but rather shortly after and some miles distant from it. This was where the Prince panics in his flight and Elcho goes to him to get orders pleading in vain with him to take the head of the remaining Highlanders and wage a guerrilla war so as to get decent terms of surrender from Cumberland. But Charles Edward is terrified, believing that he will be betrayed for the £30,000 promised by the Government and insists on fleeing to France and safety. There must have been a flaming row of which there are echoes in Padre Cordara (the narrative put together in Italy soon after the collapse of the Rising). Sir Walter Scott's mistake was no doubt due to his not having been favoured with a sight of the *Journal*.

Where Henrietta Tayler is right is to point out that the words do not appear in either the *Narrative*, or the *Journal*. But is was unlikely that they should do so, for it was a polite society from which swear words were banished as is shown by the delicate fashion Sir Walter relates the same incident in *Tales of a Grandfather*: 'Lord Elcho turned from him with a bitter execration and declared he would never see his face again!'

This misleading introduction is followed by a faithful transcription of that part of the English translation of the *Journal* which describes the '45, ending with Charles Edward's refusal to receive Elcho in Paris, but omitting the following passage which comes a little later. 'On the day the Prince refused to see me all the Scotsmen then in Paris came to see me to tell me of their disapproval of his conduct.' The Tayler article is sprinkled with footnotes tending to show that what Elcho writes is not true. In fact the whole purpose of the Henrietta Tayler exercise seems to be to discredit a valuable document which shows the Bonnie Prince in an unfavourable light. If so, she has succeeded and deprived British and indeed European historians of a valuable insight on an important episode of 18th century history.

I have often wondered what led this highly respected historian, who has added so much to our knowledge of Jacobitism to behave in such a strange fashion. Did she consciously wish to discredit a document which throws so devastating a light on her beloved Prince, or was the Prince's charm still effective after two centuries?

Let us end this book with the words of Sir Henry Stuart of Allanton who claimed in 1832 to be better informed about Elcho than was any member of his own family. 'I truly believe that there was not a more honourable, noble, brave and high-spirited gentleman, though a little irritable and eccentric', a fine tribute from one whose sympathies apparently lay with the Stuart cause.

Appendix

1.   The Prince in the immediate aftermath of Culloden

From Elcho's Journal (Translation)

The Prince came to a halt four miles from the field of battle where I found him in a desperate state. Having always been flattered with false hopes that the Duke of Cumberland's army would take flight as had those of Cope and Hawley, he came to believe that all that had happened was due to treachery, and he became afraid of all the Scots whom he believed were capable of delivering him up so as to obtain peace and the £30,000 placed on his head. He consulted no one, and indeed spoke to no one except the Irish who were still with him. He asked them if all their officers had obtained a superior rank which might prove useful on their return to France. He appeared to be only concerned with their lot and not at all about the fate of the Scots. Seeing that the number of Scottish officers was increasing, he ordered them off to a village a mile away where he would send his orders.

I remained on and asked him if he had any orders for me. He told me I could go wherever I liked; as for himself, he was about to leave for France. I said I was surprised by a resolution so little worthy of a prince of his birth; that it was unworthy of him to have got all these people to sacrifice themselves for him and then to abandon them because he may have lost a thousand men in the battle; that he ought to remain and place himself at the head of the 9000 men who remained, and live and die with them. I pointed out that he would still have an army of 9000 men in spite of his losses; despite everything his position was better now than it had been on his arrival. I also pointed out that finding themselves without a leader, his followers would disperse and thus fall into the vengeful hands of the Duke of Cumberland. All these arguments made no impression upon him and he told me that his intention was to seek safety in France. Upon which I left resolved never to have anything more to do with him.

2. From Sir Walter Scott's Journal for February 1826

Yesterday I had an anecdote from old Sir James Steuart Denham, which is worth writing down. His uncle, Lord Elcho, was, as is well known, engaged in the affair of 1745. He was dissatisfied with the conduct of matters from beginning to end. But after the left wing of the Highlanders was repulsed and broken at Culloden, Elcho rode up to the Chevalier and told him all was lost, and that nothing remained except to charge at the head of two thousand men, who were still unbroken, and either turn the fate of the day or die sword in hand, as became his pretensions. The Chevalier gave him some evasive answer, and turning his horse's head, rode off the field. Lord Elcho called after him (I write the very words) 'There you go for a damned cowardly Italian,' and never would see him again, though he lost his property and remained an exile in the cause. Lord Elcho left two copies of his memoirs, one with Sir James Steuart's family, one with Lord Wemyss. This is better evidence than the romance of Chevalier Johnstone; and I have little doubt it is true.

Sources and Bibliography

The principal sources for this book are two original works by David, Lord Elcho; his *Journal*, translated by Alice Wemyss from the original manuscript in French and *A Short Account of the Affairs of Scotland* known as the *Narrative* edited by Hon E Charteris and published in Edinburgh in 1907.

MANUSCRIPT SOURCES

Archives communales de Bôle (Archives cantonales de Neuchâtel)

Cumberland Papers: United Services Museum, Edinburgh Castle

Dossier: particulier Wemyss (Archives cantonales)

Dossier: Margaret Wemyss - Elcho's daughter (Archives cantonales)

Five letters from Lord Wemyss to the Banneret Osterwald 18-23 Sept 1781 & 28 Nov 1782 (Mss 1229 Bibliothèque de Neuchâtel)

Lord Elcho to the wife of Prince Charles Edward (Jan 1777)

Memoire d'un Ecossais (Lochiel) April 1747 A E C D Ag 82 Reproduced in full as an appendix to *Locheil of the '45* by John Sibbald Gibson (Edinburgh University Press, 1994)

MSSL (Affaires Etrangères) Angleterre 76 (re Sir J Hynde Cotton)

MSS 18 letters between Captain Wemyss, Lord Wemyss & Sir Henry Stewart of Allanton re the publication of the 'Narrative' (Gosford House Papers)

Prince Charles Edward to Duncan Cant [Elcho] 16 March 1744 (Stuart MSS Vol 256/134)

The Jacobite Correspondence of the Atholl Family (Abbotsford Club 1840)

The Woodhouselie MSS W R Chambers, Edinburgh 1907

PRINTED SOURCES

Allardyce, Col. James ed. *Historical Papers relating to the Jacobite Period* (1895)

Anon (by a contemporary) *History of the Rebellion in the years 1745 and 1746*, Roxburghe Club, London, 1944

Argenson (Marquis d') *Journal et Mémoires 1747-1749* (1897)

Balfour Paul, J *History of the Company of Royal Archers* (1975)

Barbier *Journal du Règne de Louis XV* Vol IV

Beer, G R *Lord Wemyss à Cotendard* (Musée Neuchatelois 1950)

Beresford-Chancellor, E *Col Charteris & the Duke of Wharton* (London 1925)

Berthoud, F *Jean Jacques Rousseau et le Pasteur de Montmollin*

Biddulf, Violet *Kitty Duchess of Queensberry* (London 1936)

Blaikie, W B *Origins of the Forty Five* (Edinburgh 1916)

Blaikie, W B *Rebellion in Fife* Account of Walter Grosset Esq in Origins of the Forty-Five

Bongie, L L *The Love of a Prince* (Vancouver 1986)

Boswell, James *Boswell on the Grand Tour 1764* (Yale edition, 1953)

Brosses, Charles des *Le Président des Brosses en Italie* (Paris 1858)

Browne, James *A History of the Highlands* 3 Vols (Edinburgh 1853)

Burton, J H *History of Scotland from the Revolution to the Extinction of the Last Jacobite Insurrection* 2 vols (London 1853)

Carlyle, Rev Alexander *Anecdotes and Characters of the Times by the Revd. Alexander Carlyle* (Oxford University Press, 1973)

Chambers, Robert *Jacobite Memoirs of the Rebellion of 1745*

Chambers, Robert *Traditions of Edinburgh* (London & Edinburgh)

Charteris, Colonel Francis *State of Great Britain* (London Magazine & Gentleman's Magazine 1732)

Charel, A *Un Aventurier religieux an XVIII siecle,* A Ramsay (Paris 1926)

Charrière, Isabelle de *Oeuvres completes* (Amsterdam)

Chevallier, C H *Maçons Ecossais au XVIII s* (1969)

Chevallier, Pierre). *Les Ducs sous L'Acacia 1724-1743* (Paris, 1968)

Cohn, J *Louis XV et les Jacobites* (Paris 1901)

Cuthell, C C *The Scottish Friend of Fredrick the Great* (London 1915)

Duke, Winifred *Lord George Murray & The Forty Five* (Aberdeen 1927)

Ewald, A C *Life and Times of Prince Charles Edward* 2 vols (1875)

Fauchier-Maganan, Adrien *The Small German Courts in the Eighteenth Century* (London 1948)

Fraser, Sir W. *Memorial of the House of Wemyss* (3 vols Edinburgh 1888)

Gibson, John S *Ships of the '45* (London 1967)

Gibson, John S *Lochiel of the '45* (Edinburgh 1994)

Gibson, John S *Edinburgh in the '45* (Edinburgh 1967)

Godet, Philippe *Madame de Charrière et ses Amis* 2 vols (Geneva 1906)

Hamilton, Marion F 'The Loch Arkaig Treasure' (Scottish Historical Society Miscellany vii 1941)

Hay, Ian *The Royal Company of Archers 1576-1951* (Edinburgh)

Henderson, Andrew *The History of the Rebellion* (1752)

Henderson, Andrew *The Edinburgh History of the Late Rebellion* (1753)

Henderson, G D *Chevalier Ramsay* (London 1953)

Home, John *History of the Rebellion in Scotland* (London 1802)

Home, John *History of the Rebellion in Scotland* (Edinburgh 1822)

Hughan, W J *The Jacobite Lodge at Rome 1735-1737* (Torquay 1910)

Hume, David *Letters* 2 vols (Oxford 1932)

Jaquart, J 'Les débuts de l'Anglomanie en France au XVIIIs' in *Mémoire de la Société d'Agriculture et Arts d'Angers* (1936)

Johnstone, Chevalier de *Memoirs of the Rebellion in 1745-46* (3rd edition London 1822)

King, William *Political & Literary Anecdotes of his own time* (1819)

Labregère-Baleix, Jacqueline *Engoulesme-Angouleme au fil de l'histoire* (Angouleme)

Lang, Andrew *Pickle the Spy* (London 1897)

Laurie, W A *History of Free Masonry, Grand Lodge of Scotland*

Le Fevre-Pontalis, G *La Mission du Marquis d'Eguilles* (Paris 1886)

Lees-Milne, James *The Last of the Stuarts* (London)

Leigh, A ed. 'Dupeyrou Seconde lettre relative à M. J J Rousseau addressée à Mylord Comte de Wemyss, Baron Elcho, etc, etc.'in *Correspondence complète de Jean Jacques Rousseau.*

Lenman, Bruce *The Jacobite Risings in Britain* (London 1980)

Lenman, B and Gibson, J S *The Jacobite Threat* (Edinburgh 1990)

Lewis, Lesley *Connaisseurs & Secret Agents in XVIII Century Rome* (1961)

Lindsay, R *Le Rite Ecossais pour l'Ecosse* (Laval 1961)

Luynes, Duc de *Les Mémoires du Duc d Luynes sur la cour de Louis XV*

Mackay, J G *A History of Fife and Kinross* (Edinburgh 1896)

Maxwell, James of Kirkconnel *Narrative of Charles Prince of Wales' Expedition in Scotland in the year 1745*, Edinburgh (Maitland Club) 1841

Mitford, Nancy *Frederick the Great* (London 1970)

Mossner, E C *The Life of David Hume* (London 1954)

Murray, John of Broughton *Memorials* (Edinburgh 1898)

McLynn, E J *The Jacobite Army in England 1745* (Edinburgh 1982)

McLynn, F J *France and the Jacobite Rising of 1745* (Edinburgh 1981)

Nordman, Claude *Les Jacobites Ecossais en France au XVIII siecle* (Universite de Lille, 1977)

Oberkirch, The Baroness *Memoirs written by herself* 3 vols. (London 1952)

O'Callaghan, J C *History of the Irish Brigades in the Service of France* (Glasgow 1870)

O'Sullivan, Sir John William *Journal of the '45 Campaign and After* (1938)

Ray, James of Whitehaven *A Complete History of the Rebellion from 1745 to 1746* (York 1749)

Pury, Abram de *Six lettres au Cousin David* (1767)

Scott, Sir Walter *Tales of a Grandfather* (London 1898)

Sinclair, John Master of *Memoirs of the Rebellion* (Abbotsford Club, Edinburgh 1858)

Speck, W A *The Butcher* (1981)

Tayler, Henrietta ed. *A Jacobite Miscellany: Letters of Magdalen Pringle* (Roxburghe Club, London 1948)

Terry, C S *The Albemarle Papers* (Spalding Club, Aberdeen 1901-2)

Tomasson, K *The Jacobite General* (London 1958)

Topham, Edward *Letters from Edinburgh 1774-1779* (Edinburgh 1971)

Tribolet, D G *Histoire de Neuchâtel et Valangin* (Neuchatel 1846)

Tripet, Maurice *Exposé de la Constitution de la Principauté de Neuchâtel et Valangin* (Colombier 1893)

Walpole, Horace *Letters* (London 1877)

Wemyss, Janet Countess of *Letters to and from.* (N.L.S)

Index

About the Saltire Society

The Saltire Society was founded in 1936 at a time when many of the distinctive features of Scotland and its culture seemed in jeopardy. Over the years its members, who have included many of Scotland's most distinguished scholars and creative artists, have fought to preserve and present the nation's cultural heritage so that Scotland might once again be a creative force in European civilisation. As well as publishing books and producing recordings the Society makes a number of national awards for excellence in fields as diverse as housing design, civil engineering, historical publication and scientific research. There are Saltire Society branches in many towns and cities in Scotland and beyond, and each year members organise dozens of lectures, seminars and conferences on important aspects of Scottish culture.

The Society has no political affiliation and welcomes as members all who share its aims. Further information from The Administrator, The Saltire Society, Fountain Close, 22 High Street, Edinburgh, EH1 ITF Telephone 0131 556 1836.

Alternatively, you can make contact by email at saltire@saltiresociety.org.uk. and visit the Society web site at www.saltire-society.demon.co.uk